Knowledge of Language

Knowledge of Language:
Its Nature, Origin, and Use

Noam Chomsky

CONVERGENCE

A Series Founded, Planned, and Edited by Ruth Nanda Anshen

PRAEGER

Westport, Connecticut
London

Library of Congress Cataloging-in-Publication Data

Chomsky, Noam.
    Knowledge of language.

    (Convergence)
    Bibliography: p.
    Includes index.
    I. Language and languages.   I. Title.
II. Series: Convergence (Praeger Publishers)
P106.C518 1986   410   85-12234
ISBN 0-275-90025-8 (alk. paper)
ISBN 0-275-91761-4 (pbk: alk. paper)

Library of Congress Catalog Card Number: 85-12234

ISBN: 0-275-90025-8
      0-275-91761-4 (pbk.)

First published in 1986

Praeger Publishers, 88 Post Road West, Westport, CT 06881
An imprint of Greenwood Publishing Group, Inc.

Printed in the United States of America

♾™
The paper used in this book complies with the
Permanent Paper Standard issued by the National
Information Standards Organization (Z39.48-1984).

20 19 18 17 16 15 14 13 12

CONVERGENCE

A Series Founded, Planned, and Edited by Ruth Nanda Anshen

Books in the Convergence Series

Contents

Convergence

Ruth Nanda Anshen

"There is no use trying," said Alice; "one *can't* believe impossible things."

"I dare say you haven't had much practice," said the Queen, "When I was your age, I always did it for half an hour a day. Why, sometimes I've believed as many as six impossible things before breakfast."

This commitment is an inherent part of human nature and an aspect of our creativity. Each advance of science brings increased comprehension and appreciation of the nature, meaning, and wonder of the creative forces that move the cosmos and created man. Such openness and confidence lead to faith in the reality of possibility and eventually to the following truth: "The mystery of the universe is its comprehensibility."

When Einstein uttered that challenging statement, he could have been speaking about our relationship with the universe. The old division of the Earth and the Cosmos into objective processes in space and time and mind in which they are mirrored is no longer a suitable starting point for understanding the universe, science, or ourselves. Science now begins to focus on the convergence of man and nature, on the framework which makes us, as living beings, dependent parts of nature and simultaneously makes nature the object of our thoughts and actions. Scientists can no longer confront the universe as objective observers. Science recognizes the participation of man with the universe. Speaking quantitatively, the universe is largely indifferent to what happens in man. Speaking qualitatively, nothing happens in man that does not have a bearing on the elements which constitute the universe. This gives cosmic significance to the person.

Nevertheless, all facts are not born free and equal. There exists a hierarchy of facts in relation to a hierarchy of values. To arrange the facts rightly, to differentiate the important from the trivial, to see their bearing in relation to each other and to evaluational criteria, requires a judgment which is intuitive as well as empirical. We need meaning in addition to information. Accuracy is not the same as truth.

Our hope is to overcome the cultural *hubris* in which we have been living. The scientific method, the technique of analyzing, explaining, and classifying, has demonstrated its inherent limitations. They arise because, by its intervention, science presumes to alter and fashion the object of its investigation. In reality, method and object can no longer be separated. The outworn Cartesian, scientific world view has ceased to be scientific in the most profound sense of the word, for a common bond links us all—man, animal, plant, and galaxy—in the unitary principle of all reality. For the self without the universe is empty.

This universe of which we human beings are particles may be defined as a living, dynamic process of unfolding. It is a breathing universe, its respiration being only one of the many rhythms of its life. It is evolution itself. Although what we observe may seem to be a community of separate, independent units, in actuality these units are made up of subunits, each with a life of its own, and the subunits constitute smaller living entities. At no level in the hierarchy of nature is independence a reality. For that which lives and constitutes matter, whether organic or inorganic, is dependent on discrete entities that, gathered together, form aggregates of new units which interact in support of one another and become an unfolding event, in constant motion, with ever-increasing complexity and intricacy of their organization.

Are there goals in evolution? Or are there only discernible patterns? Certainly there is a law of evolution by which we can explain the emergence of forms capable of activities which are indeed novel. Examples may be said to be the origin of life, the emergence of individual consciousness, and the appearance of language.

The hope of the concerned authors in Convergence is that they will show that evolution and development are interchangeable and that the entire system of the interweaving of man, nature, and the universe constitutes a living totality. Man is searching for his legitimate place in this unity, this cosmic scheme of things. The meaning of this cosmic scheme—if indeed we can impose meaning on the mystery and majesty of nature—and the extent to which we can assume responsibility in it as uniquely intelligent beings, are supreme questions for which this Series seeks an answer.

Inevitably, toward the end of a historical period, when thought and custom have petrified into rigidity and when the elaborate machinery of civilization opposes and represses our more noble qualities, life stirs again beneath the hard surface. Nevertheless, this attempt to define the purpose of Convergence is set forth with profound trepidation. We are living in a period of extreme darkness. There is moral atrophy, destructive radiation within us, as we watch the collapse of values hitherto cherished—but now betrayed. We seem to be face to face with an apocalyptic destiny. The anomie, the chaos, surrounding us produces an almost lethal distintegration of the person, as well as ecological and demographic disaster. Our situation is desperate. And there is no glossing over the deep and unresolved tragedy that fills our lives. Science now begins to question its premises and tells us not only what *is*, but what *ought* to be; *p*rescribing in addition to *d*escribing the realities of life, reconciling order and hierarchy.

My introduction to Convergence is not to be construed as a prefatory essay to each individual volume. These few pages attempt to set forth the general aim and purpose of this Series. It is my hope that this statement will provide the reader with a new orientation in his thinking, one more specifically defined by these scholars who have been invited to participate in this intellectual, spiritual, and moral endeavor so desperately needed in our time. These scholars recognize the relevance of the nondiscursive experience of life which the discursive, analytical method alone is unable to convey.

The authors invited to Convergence Series acknowledge a structural kinship between subject and object, between living and nonliving matter, the immanence of the past energizing the present and thus bestowing a promise for the future. This kinship has long been sensed and experienced by mystics. Saint Francis of Assisi described with extraordinary beauty the truth that the more we know about nature, its unity with all life, the more we realize that we are one family, summoned to acknowledge the intimacy of our familial ties with the universe. At one time we were so anthropomorphic as to exclude as inferior such other aspects of our relatives as animals, plants, galaxies, or other species—even inorganic matter. This only exposed our provincialism. Then we believed there were borders beyond which we could not, must not, trespass. These frontiers have never existed. Now we are beginning to recognize, even take pride in, our neighbors in the Cosmos.

Human thought has been formed through centuries of man's consciousness, by perceptions and meanings that relate us to nature. The smallest living entity, be it a molecule or a particle, is at the same time present in the structure of the Earth and all its inhabitants, whether human or manifesting themselves in the multiplicity of other forms of life.

Today we are beginning to open ourselves to this evolved experience of consciousness. We keenly realize that man has intervened in the evolutionary process. The future is contingent, not completely prescribed, except for the immediate necessity to evaluate in order to live a life of integrity. The specific gravity of the burden of change has moved from genetic to cultural evolution. Genetic evolution itself has taken millions of years; cultural evolution is a child of no more than twenty or thirty thousand years. What will be the future of our evolutionary course? Will it be cyclical in the classical sense? Will it be linear in the modern sense? Yet we know that the laws of nature are not linear. Certainly, life is more than mere endless repetition. We must restore the importance of each moment, each deed. This is impossible if the future is nothing but a mechanical extrapolation of the past. Dignity becomes possible only with choice. The choice is ours.

In this light, evolution shows man arisen by a creative power inherent in the universe. The immense ancestral effort that has borne man invests him with a cosmic responsibility. Michelangelo's image of Adam created at God's command becomes a more intelligent symbol of man's position in the world than does a description of man as a chance aggregate of atoms or cells. Each successive stage of emergence is more comprehensive, more meaningful, more fulfilling, and more converging, than the last. Yet a higher faculty must always operate through the levels that are below it. The higher faculty must enlist the laws controlling the lower levels in the service of higher principles, and the lower level which enables the higher one to operate through it will always limit the scope of these operations, even menacing them with possible failure. All our higher endeavors must work through our lower forms and are necessarily exposed thereby to corruption. We may thus recognize the cosmic roots of tragedy and our fallible human condition. Language itself as the power of universals, is the basic expression of man's ability to transcend his environment and to transmute tragedy into a moral and spiritual triumph.

This relationship, this convergence, of the higher with the lower applies again when an upper level, such as consciousness or freedom, endeavors to reach beyond itself. If no higher level can be accounted for by the operation of a lower level, then no effort of ours can be truly creative in the sense of establishing a higher principle not intrinsic to our initial condition. And establishing such a principle is what all great art, great thought, and great action must aim at. This is indeed how these efforts have built up the heritage in which our lives continue to grow.

Has man's intelligence broken through the limits of his own powers? Yes and no. Inventive efforts can never fully account for their success, but the story of man's evolution testifies to a creative power that goes beyond that which we can account for in ourselves. This power can make us surpass ourselves. We exercise some of it in the simple act of acquiring knowledge and holding it to be true. For, in doing so, we strive for intellectual control over things outside ourselves, in spite of our manifest incapacity to justify this hope. The greatest efforts of the human mind amount to no more than this. All such acts impose an obligation to strive for the ostensibly impossible, representing man's search for the fulfillment of those ideals which, for the moment, seem to be beyond his reach. For the good of a moral act is inherent in the act itself and has the power to ennoble the person who performs it. Without this moral ingredient there is corruption.

The origins of one person can be envisaged by tracing that person's family tree all the way back to the primeval specks of protoplasm in which his first origins lie. The history of the family tree converges with everything that has contributed to the making of a human being. This segment of evolution is on a par with the history of a fertilized egg developing into a mature person, or the history of a plant growing from a seed; it includes everything that caused that person, or that plant, or that animal, or even that star in a galaxy, to come into existence. Natural selection plays no part in the evolution of a single human being. We do not include in the mechanism of growth the possible adversities which did not befall it and hence did not prevent it. The same principle of development holds for the evolution of a single human being; nothing is gained in understanding this evolution by considering the adverse chances which might have prevented it.

In our search for a reasonable cosmic view, we turn in the first place to common understanding. Science largely relies for its subject matter on a common knowledge of things. Concepts of life and death, plant and animal, health and sickness, youth and age, mind and body, machine and technical processes, and other innumerable and equally important things are commonly known. All these concepts apply to complex entities, whose reality is called into question by a theory of knowledge which claims that the entire universe should ultimately be represented in all its aspects by the physical laws governing the inanimate substrate of nature. "Technological inevitability" has alienated our relationship with nature, with work, with other human beings, with ourselves. Judgment, decision, and freedom of choice, in other words *knowledge* which contains a moral imperative, cannot be ordered in the form that some technological scientists believe. For there is no mechanical ordering, no exhaustive set of permutations or combinations that can perform the task. The power which man has achieved through technology has been transformed into spiritual and moral impotence. Without the insight into the nature of *being*, more important than *doing*, the soul of man is imperilled. And those self-transcendent ends that ultimately confer dignity, meaning and identity on man and his life constitute the only final values worth pursuing. The pollution of consciousness is the result of mere technological efficiency. In addition, the authors in this Series recognize that the computer in itself can process information—not meaning. Thus we see on the stage of life no moral actors, only anonymous events.

Our new theory of knowledge, as the authors in this Series try to demonstrate, rejects this claim and restores our respect for the immense range of common knowledge acquired by our experience of convergence. Starting from here, we sketch out our cosmic perspective by exploring the wider implications of the fact that all knowledge is acquired and possessed by relationship, coalescense, convergence.

We identify a person's physiognomy by depending on our awareness of features that we are unable to specify, and this amounts to a convergence in the features of a person for the purpose of comprehending their joint meaning. We are also able to read in the features and behavior of a person the presence of moods, the gleam of intelligence, the response to animals or a sunset or a fugue by Bach, the signs of sanity, human responsibility, and experience. At a lower level, we comprehend by a similar mechanism the body of a person and understand the functions of the physiological mechanism. We know that even physical theories constitute in this way the processes of inanimate nature. Such are the various levels of knowledge acquired and possessed by the experience of convergence.

The authors in this Series grasp the truth that these levels form a hierarchy of comprehensive entities. Inorganic matter is comprehended by physical laws; the mechanism of physiology is built on these laws and enlists them in its service. Then, the intelligent behavior of a person relies on the healthy functions of the body and, finally, moral responsibility relies on the faculties of intelligence directing moral acts.

We realize how the operations of machines, and of mechanisms in general, rely on the laws of physics but cannot be explained, or accounted for, by these laws. In a hierarchic sequence of comprehensive levels, each higher level is related to the levels below it in the same way as the operations of a machine are related to the particulars, obeying the laws of physics. We cannot explain the operations of an upper level in terms of the particulars on which its operations rely. Each higher level of integration represents, in this sense, a higher level of existence, not completely accountable by the levels below it yet including these lower levels implicitly.

In a hierarchic sequence of comprehensive levels each higher level is known to us by relying on our awareness of the particulars on the level below it. We are conscious of each level by internalizing its particulars and mentally performing the integration that constitutes it. This is how all experience, as well as all knowledge, is based on convergence, and this is how the consecutive stages of convergence form a continuous transition from the understanding of the inorganic, the inanimate, to the comprehension of man's moral responsibility and participation in the totality, the organismic whole, of all reality. The sciences of the subject-object relationship thus pass imperceptibly into the metascience of the convergence of the subject and object interrelationship, mutually altering each other. From the minimum of convergence, exercised in a physical observation, we move without a break to the maximum of convergence, which is a total commitment.

"The last of life, for which the first was made, is yet to come." Thus, Convergence has summoned the world's most concerned thinkers to rediscover the experience of *feeling*, as well as of thought. The convergence of all forms of reality presides over the possible fulfillment of self-awareness—not the isolated, alienated self, but rather the participation in the life process with other lives and other forms of life. Convergence is a cosmic force and may possess liberating powers allowing man to become what he is, capable of freedom, justice, love. Thus man experiences the meaning of grace.

A further aim of this Series is not, nor could it be, to disparage science. The authors themselves are adequate witness to this fact. Actually, in viewing the role of science, one arrives at a much more modest judgment of its function in our whole body of knowledge. Original knowledge was probably not acquired by us in the active sense; most of it must have been given to us in the same mysterious way we received our consciousness. As to content and usefulness, scientific knowledge is an infinitesimal fraction of natural knowledge. Nevertheless, it is knowledge whose structure is endowed with beauty because its abstractions satisfy our urge for specific knowledge much more fully than does natural knowledge, and we are justly proud of scientific knowledge because we can call it our own creation. It teaches us clear thinking, and the extent to which clear thinking helps us to order our sensations is a marvel which fills the mind with ever new and increasing admiration and awe. Science now begins to include the realm of human values, lest even the memory of what it means to be human be forgotten. In fact, it may well be that science has reached the limits of the knowable and may now be required to recognize its inability to penetrate into the caprice and the mystery of the soul of the atom.

Organization and energy are always with us, wherever we look, on all levels. At the level of the atom organization becomes indistinguishable from form, from order, from whatever the forces are that held the spinning groups of ultimate particles together in their apparent solidity. And now that we are at the atomic level, we find that modern physics has recognized that these ultimate particles are primarily electrical charges, and that mass is therefore a manifestation of energy. This has often been misinterpreted by idealists as meaning that matter has somehow been magicked away as if by a conjuror's wand. But nothing could be more untrue. It is impossible to transform matter into spirit just by making it thin. Bishop Berkeley's views admit of no refutation but carry no conviction nevertheless. However, something has happened to matter. It was only separated from form because it seemed too simple. Now we realize that, and this is a revolutionary change; we cannot separate them. We are now summoned to cease speaking of Form and Matter and begin to consider the convergence of Organization and Energy. For the largest molecule we know and the smallest living particles we know overlap. Such a cooperation, even though far down at the molecular level, cannot but remind us of the voluntary cooperation of individual human beings in maintaining patterns of society at levels of organization far higher. The tasks of Energy and Organization in the making of the universe and ourselves are far from ended.

No individual destiny can be separated from the destiny of the universe. Alfred North Whitehead has stated that every event, every step or process in the universe, involves both effects from past situations and the anticipation of future potentialities. Basic for this doctrine is the assumption that the course of the universe results from a multiple and never-ending complex of steps developing out of one another. Thus, in spite of all evidence to the contrary, we conclude that there is a continuing and permanent energy of that which is not only man but all life. For not an atom stirs in matter, organic and inorganic, that does not have its cunning duplicate in mind. And faith in the convergence of life with all its multiple manifestations creates its own verification.

We are concerned in this Series with the unitary structure of all nature. At the beginning, as we see in Hesiod's *Theogony* and in the Book of Genesis, there was a primal unity, a state of fusion in which, later, all elements become separated but then merge again. However, out of this unity there emerge, through separation, parts of opposite elements. These opposites intersect or reunite, in meteoric phenomena or in individual living things. Yet, in spite of the immense diversity of creation, a profound underlying convergence exists in all nature. And the principle of the conservation of energy simply signifies that there is a *something* that remains constant Whatever fresh notions of the world may be given us by future experiments, we are certain beforehand that something remains unchanged which we may call *energy*. We now do not say that the law of nature springs from the invariability of God, but with that curious mixture of arrogance and humility which scientists have learned to put in place of theological terminology, we say instead that the law of conservation is the physical expression of the elements by which nature makes itself understood by us.

The universe is our home. There is no other universe than the universe of all life including the mind of man, the merging of life with life. Our consciousness is evolving, the primordial principle of the unfolding of that which is implied or contained in all matter and spirit. We ask: Will the central mystery of the cosmos, as well as man's awareness of and participation in it, be unveiled, although forever receding, asymptotically? Shall we perhaps be able to see all things, great and small, glittering with new light and reborn meaning, ancient but now again relevant in an iconic image which is related to our own time and experience?

The cosmic significance of his panorama is revealed when we consider it as the stages of an evolution that has achieved the rise of man and his consciousness. This is the new plateau on which we now stand. It may seem obvious that the succession of changes, sustained through a thousand million years, which have transformed microscopic specks of protoplasm into the human race, has brought forth, in so doing, a higher and altogether novel kind of being capable of compassion, wonder, beauty and truth, although each form is as precious, as sacred, as the other. The interdependence of everything with everything else in the totality of being includes a participation of nature in history and demands a participation of the universe.

The future brings us nothing, gives us nothing; it is we who in order to build it have to give it everything, our very life. But to be able to give, one has to possess; and we possess no other life, no living sap, than the treasures stored up from the past and digested, assimilated, and created afresh by us. Like all human activities, the law of growth, of evolution, of convergence draws its vigor from a tradition which does not die.

At this point, however, we must remember that the law of growth, of evolution, has both a creative and a tragic nature. This we recognize as a degenerative process, as devolution. Whether it is the growth of a human soul or the growth of a living cell or of the universe, we are confronted not only with fulfillment but with sacrifice, with increase and decrease, with enrichment and diminution. Choice and decision are necessary for growth and each choice, each decision, excludes certain potentialities, certain potential realities. But since these unactualized realities are part of us, they possess a right and command of their own. They must avenge themselves for their exclusion from existence. They may perish and with them all the potential powers of their existence, their creativity. Or they may not perish but remain unquickened within us, repressed, lurking, ominous, swift to invade in some disguised form our life process, not as a dynamic, creative, converging power, but as a necrotic, pathological force. If the diminishing and the predatory processes co-mingle, atrophy and even death in every category of life ensue. But if we possess the maturity and the wisdom to accept the necessity of choice, of decision, or order and hierarchy, the inalienable right of freedom and autonomy, then, in spite of its tragedy, its exclusiveness, the law of growth endows us with greatness and a new moral dimension.

Convergence is committed to the search for the deeper meanings of science, philosophy, law, morality, history, technology, in fact all the disciplines in a trans-disciplinary frame of reference. This Series aims to expose the error in that form of science which creates an unreconcilable dichotomy between the observer and the participant, thereby destroying the uniqueness of each discipline by neutralizing it. For in the end we would know everything but *understand nothing*, not being motivated by concern for any question. This Series further aims to examine relentlessly the ultimate premises on which work in the respective fields of knowledge rests and to break through from these into the universal principles which are the very basis of all specialist information. More concretely, there are issues which wait to be examined in relation to, for example, the philosophical and moral meanings of the models of modern physics, the question of the purely physico-chemical processes versus the postulate of the irreducibility of life in biology. For there is a basic correlation of elements in nature, of which man is a part, which cannot be separated, which compose each other, which converge, and alter each other mutually.

Certain mysteries are now known to us: the mystery, in part, of the universe and the mystery of the mind have been in a sense revealed out of the heart of darkness. Mind and matter, mind and brain, have converged; space, time, and motion are reconciled; man, consciousness, and the universe are reunited since the atom in a star is the same as the atom in man. We are homeward bound because we have accepted our convergence with the Cosmos. We have reconciled observer and participant. For at last we know that time and space are modes by which we think, but not conditions in which we live and have our being. Religion and science meld; reason and feeling merge in mutual respect for each other, nourishing each other, deepening, quickening, and enriching our experiences of the life process. We have heeded the haunting voice in the Whirlwind.

The Möbius Strip

The symbol found on the cover of each volume in Convergence is the visual image of *convergence*—the subject of this Series. It is a mathematical mystery deriving its name from Augustus Möbius, a German mathematician who lived from 1790 to 1868. The topological problem still remains unsolved mathematically.

The Möbius Strip has only one continuous surface, in contrast to a cylindrical strip, which has two surfaces—the inside and the outside. An examination will reveal that the Strip, having one continuous edge, produces *one* ring, twice the circumference of the original Strip with one half of a twist in it, which eventually *converges with itself.*

Since the middle of the last century, mathematicians have increasingly refused to accept a "solution" to a mathematical problem as "obviously true," for the "solution" often then becomes the problem. For example, it is certainly obvious that every piece of paper has two sides in the sense that an insect crawling on one side could not reach the other side without passing around an edge or boring a hole through the paper. Obvious—but false!

The Möbius Strip, in fact, presents only one mono-dimensional, continuous ring having no inside, no outside, no beginning, no end. Converging with itself it symbolizes the structural kinship, the intimate relationship between subject and object, matter and energy, demonstrating the error of any attempt to bifurcate the observer and participant, the universe and man, into two or more systems of reality. All, all is unity.

I am indebted to Fay Zetlin, Artist-in-Residence at Old Dominion University in Virginia, who sensed the principle of convergence, of emergent transcendence, in the analogue of the Möbius Strip. This symbol may be said to crystallize my own

continuing and expanding explorations into the unitary structure of all reality. Fay Zetlin's drawing of the Möbius Strip
constitutes the visual image of this effort to emphasize the
experience of convergence.

R.N.A.

Preface

For many years, I have been intrigued by two problems concerning human knowledge. The first is the problem of explaining how we can know so much given that we have such limited evidence. The second is the problem of explaining how we can know so little, given that we have so much evidence. The first problem we might call "Plato's problem," the second, "Orwell's problem," an analogue in the domain of social and political life of what might be called "Freud's problem."

The essence of Plato's problem was well expressed by Bertrand Russell in his later work when he raised the question: "How comes it that human beings, whose contacts with the world are brief and personal and limited, are nevertheless able to know as much as they do know?" In certain domains of thought and understanding, our knowledge is vast in scope, highly specific and richly articulated in character, and in large measure shared with others who have similar backgrounds and experience. The same is true of systems of belief and expectation, modes of interpretation and integration of experience, and more generally what we may call "cognitive systems," only parts of which qualify as actual knowledge. The problem that arises when we consider the matter with a little care is one of "poverty of the stimulus." Although our cognitive systems surely reflect our experience in some manner, a careful specification of the properties of these systems on one hand, and of the experience that somehow led to their formation on the other, shows that the two are separated by a considerable gap, in fact, a chasm. The problem is to account for the specificity and the richness of the cognitive systems that arise in the individual on the basis of the limited information available. Cognitive systems result from the interaction of experience and the organism's method of constructing and dealing with it, including analytic mechanisms and the intrinsic determinants of maturation and cognitive growth. The problem, then, is to determine the innate endowment that serves to bridge the gap between experience and knowledge attained—or cognitive systems attained, abstracting from the truth-requirement for knowledge and generalizing to other systems that involve belief, understanding, interpretation, and perhaps more.

The study of human language is particularly interesting in this regard. In the first place, it is a true species property and one central to human thought and understanding. Furthermore, in the case of language we can proceed rather far toward characterizing the system of knowledge attained—knowledge of English, of Japanese, etc.—and determining the evidence that was available to the child who gained this knowledge; we also have a wide range of evidence available about the variety of attainable systems. We are thus in a good position to ascertain the nature of the biological endowment that constitutes the human "language faculty," the innate component of the mind/brain that yields knowledge of language when presented with linguistic experience, that converts experience to a system of knowledge.

Much of the interest of the study of language, in my opinion, lies in the fact that it offers an approach to Plato's problem in a domain that is relatively well circumscribed and open to inspection and inquiry, and at the same time deeply integrated in human life and thought. If we can discover something about the principles that enter into the construction of this particular cognitive system, the principles of the language faculty, we can progress toward a solution for at least one special and quite important case of Plato's problem. We can then ask whether these principles generalize to other cases, or if not, whether an approach that meets with a degree of explanatory success in the case of human language can at least serve as a suggestive model for similar inquiries in other cognitive domains. My own belief is that the principles do not generalize, that they are in crucial respects specific to the language faculty, but that the approach may indeed be suggestive elsewhere, both in its achievements and their apparent boundaries. The following chapters are primarily concerned with the question of what we may be able to learn about Plato's problem from the study of human language and how this study finds its place in the more general inquiry into cognitive systems, their character, and development. Chapters 1, 2, and 4 are concerned primarily with general and conceptual issues. Chapter 3, which is considerably more technical (particularly sections 3.4.3, 3.4.4, and 3.5.2)[1], introduces and develops some ideas that figure prominently in current research, which has taken a rather new turn in the past few years.

Plato's problem, then, is to explain how we know so much, given that the evidence available to us is so sparse. Orwell's problem is to explain why we know and understand so little, even though the evidence available to us is so rich. Like many other twentieth-century intellectuals, Orwell was impressed with the ability of totalitarian systems to instill beliefs that are firmly held and widely accepted although they are completely without foundation and often plainly at variance with obvious facts about the world around us. The problem is far broader, as the history of religious dogma suffices to show. To solve Orwell's problem we must discover the institutional and other factors that block insight and understanding in crucial areas of our lives and ask why they are effective.

In the modern era, the cult of state worship has frequently taken on the character of earlier forms of religious faith, not only in totalitarian states. In the latter, the mechanisms used to induce passivity and conformism are relatively transparent: ultimately, some form of violence employed or threatened under highly visible centralized control. But I think it has been amply demonstrated that in democratic societies where violence is rarely used to ensure obedience, Orwell's problem nevertheless arises. Thousands of pages of detailed documentation have demonstrated beyond any reasonable doubt that in these societies too, the doctrines of the state religion are firmly implanted and widely believed, in utter defiance of plain fact, particularly by the intelligentsia who construct and propagate these doctrines, those who take on the task of "manufacture of consent" (Walter Lippman) or "engineering of consent" (Edward Bernays), a task that many have regarded as essential in societies that can no longer impose conformity and obedience by violence. Such demonstrations, whatever their force, have essentially zero effect in the mainstream of respectable intellectual life, because the state religion naturally excludes investigation or understanding of the actual functioning of dominant institutions on the Orwellian principle that Ignorance is Strength.

This case of Orwell's problem is considerably more challenging than the one that is usually considered——by Orwell himself, in particular——because the mechanisms are more subtle and complex. For obvious reasons, it is also a far more important case for citizens of the democratic societies, and we can therefore predict from the principles of the state religion that it will rarely be investigated and that the occasional violation of the rules will not be welcomed with great enthusiasm.

I had originally intended to include here a detailed investigation of Orwell's problem, concentrating on the more interesting and more important case of the democratic societies, but decided against it for several reasons, one being that the character of inquiry into these two problems is so different. In the case of Plato's problem, the questions ultimately belong to the sciences, although many conceptual questions arise, including some that have long been troublesome in one or another form. The problem is to discover explanatory principles, often hidden and abstract, to make some sense of phenomena that seem on the surface chaotic, discordant, lacking any meaningful pattern. The study of Orwell's problem is quite different. The patterns that lie behind the most important phenomena of political, economic, and social life are not very difficult to discern, although much effort is devoted toward obscuring the fact; and the explanation for what will be observed by those who can free themselves from the doctrines of the faith is hardly profound or difficult to discover or comprehend. The study of Orwell's problem, then, is primarily a matter of accumulating evidence and examples to illustrate what should be fairly obvious to a rational observer even on superficial inspection, to establish the conclusion that power and privilege function much as any rational mind would expect, and to exhibit the mechanisms that operate to yield the results that we observe. Furthermore, the evidence and examples accumulated and the principles under which they fall will, virtually by definition, be unintelligble, misconstrued, distorted, dismissed, or otherwise rendered irrelevant, however powerful the case that is made with regard to the highly systematic behavior of the state and other dominant institutions, including the ideological institutions. The correctness of the (not particularly profound) thesis it attempts to verify and establish virtually guarantees the pointlessness of the effort, in this case.

I have discussed these matters elsewhere,[2] and expect to do so again, but the context of an inquiry into the nature of language is perhaps not the appropriate place, despite the widespread belief, which I personally share only in part, that misuse or control of language is a central feature of the problem. I have, however, included a brief appendix touching on the question, a revised version of an article that appeared in *Cambio* (Spain),[3] which I expect to publish in an extended and documented version elsewhere.

Plato's problem is deep and intellectually exciting; Orwell's problem, in contrast, seems to me much less so. But unless we can come to understand Orwell's problem and to recognize its significance in our own social and cultural life, and to overcome it, the chances are slim that the human species will survive long enough to discover the answer to Plato's problem or others that challenge the intellect and the imagination.

NOTES

1 For comment on an earlier draft of this material, I am indebted to Joseph Aoun and Kenneth Safir, among others.

2 For example, in *The Political Economy of Human Rights* (Boston: South End, 1979; with Edward S. Herman), *Towards a New Cold War* (New York: Pantheon, 1982), *The Fateful Triangle* (South End: Boston, 1983), and several earlier books beginning with *American Power and the New Mandarins* (New York: Pantheon, 1969). See also Edward S. Herman, *The Real Terror Network* (Boston: South End, 1982).

3 16–23 April, 1984. See also *Thoreau Quarterly*, Fall 1984, containing the transcript of a talk of mine that is very close in content to the *Cambio* article and of the ensuing discussion, at a conference of U.S. journalists.

Knowledge of Language

1 Knowledge of Language as a Focus of Inquiry

The study of language has a long and rich history, extending over thousands of years. This study has frequently been understood as an inquiry into the nature of mind and thought on the assumption that "languages are the best mirror of the human mind" (Leibniz). A common conception was that "with respect to its *substance* grammar is one and the same in all languages, though it does vary *accidentally*" (Roger Bacon). The invariant "substance" was often taken to be the mind and its acts; particular languages use various mechanisms—some rooted in human reason, others arbitrary and adventitious—for the expression of thought, which is a constant across languages. One leading eighteenth century rational grammarian defined "general grammar" as a deductive science concerned with "the immutable and general principles of spoken or written language" and their consequences; it is "prior to all languages," because its principles "are the same as those that direct human reason in its intellectual operations" (Beauzée). Thus, "the science of language does not differ at all from the science of thought." "Particular grammar" is not a true "science" in the sense of this rationalist tradition because it is not based solely on universal necessary laws; it is an "art" or technique that shows how given languages realize the general principles of human reason. As John Stuart Mill later expressed the same leading idea, "The principles and rules of grammar are the means by which the forms of language are made to correspond with the universal forms of thought.... The structure of every sentence is a lesson in logic." Others, particularly during the

1

Romantic period, argued that the nature and content of thought are determined in part by the devices made available for its expression in particular languages. These devices may include contributions of individual genius that affect the "character" of a language, enriching its means of expression and the thoughts expressed without affecting its "form," its sound system and rules of word and sentence formation (Humboldt).

With regard to the acquisition of knowledge, it was widely held that the mind is not "so much to be filled therewith from without, like a vessel, as to be kindled and awaked" (Ralph Cudworth); "The growth of knowledge...[rather resembles]... the growth of Fruit; however external causes may in some degree cooperate, it is the internal vigour, and virtue of the tree, that must ripen the juices to their just maturity" (James Harris).[1] Applied to language, this essentially Platonistic conception would suggest that knowledge of a particular language grows and matures along a course that is in part intrinsically determined, with modifications reflecting observed usage, rather in the manner of the visual system or other bodily "organs" that develop along a course determined by genetic instructions under the triggering and shaping effects of environmental factors.

With the exception of the relativism of the Romantics, such ideas were generally regarded with much disapproval in the mainstream of linguistic research by the late nineteenth century and on through the 1950s. In part, this attitude developed under the impact of a rather narrowly construed empiricism and later behaviorist and operationalist doctrine. In part, it resulted from the quite real and impressive successes of historical and descriptive studies conducted within a narrower compass, specifically, the discovery of "sound laws" that provided much understanding of the history of languages and their relationships. In part, it was a natural consequence of the investigation of a much richer variety of languages than were known to earlier scholars, languages that appeared to violate many of the allegedly a priori conceptions of the earlier rationalist tradition.[2] After a century of general neglect or obloquy, ideas resembling those of the earlier tradition re-emerged (initially, with virtually no awareness of historical antecedents) in the mid-1950s, with the development of what came to be called "generative grammar"—again, reviving a long-lapsed and largely forgotten tradition.[3]

The generative grammar of a particular language (where "generative" means nothing more than "explicit") is a theory that is concerned with the form and meaning of expressions of this language. One can imagine many different kinds of approach to such questions, many points of view that might be adopted in dealing with them. Generative grammar limits itself to certain elements of this larger picture. Its standpoint is that of individual psychology. It is concerned with those aspects of form and meaning that are determined by the "language faculty," which is understood to be a particular component of the human mind. The nature of this faculty is the subject matter of a general theory of linguistic structure that aims to discover the framework of principles and elements common to attainable human languages; this theory is now often called "universal grammar" (UG), adapting a traditional term to a new context of inquiry. UG may be regarded as a characterization of the genetically determined language faculty. One may think of this faculty as a "language acquisition device," an innate component of the human mind that yields a particular language through interaction with presented experience, a device that converts experience into a system of knowledge attained: knowledge of one or another language.

The study of generative grammar represented a significant shift of focus in the approach to problems of language. Put in the simplest terms, to be elaborated below, the shift of focus was from behavior or the products of behavior to states of the mind/brain that enter into behavior. If one chooses to focus attention on this latter topic, the central concern becomes knowledge of language: its nature, origins, and use.

The three basic questions that arise, then, are these:

(i)   What constitutes knowledge of language?   (1)
(ii) How is knowledge of language acquired?
(iii) How is knowledge of language put to use?

The answer to the first question is given by a particular generative grammar, a theory concerned with the state of the mind/brain of the person who knows a particular language. The answer to the second is given by a specification of UG along with an account of the ways in which its principles interact with experience to yield a particular language; UG is a theory of the "initial state" of the language faculty, prior to any linguistic experience. The answer to the third question would be a theory of how the knowledge of language attained enters into the expression of thought and the understanding of presented specimens of language, and derivatively, into communication and other special uses of language.

So far, this is nothing more than the outline of a research program that takes up classical questions that had been put aside for many years. As just described, it should not be particularly controversial, since it merely expresses an interest in certain problems and offers a preliminary analysis of how they might be confronted, although as is often the case, the initial formulation of a problem may prove to be far-reaching in its implications, and ultimately controversial as it is developed.

Some elements of this picture may appear to be more controversial than they really are. Consider, for example, the idea that there is a language faculty, a component of the mind/brain that yields knowledge of language given presented experience. It is not at issue that humans attain knowledge of English, Japanese, and so forth, while rocks, birds, or apes do not under the same (or indeed any) conditions. There is, then, some property of the mind/brain that differentiates humans from rocks, birds, or apes. Is this a distinct "language faculty" with specific structure and properties, or, as some believe, is it the case that humans acquire language merely by applying generalized learning mechanisms of some sort, perhaps with greater efficiency or scope than other organisms? These are not topics for speculation or *a priori* reasoning but for empirical inquiry, and it is clear enough how to proceed: namely, by facing the questions of (1). We try to determine what is the system of knowledge that has been attained and what properties must be attributed to the initial state of the mind/brain to account for its attainment. Insofar as these properties are language-specific, either individually or in the way they are organized and composed, there is a distinct language faculty.

Generative grammar is sometimes referred to as a theory, advocated by this or that person. In fact, it is not a theory any more than chemistry is a theory. Generative grammar is a topic, which one may or may not choose to study. Of course, one can adopt a point of view from which chemistry disappears as a discipline (perhaps it is all done by angels with mirrors). In this sense, a decision to study chemistry does stake out a position on matters of fact. Similarly, one may argue that the topic of generative grammar does not exist, although it is hard to see how to make this position minimally plausible. Within the study of generative grammar there have been many changes and differences of opinion, often reversion to ideas that had been abandoned and were later reconstructed in a different light. Evidently, this is a healthy phenomenon indicating that the discipline is alive, although it is sometimes, oddly, regarded as a serious deficiency, a sign that something is wrong with the basic approach. I will review some of these changes as we proceed.

In the mid-1950s, certain proposals were advanced as to the form that answers to the questions of (1) might take, and a research program was inaugurated to investigate the adequacy of these proposals and to sharpen and apply them. This program was one of the strands that led to the development of the cognitive sciences in the contemporary sense, sharing with other approaches the belief that certain aspects of the mind/brain can be usefully construed on the model of computational systems of rules that form and modify representations, and that are put to use in interpretation and action. From its origins (or with a longer perspective, one might say "its reincarnation") about 30 years ago, the study of generative grammar was undertaken with an eye to gaining some insight into the nature and origins of systems of knowledge, belief, and understanding more broadly, in the hope that these general questions could be illuminated by a detailed investigation of the special case of human language.

This research program has since been running its course, along a number of different paths. I will be concerned here with only one of these, with the problems it faced and the steps that were taken in an effort to deal with them. During the past 5–6 years, these efforts have converged in a somewhat unexpected way, yielding a rather different conception of the nature of language and its mental representation, one that offers interesting answers to a range of empirical questions and opens a variety of new ones to inquiry while suggesting a rethinking of the character of others. This is what accounts for an unmistakable sense of energy and anticipation—and also uncertainty—which is reminiscent of the period when the study of generative grammar in the modern sense was initiated about 30 years ago.

Some of the work now being done is quite different in character from what had previously been possible as well as considerably broader in empirical scope, and it may be that results of a rather new kind are within reach, or at least within sight. I would like to try to explain why this may be so, beginning with some remarks about goals, achievements, and failures of the past years.

To avoid misunderstanding, I am not speaking here about all of the study of language but rather of generative grammar, and even here I will not attempt anything like a real history of the course of research but rather will give a somewhat idealized picture that is in part clearer in retrospect than it was at the time. Furthermore, what I am describing has represented a minority position throughout, and probably still does, although in my view it is the correct one. A number of different current approaches share properties of the sort discussed here and may be intertranslatable to a considerable extent. I will not consider this important topic here and will also make no effort to survey the range of ideas, often conflicting, that fall within the particular tendency that I will discuss—what is now sometimes called "government-binding (GB) theory."

I want to consider, then, two major conceptual shifts, one that inaugurated the contemporary study of generative grammar, and a second, more theory-internal, that is now in process and that offers some new perspectives on traditional problems.[4]

Traditional and structuralist grammar did not deal with the questions of (1), the former because of its implicit reliance on the unanalyzed intelligence of the reader, the latter because of its narrowness of scope. The concerns of traditional and generative grammar are, in a certain sense, complementary: a good traditional or pedagogical grammar provides a full list of exceptions (irregular verbs, etc.), paradigms and examples of regular constructions, and observations at various levels of detail and generality about the form and meaning of expressions. But it does not examine the question of how the reader of the grammar uses such information to attain the knowledge that is used to form and interpret new expressions, or the question of the nature and elements of this knowledge: essentially the questions of (1), above. Without too much exaggeration, one could describe such a grammar as a structured and organized version of the data presented to a child learning a language, with some general commentary and often insightful observations. Generative grammar, in contrast, is concerned primarily with the intelligence of the reader, the principles and procedures brought to bear to attain full knowledge of a language. Structuralist theories, both in the European and American traditions, did concern themselves with analytic procedures for deriving aspects of grammar from data, as in the procedural theories of Nikolay Trubetzkoy, Zellig Harris, Bernard Bloch, and others, but primarily in the areas of phonology and morphology. The procedures suggested were seriously inadequate and in any event could not possibly be understood (and were not intended) to provide an answer to question (1ii), even in the narrower domains where most work was concentrated. Nor was there an effort to determine what was involved in offering a comprehensive account of the knowledge of the speaker/hearer.

As soon as these questions were squarely faced, a wide range of new phenomena were discovered, including quite simple ones that had passed unnoticed, and severe problems arose that had previously been ignored or seriously misunderstood. A standard belief 30 years ago was that language acquisition is a case of "overlearning." Language was regarded as a habit system, one that was assumed to be much overdetermined by available evidence. Production and interpretation of new forms was taken to be a straightforward matter of analogy, posing no problems of principle.[5] Attention to the questions of (1) quickly reveals that exactly the opposite is the case: language poses in a sharp and clear form what has sometimes been called "Plato's problem," the problem of "poverty of stimulus," of accounting for the richness, complexity, and specificity of shared knowledge, given the limitations of the data available. This difference of perception concerning where the problem lies—overlearning or poverty of evidence—reflects very clearly the effect of the shift of focus that inaugurated the study of generative grammar.

A great many examples have been given over the years to illustrate what clearly is the fundamental problem: the problem of poverty of evidence. A familiar example is the structure-dependence of rules, the fact that without instruction or direct evidence, children unerringly use computationally complex structure-dependent rules rather than computationally simple rules that involve only the predicate "leftmost" in a linear sequence of words.[6] To take some other examples, to which we will return, consider sentences (2)–(7):

I wonder who [the men expected to see them]   (2)
[the men expected to see them]   (3)
John ate an apple   (4)
John ate   (5)
John is too stubborn to talk to Bill   (6)
John is too stubborn to talk to   (7)

Both (2) and (3) include the clause bounded by brackets, but only in (2) may the pronoun *them* be referentially dependent on the antecedent *the men*; in (3) the pronoun is understood as referring in some manner indicated in the situational or discourse context, but not to the men. Numerous facts of this sort, falling under what is now generally called "binding theory," are known without relevant experience to differentiate the cases. Such facts pose a serious problem that was not recognized in earlier work: How does every child know, unerringly, to interpret the clause differently in the two cases? And why does no pedagogic grammar have to draw the learner's attention to such facts (which were, in fact, noticed only quite recently, in the course of the study of explicit rule systems in generative grammar)?

Turning to examples (4)–(7), sentence (5) means that John ate something or other, a fact that one might explain on the basis of a simple inductive procedure: *ate* takes an object, as in (4), and if the object is missing, it is understood as arbitrary. Applying the same inductive procedure to (6) and (7), it should be that (7) means that John is so stubborn that he (John) will not talk to some arbitrary person, on the analogy of (6). But the meaning is, in fact, quite different: namely, that John is so stubborn that some arbitrary person won't talk to him (John). Again, this is known without training or relevant evidence.[7]

The situation is, in fact, more complex. Although plausible, the inductive procedure suggested for the relatively straightforward examples (4)–(5) does not seem correct. As noted by Howard Lasnik, the word *eat* has a somewhat different meaning in its intransitive usage, something like *dine*. One can say "John ate his shoe," but "John ate" cannot be understood to include this case. The observation is general for such cases. The intransitive forms differ from normal intransitives in other respects; for example, we can form "the dancing bear" (corresponding to "the bear that dances"), but not "the eating man" (corresponding to "the man who eats").[8] Such facts pose further problems of poverty of stimulus.

Children do not make errors about the interpretation of such sentences as (6)–(7) past a certain stage of development, and if they did, the errors would largely be uncorrectable. It is doubtful that even the most compendious traditional or teaching grammar notes such simple facts as those illustrated in (2)–(7), and such observations lie far beyond the domain of structural grammars. A wide variety of examples of this sort immediately come to attention when one faces the questions formulated in (1).

Knowledge of language is often characterized as a practical ability to speak and understand, so that questions (1i) and (1iii) are closely related, perhaps identified. Ordinary usage makes a much sharper distinction between the two questions, and is right to do so. Two people may share exactly the same knowledge of language but differ markedly in their ability to put this knowledge to use. Ability to use language may improve or decline without any change in knowledge. This ability may also be impaired, selectively or in general, with no loss of knowledge, a fact that would become clear if injury leading to impairment recedes and lost ability is recovered. Many such considerations support the commonsense assumption that knowledge cannot be properly described as a practical ability. Furthermore, even if this view could somehow be maintained, it would leave open all of the serious questions. Thus, what is the nature of the "practical ability" manifested in our interpretation of the sentences (2)–(7), how is it properly described, and how is it acquired?

Often it is not immediately obvious what our knowledge of language entails in particular cases, a fact illustrated even with short and simple sentences such as (8)–(10):

his wife loves her husband   (8)
John is too clever to expect us to catch Bill   (9)
John is too clever to expect us to catch   (10)

In the case of (8), it takes some thought to determine whether *his* can be referentially dependent on *her husband* if *her* is dependent on *his wife*—that is, if the reference of either *he* or *she* is not somehow contextually indicated.[9] Examples (9) and (10) are, in fact, analogous to (6) and (7), respectively, but again, it takes some thought to discover that (10) means that John is so clever that an arbitrary person cannot expect us to catch him (John), although it is clear at once that it does not mean that John is so clever that he (John) cannot catch some arbitrary person, on the analogy of (9) (and (4), (5)). Our abilities seem limited somehow in such cases (and there are far more complex ones), but it would make little sense to speak of our knowledge of language as "limited" in any comparable way.

Suppose we insist on speaking of knowledge of language as a practical ability to speak and understand. Then normal usage must be revised in numerous cases such as those just discussed. Suppose that Jones takes a public speaking course and improves his ability to speak and understand without any change in his knowledge of English, as we would describe the situation in normal usage. We must now revise this common-sense usage and say, rather, that Jones has improved his $ability_1$ to use his $ability_2$ to speak and understand; similar translations are required in the other cases. But the two occurrences of "ability" in this description are hardly more than homonyms. $Ability_1$ is ability in the normal sense of the word: it can improve or decline, can be inadequate to determine consequences of knowledge, and so on. $Ability_2$, however, remains stable while our ability to use it changes, and we have this kind of "ability" even when we are unable to detect what it entails in concrete cases. In short, the neologism "$ability_2$" is invested with all the properties of knowledge. Note that there are cases when we do speak of abilities that we cannot put to use: for example, the case of swimmers who cannot swim because their hands are tied, although they retain the ability to swim. The cases in question are not of this sort, however.

The purpose of the attempt to reduce knowledge to ability is, presumably, to avoid problematic features that seem to inhere in the concept of knowledge, to show that these can be explained in dispositional or other terms more closely related to actual behavior (whether this is possible even in the case of $ability_1$, the normal sense, is another question). But nothing of the sort is achieved by this departure from ordinary usage; the problems remain, exactly as before, now embedded in terminological confusion. The task of determining the nature of our knowledge (= ability$_2$), and accounting for its origins and use, remains exactly as challenging as before, despite the terminological innovations.

Other examples similar to (8)–(10) raise further questions. Consider the following sentences:

> John is too stubborn to expect anyone to talk (11)
> to Bill

> John is too stubborn to visit anyone who talked (12)
> to Bill

Suppose we delete *Bill* from (11) and (12), yielding (13) and (14), respectively:

> John is too stubborn to expect anyone to talk to (13)

> John is too stubborn to visit anyone who talked to (14)

Sentence (13) is structurally analogous to (10), and is understood in the same manner: it means that John is so stubborn that an arbitrary person would not expect anyone to talk to him (John). "By analogy," then, we would expect sentence (14) to mean that John is so stubborn that an arbitrary person would not visit anyone who talked to him (John). But it does not have that meaning; in fact, it is gibberish. Here we have a double failure of analogy. Sentence (14) is not understood "on the analogy" of (4), (5), (6), (9), and (12) (hence meaning that John is so stubborn that he (John) would not visit anyone who talked to some arbitrary person), nor is it understood "on the analogy" of (7), (10), and (13); rather, it has no interpretation at all. And while the status of (11), (12), and (14) is immediately obvious, it takes some thought or preparation to see that (13) has the interpretation it does have, and thus to determine the consequences of our knowledge in this case.

Again, these are facts that we know, however difficult it may be to determine that our system of knowledge has these consequences. We know these facts without instruction or even direct evidence, surely without correction of error by the speech community. It would be absurd to try to teach such facts as these to people learning English as a second language, just as no one taught them to us or even presented us with evidence that could yield this knowledge by any generally reliable procedure. This is knowledge without grounds, without good reasons or support by reliable procedures in any general or otherwise useful sense of these notions. Were we to insist that knowledge is a kind of ability, we would have to claim that we lack the ability to understand "John is too stubborn to talk to" as meaning "John is too stubborn to talk to someone or other" (on the analogy of "John ate an apple"—"John ate"), and that we lack the ability to understand (14) on the analogy of "John ate an apple"—"John ate" (so that it means that John is too stubborn to visit anyone who talked to someone or other) or on the analogy of "John is too stubborn to talk to," with the "inversion strategy" that we somehow use in this case (so that (14) means that John is too stubborn for someone or other to visit anyone who talked to him, John). But these would be odd claims, to say the least. These are not failures of ability. It is not that we are too weak, or lack some special skill that could be acquired. We are perfectly capable of associating the sentence (14), for example, with either of the two meanings that would be provided "by analogy" (or others), but we know that these are not the associations that our knowledge of the language provides; ability is one thing, knowledge something quite different. The system of knowledge that has somehow developed in our minds has certain consequences, not others; it relates sound and meaning and assigns structural properties to physical events in certain ways, not others.

It seems that there is little hope in accounting for our knowledge in terms of such ideas as analogy, induction, association, reliable procedures, good reasons, and justification in any generally useful sense, or in terms of "generalized learning mechanisms" (if such exist). And it seems that we should follow normal usage in distinguishing clearly between knowledge and ability to use that knowledge. We should, so it appears, think of knowledge of language as a certain state of the mind/brain, a relatively stable element in transitory mental states once it is attained; furthermore, as a state of some distinguishable faculty of the mind—the language faculty—with its specific properties, structure, and organization, one "module" of the mind.[10]

NOTES

1. On these and many other discussions, primarily in the seventeenth–nineteenth centuries, see Chomsky (1966). For discussion of some misinterpretation of this work, see Bracken (1984).

2. The alleged *a priorism* of work in this tradition has often been exaggerated. See Chomsky (1966) and more recent work for discussion of this point.

3. The tradition, in this case, is a different one, represented in its most advanced form in the early work of the Indian grammarians 2,500 years ago. See Kiparsky (1982). A modern counterpart is Bloomfield (1939), which was radically different in character from the work of the period and inconsistent with his own theories of language, and remained virtually without influence or even awareness despite Bloomfield's great prestige.

4. See Newmeyer (1980) for one view of the history of this period prior to the second major conceptual shift; and for some more personal comments, the introduction to Chomsky (1975a), a somewhat abbreviated version of a 1956 revision of a 1955 manuscript, both unpublished. See Lightfoot (1982) and Hornstein and Lightfoot (1981) for discussion of the general backgrounds for much current work, and Radford (1981) for an introduction to the work that led to the second conceptual shift. See Chomsky (1981) for a more technical presentation of some of the ideas that entered into this conceptual shift and van Riemsdijk and Williams (1985) for an introductory study of this current work.

5. Although basically adopting this point of view, W.V. Quine, however, argued that there is a very severe, in fact, insuperable problem of underdetermination affecting all aspects of language and grammar, and much of psychology more generally (Quine, 1960, 1972). I do not think that he succeeded in showing that some novel form of indeterminacy affects the study of language beyond the normal underdetermination of theory by evidence; his own formulations of the thesis furthermore involve internal inconsistency (see Chomsky, 1975b, 1980b). There seems no reason on these grounds, then, to distinguish linguistics or psychology in principle from the natural sciences in accordance with what Hockney (1975) calls Quine's "bifurcation

thesis." A similar conclusion is reached by Putnam (1981) in his abandonment of metaphysical realism on Quinean grounds. His step also abandons the bifurcation thesis, although in the opposite direction.

6. See Chomsky (1975a). See Crain and Nakayama (1984) for empirical study of this question with 3–5-year-old children.

7. The reaction to such phenomena, also unnoticed until recently, again illustrates the difference of outlook of structuralist-descriptive and generative grammar. For some practitioners of the former, the statement of the facts, which is straightforward enough once they are observed, is the answer—nothing else is necessary; for the latter, the statement of the facts poses the problem to be solved. Cf. Ney (1983), particularly, his puzzlement about the "peculiar view of grammar [that] unnecessarily complicates the whole matter" by seeking an explanation for the facts. Note that there is no question of right or wrong here, but rather of topic of inquiry.

8. In early work, such facts were used to motivate an analysis of intransitives such as *eat* as derived from corresponding transitives by a system of ordered rules that excluded the unwanted cases; see Chomsky (1962).

9. On structures of this type, and problems of binding theory, more generally, see Higginbotham (1938a), among much other work.

10. See Fodor (1983). But it is too narrow to regard the "language module" as an input system in Fodor's sense, if only because it is used in speaking and thought. We might consider supplementing this picture by adding an "output system," but plainly this must be linked to the input system; we do not expect a person to speak only English and understand only Japanese. That is, the input and output systems must each access a fixed system of knowledge. The latter, however, is a central system which has essential problems of modularity, a fact that brings the entire picture into question. Furthermore, even regarded as an input system, the language module does not appear to have the property of rapidity of access that Fodor discusses, as indicated by (8)–(14). Note also that even if Fodor is right in believing that there is a sharp distinction between modules in his sense and "the rest," which is holistic in several respects, it does not follow that the residue is unstructured. In fact, this seems highly unlikely, if only because of the "epistemic boundedness" that he notes. Many other questions arise concerning Fodor's very intriguing discussion of these issues, which I will not pursue here.

2   Concepts of Language

2.1   THE COMMONSENSE CONCEPT AND DEPARTURES FROM IT

Let us turn now to the questions of (1) of Chapter 1. To begin with, let us distinguish the intuitive, pretheoretic commonsense notion of language from various technical concepts that have been proposed with the intent of developing an eventual science of language. Let us call the latter "scientific approaches" to language, with an eye directed more toward a possible future than a present reality, some might argue. The scientific approaches, I believe without exception, depart from the commonsense notion in several ways; these departures also affect the concepts of knowledge or understanding of language, use of language, rule of language, rule-guided linguistic behavior, and others.

In the first place, the commonsense notion of language has a crucial sociopolitical dimension. We speak of Chinese as "a language," although the various "Chinese dialects" are as diverse as the several Romance languages. We speak of Dutch and German as two separate languages, although some dialects of German are very close to dialects that we call "Dutch" and are not mutually intelligible with others that we call "German." A standard remark in introductory linguistics courses is that a language is a dialect with an army and a navy (attributed to Max Weinreich). That any coherent account can be given of "language" in this sense is doubtful; surely, none has been offered or even seriously attempted. Rather, all scientific approaches have simply abandoned these elements of what is called "language" in common usage.[1]

15

The commonsense notion also has a normative-teleological element that is eliminated from scientific approaches. I do not refer here to prescriptive grammar but to something else. Consider the way we describe a child or a foreigner learning English. We have no way of referring directly to what that person knows: It is not English, nor is it some other language that resembles English. We do not, for example, say that the person has a perfect knowledge of some language L, similar to English but still different from it. What we say is that the child or foreigner has a "partial knowledge of English," or is "on his or her way" toward acquiring knowledge of English, and if they reach the goal, they will then know English. Whether or not a coherent account can be given of this aspect of the commonsense terminology, it does not seem to be one that has any role in an eventual science of language.

I will follow standard practice in disregarding these aspects of the commonsense notions of language and the associated notions of rule-following and so forth, although the departure should be noted, and one may ask whether it is entirely innocent.

Modern linguistics commonly avoided these questions by considering an idealized "speech community" that is internally consistent in its linguistic practice.[2] For Leonard Bloomfield, for example, a language is "the totality of utterances that can be made in a speech community," regarded as homogeneous (Bloomfield, 1928/1957). In other scientific approaches, the same assumption enters in one or another form, explicitly or tacitly, in identification of the object of inquiry. No attempt is made to capture or formulate any concept with the sociopolitical or normative-teleogical aspects of informal usage of the term "language." The same is true of approaches that understand language to be a social product in accordance with the Saussurean concept of "langue."

Of course, it is understood that speech communities in the Bloomfieldian sense—that is, collections of individuals with the same speech behavior[3]—do not exist in the real world. Each individual has acquired a language in the course of complex social interactions with people who vary in the ways in which they speak and interpret what they hear and in the internal representations that underlie their use of language. Structural linguistics abstracted from these facts in its attempts at theory construction; we also abstract from these facts in posing questions (1) of Chapter 1, considering only the case of a person presented with uniform experience in an ideal Bloomfieldian speech community with no dialect diversity and no variation among speakers.

We should also make note of a more subtle theory-internal assumption: The language of the hypothesized speech community, apart from being uniform, is taken to be a "pure" instance of UG in a sense that must be made precise, and to which we will return. We exclude, for example, a speech community of uniform speakers, each of whom speaks a mixture of Russian and French (say, an idealized version of the nineteenth-century Russian aristocracy). The language of such a speech community would not be "pure" in the relevant sense, because it would not represent a single set of choices among the options permitted by UG but rather would include "contradictory" choices for certain of these options.

Questions (1) of Chapter 1, then, arise initially under these idealizations, and the same is true, in effect, of other approaches to language, although the fact is often not explicitly recognized and may even sometimes be denied.

The legitimacy of these idealizations has sometimes been questioned, but on dubious grounds.[4] Indeed, they seem indispensable. Surely there is some property of mind P that would enable a person to acquire a language under conditions of pure and uniform experience, and surely P (characterized by UG) is put to use under the real conditions of language acquisition. To deny these assumptions would be bizarre indeed: It would be to claim either that language can be learned only under conditions of diversity and conflicting evidence, which is absurd, or that the property P exists—there exists a capacity to learn language in the pure and uniform case—but the actual learning of language does not involve this capacity. In the latter case, we would ask why P exists; is it a "vestigial organ" of some sort? The natural approach, and one that I think is tacitly adopted even by those who deny the fact, is to attempt to determine the real property of mind P, and then ask how P functions under the more complex conditions of actual linguistic diversity. It seems clear that any reasonable study of the nature, acquisition, and use of language in real life circumstances must accept these assumptions and then proceed on the basis of some tentative characterization of the property of mind P. In short, the idealizations made explicit in more careful work are hardly controversial; they isolate for examination a property of the language faculty the existence of which is hardly in doubt, and which is surely a crucial element in actual language acquisition.

By making these idealizations explicit and pursuing our inquiry in accordance with them, we do not in any way prejudice the study of language as a social product. On the contrary, it is difficult to imagine how such studies might fruitfully progress without taking into account the real properties of mind that enter into the acquisition of language, specifically, the properties of the initial state of the language faculty characterized by UG.

Note also that the study of language and UG, conducted within the framework of individual psychology, allows for the possibility that the state of knowledge attained may itself include some kind of reference to the social nature of language. Consider, for example, what Putnam (1975) has called "the division of linguistic labor." In the language of a given individual, many words are semantically indeterminate in a special sense: The person will defer to "experts" to sharpen or fix their reference. Suppose, for example, that someone knows that yawls and ketches are sailing vessels but is unsure of the exact reference of the words "yawl" and "ketch," leaving it to specialists to fix this reference. In the lexicon of this person's language, the entries for "yawl" and "ketch" will be specified to the extent of his or her knowledge, with an indication that details are to be filled in by others, an idea that can be made precise in various ways but without going beyond the study of the system of knowledge of language of a particular individual. Other social aspects of language can be regarded in a like manner—although this is not to deny the possibility or value of other kinds of study of language that incorporate social structure and interaction. Contrary to what is sometimes thought, no conflicts of principle or practice arise in this connection.

We are also assuming another idealization: That the property of mind described by UG is a species characteristic, common to all humans. We thus abstract from possible variation among humans in the language faculty. It is plausible to suppose that apart from pathology (potentially an important area of inquiry), such variation as there may be is marginal and can be safely ignored across a broad range of linguistic investigation. Again, the assumption is conventional, though generally explicit, in scientific in scientific approaches. Weaker assumptions than strict identity would suffice for the discussion below, but this stronger assumption seems a reasonable one, to a very good approximation, and I will keep to it here.

2.2 EXTERNALIZED LANGUAGE

Scientific approaches to language, in the sense of the term used earlier, have developed various technical notions of language to replace the commonsense notion. The term "grammar" has also been used in a variety of ways. In conventional usage, a grammar is a description or theory of a language, an object constructed by a linguist. Let us keep to this usage. Then associated with the various technical notions of language there are corresponding notions of grammar and of universal grammar (UG).

Structural and descriptive linguistics, behavioral psychology, and other contemporary approaches tended to view a language as a collection of actions, or utterances, or linguistic forms (words, sentences) paired with meanings, or as a system of linguistic forms or events. In Saussurean structuralism, a language (*langue*) was taken to be a system of sounds and an associated system of concepts; the notion of sentence was left in a kind of limbo, perhaps to be accommodated within the study of language use. For Bloomfield, as noted earlier, a language is "the totality of utterances that can be made in a speech community." The American variety of structural-descriptive linguistics that was heavily influenced by Bloomfield's ideas furthermore concentrated primarily on sound and word structure, apart from various proposals, notably those of Zellig Harris, as to how larger units (phrases) could be constructed by analytic principles modelled on those introduced for phonology and morphology.[5] Many researchers today adopt a position of the sort lucidly developed by David Lewis, who defines a language as a pairing of sentences and meanings (the latter taken to be set-theoretic constructions in terms of possible worlds) over an infinite range, where the language is "used by a population" when certain regularities "in action or belief" hold among the population with reference to the language, sustained by an interest in communication.[6]

Let us refer to such technical concepts as instances of "externalized language" (E-language), in the sense that the construct is understood independently of the properties of the mind/brain. Under the same rubric we may include the notion of language as a collection (or system) of actions or behaviors of some sort. From a point of view such as this, a grammar is a collection of descriptive statements concerning the E-language, the actual or potential speech events (perhaps along with some account of their context of use or semantic content). In technical terms, the grammar may be regarded as a function that enumerates the elements of the E-language. Sometimes, grammar has been regarded as a property of E-language, as in Bloomfield's remark that a grammar is "the meaningful arrangement of forms in a language" (Bloomfield, 1933). Despite appearances, the problem of accounting for the unbounded character of the E-language and the person's knowledge of language including this fundamental property is not squarely addressed in such approaches, a matter to which we will return.

The E-language is now understood to be the real object of study. Grammar is a derivative notion; the linguist is free to select the grammar one way or another as long as it correctly identifies the E-language. Apart from this consideration, questions of truth and falsity do not arise. Quine, for example, has argued that it is senseless to take one grammar rather than another to be "correct" if they are extensionally equivalent, characterizing the same E-language, for him a set of expressions (Quine, 1972). And Lewis doubts that there is any way "to make objective sense of the assertion that a grammar G is used by a population P whereas another grammar G', which generates the same language as G, is not."

The notion of E-language is familiar from the study of formal systems, as is the conclusion just cited: In the case of the "language of arithmetic," for example, there is no objective sense to the idea that one set of rules that generates the well-formed formulas is correct and another wrong.

As for UG, to the extent that such a study was recognized as legitimate, this theory would consist of statements that are true of many or all human languages, perhaps a set of conditions satisfied by the E-languages that count as human languages. Some appeared to deny the possibility of the enterprise, for example, Martin Joos, who put forth what he called the "Boasian" view that "languages could differ from each other without limit and in unpredictable ways," echoing William Dwight Whitney's reference to "the infinite diversity of human speech" and Edward Sapir's notion that "language is a human activity that varies without assignable limit."[7] Such statements reflect a fairly broad consensus of the time. Although they could hardly have been intended literally, they did express a relativistic impulse that denigrated the study of UG. More precisely, it cannot be that human language varies without assignable limit, although it might be true that it is "infinitely diverse"; it is an empirical question of some interest whether UG permits an infinite variety of possible languages (or a variety that is infinite in more than structurally trivial respects, say, with no bound on vocabulary), or only a finite diversity.[8]

Nevertheless, significant contributions were made to UG in our sense within these traditions. For example, the theory of distinctive features in phonology, which greatly influenced structuralist studies in other fields, postulated a fixed inventory of "atomic elements" from which phonological systems could be drawn, with certain general laws and implicational relations governing the choice. And it was generally assumed that such notions as topic and comment, or subject and predicate, were universal features of language, reflecting the fact that a declarative sentence is about something and says something about it. Later, important work on linguistic universals was conducted by Joseph Greenberg and others, yielding many generalizations that require explanation, for example, the fact that if a language has subject-object-verb order, it will tend to have postpositions rather than prepositions, and so on.

Along these lines, then, we may develop a certain technical concept of language (E-language), and an associated concept of grammar and UG, as a basis for a scientific study of language. Many different specific ideas fall roughly within this general framework.

2.3 INTERNALIZED LANGUAGE

A rather different approach was taken, for example, by Otto Jespersen, who held that there is some "notion of structure" in the mind of the speaker "which is definite enough to guide him in framing sentences of his own," in particular, "free expressions" that may be new to the speaker and to others.[9] Let us refer to this "notion of structure" as an "internalized language" (I-language). The I-language, then, is some element of the mind of the person who knows the language, acquired by the learner, and used by the speaker-hearer.

Taking language to be I-language, the grammar would then be a theory of the I-language, which is the object under investigation. And if, indeed, such a "notion of structure" exists, as Jespersen held, then questions of truth and falsity arise for grammar as they do for any scientific theory. This way of approaching the questions of language is radically different from the one sketched above and leads to a very different conception of the nature of the inquiry.

Let us return now to the point of view outlined in Chapter 1. Knowing the language L is a property of a person H; one task of the brain sciences is to determine what it is about H's brain by virtue of which this property holds. We suggested that for H to know the language L is for H's mind/brain to be in a certain state; more narrowly, for the language faculty, one module of this system, to be in a certain state S_L.[10] One task of the brain sciences, then, is to discover the mechanisms that are the physical realization of the state S_L.

Suppose we analyze the notion "H knows language L" in relational terms, that is, as involving a relation R (knowing, having, or whatever) holding between H and an abstract entity L. One might question this move; we speak of a person as knowing U.S. history without assuming that there is an entity, U.S. history, that the person knows, or knows in part. Let us, however, assume the move to be legitimate in this case. The assumption will be justified to the extent that this move contributes to providing insight into the questions that primarily concern us, those of (1) of Chapter 1; this would be the case, for example, if there are significant principles governing the set of postulated entities L. Suppose that we proceed further to regard talk of mind as talk about the brain undertaken at a certain level of abstraction at which we believe, rightly or wrongly, that significant properties and explanatory principles can be discovered. Then statements about R and L belong to the theory of mind, and one task of the brain sciences will be to explain what it is about H's brain (in particular, its language faculty) that corresponds to H's knowing L, that is, by virtue of which R(H, L) holds and the statement that R(H, L) is true.

It is natural to take L to be I-language, Jespersen's "notion of structure," regarding this as an entity abstracted from a state of the language faculty, the latter being one component of the mind. Then, for H to know L is for H to have a certain I-language. The statements of a grammar are statements of the theory of mind about the I-language, hence statements about structures of the brain formulated at a certain level of abstraction from mechanisms. These structures are specific things in the world, with their specific properties. The statements of a grammar or the statement that R(H, L) are similar to statements of a physical theory that characterizes certain entities and their properties in abstraction from whatever may turn out to be the mechanisms that account for these properties: say, a nineteenth-century theory about valence or properties expressed in the periodic table. Statements about I-language or the statement that R(H, L) (for various choices of H and L) are true or false, much in the way that statements about the chemical structure of benzene, or about the valence of oxygen, or about chlorine and fluorine being in the same column of the periodic table are true or false. The I-language L may be the one used by a speaker but not the I-language L', even if the two generate the same class of expressions (or other formal objects) in whatever precise sense we give to this derivative notion; L' may not even be a possible human I-language, one attainable by the language faculty.

UG now is construed as the theory of human I-languages, a system of conditions deriving from the human biological endowment that identifies the I-languages that are humanly accessible under normal conditions. These are the I-languages L such that R(H, L) may be true (for normal H, under normal conditions).[11]

Of course, there is no guarantee that this way of approaching the problems of (1) in Chapter 1 is the correct one. This approach may turn out to be thoroughly misguided, even if it achieves substantial success—just as a theory of valence, etc. might have turned out to be completely off the track, despite its substantial success in nineteenth-century chemistry. It is always reasonable to consider alternative approaches, if they can be devised, and this will remain true no matter what successes are achieved. The situation does not seem different in principle from what we find in other areas of empirical inquiry. I will suggest directly that in certain fundamental respects early ideas about I-language were misguided and should be replaced by a rather different conception, although one formulated in the same general framework. The reasons, however, do not derive from any incoherence or flaw in the general approach but rather from empirical considerations of description and explanation.

2.4   THE SHIFT OF FOCUS FROM E-LANGUAGE TO I-LANGUAGE

2.4.1   On the Reasons for the Shift of Focus

In Chapter 1, we saw that the study of generative grammar shifted the focus of attention from actual or potential behavior and the products of behavior to the system of knowledge that underlies the use and understanding of language, and more deeply, to the innate endowment that makes it possible for humans to attain such knowledge. The shift in focus was from the study of E-language to the study of I-language, from the study of language regarded as an externalized object to the study of the system of knowledge of language attained and internally represented in the mind/brain. A generative grammar is not a set of statements about externalized objects constructed in some manner. Rather, it purports to depict exactly what one knows when one knows a language: that is, what has been learned, as supplemented by innate principles. UG is a characterization of these innate, biologically determined principles, which constitute one component of the human mind—the language faculty.

With this shift of focus, we at once face the questions (1) of Chapter 1. In the earliest work, the answer to (1i) was taken to be that knowledge of language is knowledge of a certain rule system; the answer to (1ii), that this knowledge arises from an initial state S_0 that converts experience to a "steady state" S_s, which incorporates an I-language. Acquisition of language is, then, a matter of adding to one's store of rules, or modifying this system, as new data are processed. Question (1iii) breaks down into two parts: a "perception problem" and a "production problem." The perception problem would be dealt with by construction of a parser that incorporates the rules of the I-language along with other elements: a certain organization of memory and access (perhaps a deterministic pushdown structure with buffer of a certain size; see Marcus, 1980), certain heuristics, and so forth. A parser should not map expressions into their structures in the way that these are associated by the I-language. For example, a parser should fail to do so in the case of so-called "garden-path sentences"[12] or sentences that overload memory for left-to-right pass, it should mirror the difficulties experienced with sentences such as (8)–(14) of Chapter 1 and so forth. The production problem is considerably more obscure; we will return to that.

The E-language that was the object of study in most of traditional or structuralist grammar or behavioral psychology is now regarded as an epiphenomenon at best. Its status is similar to that of other derivative objects, say, the set of rhyming pairs, which is also determined by the I-language that constitutes the system of knowledge attained. One might argue that the status of the E-language is considerably more obscure than that of the set of rhyming pairs, since the latter is determined in a fairly definite way by the I-language whereas the bounds of E-language can be set one way or another, depending on some rather arbitrary decisions as to what it should include.

Summarizing, then, we have the following general picture. The language faculty is a distinct system of the mind/brain, with an initial state S_0 common to the species (to a very close first approximation, apart from pathology, etc.) and apparently unique to it in essential respects.[13] Given appropriate experience, this faculty passes from the state S_0 to some relatively stable steady state S_s, which then undergoes only peripheral modification (say, acquiring new vocabulary items). The attained state incorporates an I-language (it is the state of having or knowing a particular I-language). UG is the theory of S_0; particular grammars are theories of various I-languages. The I-languages that can be attained with S_0 fixed and experience varying are the attainable human languages, where by "language" we now mean I-language. The steady state has two components that can be distinguished analytically, however, they may be merged and intertwined: a component that is specific to the language in question and the contribution of the initial state. The former constitutes what is "learned"—if this is the appropriate concept to employ in accounting for the transition from the initial to the mature state of the language faculty; it may well not be.[14]

The system of knowledge attained—the I-language— assigns a status to every relevant physical event, say, every sound wave. Some are sentences with a definite meaning (literal, figurative, or whatever). Some are intelligible with, perhaps, a definite meaning, but are ill-formed in one way or another ("the child seems sleeping"; "to whom did you wonder what to give?" in some dialects; "who do you wonder to whom gave the book?" in all dialects). Some are well formed but unintelligible. Some are assigned a phonetic representation but no more; they are identified as possible sentences of some language, but not mine. Some are mere noise. There are many possibilities. Different I-languages will assign status differently in each of these and other categories. The notion of E-language has no place in this picture. There is no issue of correctness with regard to E-languages, however characterized, because E-languages are mere artifacts. We can define "E-language" in one way or another or not at all, since the concept appears to play no role in the theory of language.

The shift of focus from E- to I-language, reviving and modifying much older traditions, was very much in order. The technical concept of E-language is a dubious one in at least two respects. In the first place, as just observed, languages in this sense are not real-world objects but are artificial, somewhat arbitrary, and perhaps not very interesting constructs. In contrast, the steady state of knowledge attained and the initial state S_0 are real elements of particular mind/brains, aspects of the physical world, where we understand mental states and representations to be physically encoded in some manner. The I-language is abstracted directly as a component of the state attained. Statements about I-language, about the steady state, and about the initial state S_0 are true or false statements about something real and definite, about actual states of the mind/

brain and their components (under the idealizations already discussed). UG and theories of I-languages, universal and particular grammars, are on a par with scientific theories in other domains; theories of E-languages, if sensible at all, have some different and more obscure status because there is no corresponding real-world object. Linguistics, conceived as the study of I-language and S_0, becomes part of psychology, ultimately biology. Linguistics will be incorporated within the natural sciences insofar as mechanisms are discovered that have the properties revealed in these more abstract studies; indeed, one would expect that these studies will be a necessary step toward serious investigation of mechanisms.[15] To put it differently, E-language, however construed, is further removed from mechanisms than I-language, at a higher order of abstraction. Correspondingly, the concept raises a host of new problems, and it is not at all clear whether they are worth addressing or trying to solve, given the artificial nature of the construct and its apparent uselessness for the theory of language.

The shift of focus is also, arguably, a shift toward the commonsense notion of language. This matter is less important than the move toward realism and also much less clear, because, as noted, all of these approaches deviate from the commonsense concept in certain respects. But it seems that when we speak of a person as knowing a language, we do not mean that he or she knows an infinite set of sentences, or sound-meaning pairs taken in extension, or a set of acts or behaviors; rather, what we mean is that the person knows what makes sound and meaning relate to one another in a specific way, what makes them "hang together," a particular characterization of a function, perhaps. The person has "a notion of structure" and knows an I-language as characterized by the linguist's grammar. When we say that it is a rule of English that objects follow verbs, as distinct from the rule of Japanese that verbs follow objects, we are not saying that this is a rule of some set of sentences or behaviors, but rather that it is a rule of a system of rules, English, an I-language. The rules of the language are not rules of some infinite set of formal objects or potential actions but are rules that form or constitute the language, like Articles of the Constitution or rules of chess (not a set of moves, but a game, a particular rule system). Of the various technical notions that have been developed in the study of language, the concept of I-language seems closer to the commonsense notion than others.

The shift of perspective from the technical concept E-language to the technical concept I-language taken as the object of inquiry is therefore a shift toward realism in two respects: toward the study of a real object rather than an artificial construct, and toward the study of what we really mean by "a language" or "knowledge of language" in informal usage (again, abstracting from sociopolitical and normative-teleological factors).

Of these two considerations, the first is the clearer and more important. It is not to be expected that the concepts that are appropriate for the description and understanding of some system of the physical world (say, I-language and S_0) will include the sometimes similar concepts of normal discourse, just as the physicist's concepts of energy or mass are not those of ordinary usage. Furthermore, many questions arise about the usage of the intuitive concepts that have no obvious relevance to the inquiry into the nature of the real objects, I-language and S_0. Suppose, for example, that a Martian with a quite different kind of mind/brain were to produce and to understand sentences of English as we do, but as investigation would show, using quite different elements and rules—say, without words, the smallest units being memorized phrases, and with a totally different rule system and UG. Would we then say that the Martian is speaking the same language? Within what limits would we say this? Similar questions arise as to whether an artificial system is exhibiting some form of intelligence or understanding. These may be reasonable questions concerning the intuitive concepts of language and the like in colloquial usage, but it is not clear that they have much bearing on the inquiry into the real-world objects, I-language and the initial state S_0.[16]

The conceptual shift from E-language to I-language, from behavior and its products to the system of knowledge that enters into behavior, was in part obscured by accidents of publishing history, and expository passages taken out of context have given rise to occasional misunderstanding.[17] Some questionable terminological decisions also contributed to misunderstanding. In the literature of generative grammar, the term "language" has regularly been used for E-language in the sense of a set of well-formed sentences, more or less along the lines of Bloomfield's definition of "language" as a "totality of utterances." The term "grammar" was then used with systematic ambiguity, to refer to what we have here called "I-language" and also to the linguist's theory of the I-language; the same was true of the term UG, introduced later with the same systematic ambiguity, referring to S_0 and the theory of S_0. Because the focus of attention was on I-language, E-language being a derivative and largely artificial construct, we find the paradoxical situation that in work devoted to language, the term "language" barely appears. In my 1965 book *Aspects of the Theory of Syntax*, for example, there is no entry for "language" in the index, but many entries under "grammar," generally referring to I-language.

It would have been preferable to use the term "language" in something closer to the intuitive sense of informal usage; that is, to use the term "language" as a technical term in place of "(generative) grammar" (in the sense of I-language) while adopting some technical term (perhaps "E-language") for what was called "language." The term "(generative) grammar" would then have naturally been used for the linguist's theory of the (I-) language, along the lines of the preceding discussion. Much confusion might have been spared in this way. I suspect that the debate in past years over the alleged problems concerning the concepts grammar and knowledge of grammar may in part be traced to these unfortunate terminological choices, which reinforced inappropriate analogies to the formal sciences and gave rise to the erroneous idea that the study of grammar poses new, complex, and perhaps intractable philosophical issues compared with the study of E-language.[18]

The misleading choice of terms was, in part, a historical accident. The study of generative grammar developed from the confluence of two intellectual traditions: traditional and structuralist grammar, and the study of formal systems. Although there are important precursors, it was not until the mid-1950s that these intellectual currents truly merged, as ideas adapted from the study of formal systems came to be applied to the far more complex systems of natural language in something approaching their actual richness, and in subsequent years, their actual variety, thus making it possible, really for the first time, to give some substance to Humboldt's aphorism that language involves "the infinite use of finite means," the "finite means" being those that constitute the I-language.

But the study of formal languages was misleading in this regard. When we study, say, the language of arithmetic, we may take it to be a "given" abstract object: an infinite class of sentences in some given notation. Certain expressions in this notation are well-formed sentences, others are not. And of the well-formed sentences, some express arithmetical truths, some do not. A "grammar" for such a system is simply some set of rules that specifies exactly the well-formed sentences. In this case, there is no further question of the correct choice of grammar, and there is no truth or falsity to the matter of choosing among such grammars. Much the same is true of alternative axiomatizations, although in this case we know that none of them will capture exactly the truths. It is easy to see how one might take over from the study of formal languages the idea that the "language" is somehow given as a set of sentences or sentence-meaning pairs, while the grammar is some characterization of this infinite set of objects, hence, it might be thought, a construct that may be selected one way or another depending on convenience or other extraneous concerns. The move is understandable, but misguided, and it has engendered much pointless discussion and controversy.

Recall Quine's conclusion, cited above (p. 20), that it is senseless to take one grammar rather than another to be "correct" if they are extensionally equivalent, and Lewis's doubts that there is any way "to make objective sense of the assertion that a grammar G is used by a population P whereas another grammar G', which generates the same language as G, is not." It is quite true that for every E-language, however we choose to define this notion, there are many grammars (i.e., many grammars, each of which is a theory of a particular I-language that, under some convention that one has adopted, determines this E-language). But this is a matter of no consequence. In the case of some formal system, say arithmetic (presumably the model in mind), we assume the class of well-formed formulas in some notation to be "given," and we select the "grammar" (the rules of formation) as we please. But the E-language is not "given." What is "given" to the child is some finite array of data, on the basis of which the child's mind (incorporating S_0) constructs an I-language that assigns a status to every expression, and that we may think of as generating some E-language under one or another stipulated convention (or we may dispense with this apparently superfluous step). What is given to the linguist are finite arrays of data from various speech communities, including much data not available to the language learner, on the basis of which the linguist will attempt to discover the nature of S_0 and of the particular I-languages attained. The account presented by Quine, Lewis, and others has the story backwards: E-languages are not given, but are derivative, more remote from data and from mechanisms than I-languages and the grammars that are theories of I-languages; the choice of E-language therefore raises a host of new and additional problems beyond those connected with grammar and I-language. Whether it is worthwhile addressing or attempting to solve these problems is not at all clear, because the concept of E-language, however construed, appears to have no significance. The belief that E-language is a fairly clear notion whereas I-language or grammar raises serious, perhaps intractable philosophical problems, is quite mistaken. Just the opposite is true. There are numerous problems concerning the notions I-language and grammar, but not the ones raised in these discussions.

It should be noted that familiar characterizations of "language" as a code or a game point correctly toward I-language, not the artificial construct E-language. A code is not a set of representations but rather a specific system of rules that assigns coded representations to message-representations. Two codes may be different, although extensionally identical in the message-code pairings that they provide. Similarly, a game is not a set of moves but rather the rule system that underlies them. The Saussurean concept of *langue*, although far too narrow in conception, might be interpreted as appropriate in this respect. The same is true of Quine's definition of a language as a "complex of present dispositions to verbal behavior" insofar as it focuses on some internal state rather than E-language, although it is unacceptable for other reasons: Thus, two individuals who speak the same language may differ radically in their dispositions to verbal behavior, and if dispositions are characterized in terms of probability of response under given conditions, then it is impossible to identify languages in these terms; and again, the fundamental question of the use and understanding of new sentences is left without any explanation. Perhaps the clearest account is Jespersen's in terms of the "notion of structure" that guides the speaker "in framing sentences of his own...," these being "free expressions."

As we have seen, these ideas became the focus of attention in the study of generative grammar, although not without controversy. Saussurean structuralism had placed Jespersen's observation about "free expressions" outside of the scope of the study of language structure, of Saussure's *langue*. Bloomfield (1933) held that when a speaker produces speech forms that he has not heard, "we say that he utters them *on the analogy* of similar forms which he has heard," a position later adopted by Quine, C.F. Hockett, and the few others who even attempted to deal with the problem. This idea is not wrong but rather is vacuous until the concept of analogy is spelled out in a way that explains why certain "analogies" are somehow valid whereas others are not, a task that requires a radically different approach to the whole question. Why, for example, are sentences (6) and (7) of Chapter 1 (p. 8) not understood "on the analogy" of (4) and (5)? Why is sentence (14) not understood "on the analogy" of *any* of the earlier examples, in fact given no interpretation at all? We can give substance to the proposal by explaining "analogy" in terms of I-language, a system of rules and principles that assigns representations of form and meaning to linguistic expressions, but no other way to do so has been proposed; and with this necessary revision in the proposal, it becomes clear that "analogy" is simply an inappropriate concept in the first place.

I have been freely using various commonsense notions such as "knowledge," "rule-following," and so forth in this account. Various questions have been raised about the legitimacy of this usage. I will put these questions off for now, returning to them in Chapter 4, but meanwhile continuing to use the terms. I think the usage here is reasonably in accord with common usage, but nothing of great moment is at stake, and one could introduce technical terms for our purposes, giving them the meaning required for this discussion.

Sometimes it has been suggested that knowledge of language should be understood on the analogy of knowledge of arithmetic, arithmetic being taken to be an abstract "Platonic" entity that exists apart from any mental structures.[19] It is not in question here that there does exist what we have called an internalized language (described by what Thomas Bever calls "a psychogrammar") and that it is a problem of the natural sciences to discover it. What is claimed is that apart from particular I-languages, there is something else additional, what we might call "P-languages" (P-English, P-Japanese, etc.), existing in a Platonic heaven alongside of arithmetic and (perhaps) set theory, and that a person who we say knows English may not, in fact, have complete knowledge of P-English, or, indeed, may not know it at all. Similarly, the best theory of the I-language, of what this person actually knows, might not be the best theory of what is selected on some grounds to be P-English.[20]

The analogy to arithmetic is, however, quite unpersuasive. In the case of arithmetic, there is at least a certain initial plausibility to a Platonistic view insofar as the truths of arithmetic are what they are, independent of any facts of individual psychology, and we seem to discover these truths somewhat in the way that we discover facts about the physical world. In the case of language, however, the corresponding position is wholly without merit. There is no initial plausibility to the idea that apart from the truths of grammar concerning the I-language and the truths of UG concerning S_0 there is an additional domain of fact about P-language, independent of any psychological states of individuals. Knowing everything about the mind/brain, a Platonist would argue, we still have no basis for determining the truths of arithmetic or set theory, but there is not the slightest reason to suppose that there are truths of language that would still escape our grasp. Of course, one can construct abstract entities at will, and we can decide to call some of them "English" or "Japanese" and to define "linguistics" as the study of these abstract objects, and thus not part of the natural sciences, which are concerned with such entities as

I-language and S_0, with grammar and universal grammar in the sense of the earlier discussion. But there seems little point to such moves.

A somewhat similar conception is advanced by Soames (1984). He distinguishes between two disciplines, psychology and linguistics, each defined by certain "Leading Questions," which are different for the two disciplines. The study of I-language and S_0, as described above, is part of psychology. However, "If one's goal is to answer the Leading Questions of linguistics, one will abstract away from psycholinguistic data that are not constitutive of languages" (and similarly, from neurophysiological data, etc.). The "Leading Questions" of linguistics include, for example, the questions, "In what ways are English and Italian alike?," "In what ways has English changed" in the course of its history?, and so forth. The concepts English and Italian are taken to be clear enough pretheoretically to give these Leading Questions content, a highly dubious assumption for reasons already discussed, and surely not one made in actual linguistic research. Again, no question is raised here about the legitimacy of the investigation of I-language and S_0; rather, the question is whether this study falls under what we will decide to call "linguistics" and whether there is, as Soames urges, "a theoretically sound, empirically significant conception of linguistics" that restricts itself to a certain stipulated domain of evidence, to facts that are "constitutive of language."

One might point out that the terminological proposals that Soames advances are a bit eccentric. It seems odd, to say the least, to define "linguistics" so as to exclude many of its major practitioners—for example, Roman Jakobson and Edward Sapir, who would surely not have agreed that what Soames regards as extralinguistic data are irrelevant to the questions of linguistics as they understood them, including the "Leading Questions," and who, in support of their analyses, adduced evidence of a sort that Soames places outside of that "constitutive of language." But putting aside terminology, the real question that arises is whether there is any reason to establish a discipline of "linguistics" that restricts itself on a priori grounds to some particular data and constructs a concept of "language" that can be studied within this choice of relevant data.

To clarify what is at stake, suppose that two proposed grammars G_1 and G_2 differ in the choice of phonological features postulated: G_1 postulates the system F_1, and G_2, the system F_2. Suppose that G_1 and G_2 are not distinguishable with respect to a data base consisting of what Soames stipulates to be the "linguistically relevant" facts. Suppose that perceptual experiments of the sort Sapir conducted in his classic work, or other more sophisticated ones, yield results that can be explained in terms of the features of F_1 but not F_2. Imagine further that studies of aphasia and child language show that language breakdown and growth can be explained along Jakobsonian lines in terms of F_1 but not F_2, and that the choice of F_1 but not F_2 provides an account for speech production and recognition, again along Jakobsonian lines. Soames agrees that there is a field of inquiry, call it "C(ognitive)-linguistics," which would use this evidence to select G_1 over G_2 as the theory of language that is represented in the mind/brains of the members of this speech community. But he proposes that there is another discipline, call it "A(bstract)-linguistics," which dismisses this evidence and regards G_1 and G_2 as equally well supported by "relevant" empirical evidence; in fact, a practitioner of A-linguistics would choose G_2 over G_1 if it were "simpler" on some general grounds. There is no doubt that Sapir and Jakobson, among many others, would have followed the path of C-linguistics in such a case, selecting G_1 as the grammar and applying this conclusion to the study of "Leading Questions" concerning the historical evolution of languages, and so on.[21]

The burden of proof clearly falls on those who believe that alongside C-linguistics, the status of which is not here in question, there is some point in developing the new discipline of A-linguistics, which not only differs from linguistics as it has actually been practiced by major figures in the field but also is radically different from anything known in the sciences: It would be regarded as strange indeed to restrict biology or chemistry in some *a priori* fashion to questions and concepts defined so as to delimit in advance the category of relevant evidence. In the sciences, at least, disciplines are regarded as conveniences, not as ways of cutting nature at its joints or as the elaboration of certain fixed concepts; and their boundaries shift or disappear as knowledge and understanding advance.[22] In this respect, the study of language as understood in the discussion above is like chemistry, biology, solar physics, or the theory of human vision. Whether the burden of proof faced by advocates of A-linguistics can be borne, I will not speculate, except to observe that even if it can, the fact would have no consequences with regard to the legitimacy or character of the enterprise we are discussing, as Soames makes clear.

Note that the issue is not the legitimacy of abstraction. It is perfectly proper to develop the subject of rational mechanics, a branch of mathematics abstracted from physics that treats planets as mass points obeying certain laws, or to develop theories that consider aspects of I-language in abstraction from their physical realization or other properties; indeed, that is the standard practice, as outlined earlier. But one is not misled thereby into believing that the subject matter of rational mechanics is an entity in a Platonic heaven, and there is no more reason to suppose that that is true in the study of language.[23]

2.4.2   The Empirical Basis for the Study of I-language

In actual practice, linguistics as a discipline is characterized by attention to certain kinds of evidence that are, for the moment, readily accessible and informative: largely, the judgments of native speakers. Each such judgment is, in fact, the result of an experiment, one that is poorly designed but rich in the evidence it provides. In practice, we tend to operate on the assumption, or pretense, that these informant judgments give us "direct evidence" as to the structure of the I-language, but, of course, this is only a tentative and inexact working hypothesis, and any skilled practioner has at his or her disposal an armory of techniques to help compensate for the errors introduced. In general, informant judgments do not reflect the structure of the language directly; judgments of acceptability, for example, may fail to provide direct evidence as to grammatical status because of the intrusion of numerous other factors. The same is true of other judgments concerning form and meaning. These are, or should be, truisms.[24]

In principle, evidence concerning the character of the I-language and initial state could come from many different sources apart from judgments concerning the form and meaning of expressions: perceptual experiments, the study of acquisition and deficit or of partially invented languages such as creoles,[25] or of literary usage or language change, neurology, biochemistry, and so on. It was one of the many contributions of the late Roman Jakobson to have emphasized this fact, in principle, and in his own work in practice. As in the case of any inquiry into some aspect of the physical world, there is no way of delimiting the kinds of evidence that might, in principle, prove relevant. The study of language structure as currently practiced should eventually disappear as a discipline as new types of evidence become available, remaining distinct only insofar as its concern is a particular faculty of the mind, ultimately the brain: its initial state and its various attainable mature states.

To be sure, the judgments of native speakers will always provide relevant evidence for the study of language, just as perceptual judgments will always provide relevant evidence for the study of human vision, although one would hope that such evidence will eventually lose its uniquely privileged status. If a theory of language failed to account for these judgments, it would plainly be a failure; we might, in fact, conclude that it is not a theory of language, but rather of something else. But we cannot know in advance just how informative various kinds of evidence will prove to be with regard to the language faculty and its manifestations, and we should anticipate that a broader range of evidence and deeper understanding will enable us to identify in just what respects informant judgments are useful or unreliable and why, and to compensate for the errors introduced under the tentative working assumption, which is indispensable, for today, and does provide us with rich and significant information.

It is important to bear in mind that the study of one language may provide crucial evidence concerning the structure of some other language, if we continue to accept the plausible assumption that the capacity to acquire language, the subject matter of UG, is common across the species. This conclusion is implicit in the research program outlined earlier. A study of English is a study of the realization of the initial state S_0 under particular conditions. Therefore, it embodies assumptions, which should be made explicit, concerning S_0. But S_0 is a constant; therefore, Japanese must be an instantiation of the same initial state under different conditions. Investigation of Japanese might show that the assumptions concerning S_0 derived from the study of English were incorrect; these assumptions might provide the wrong answers for Japanese, and after correcting them on this basis we might be led to modify the postulated grammar of English. Because evidence from Japanese can evidently bear on the corrrectness of a theory of S_0, it can have indirect—but very powerful—bearing on the choice of the grammar that attempts to characterize the I-language attained by a speaker of English. This is standard practice in the study of generative grammar. For this reason alone it is quite wrong to suppose that there are no grounds to choose among "extensionally equivalent grammars" for a "given language" (see pp. 20, 30–1): One of these might, for example, require a theory of S_0 that is demonstrably inadequate for some other language.

On the highly relativistic assumptions of certain varieties of descriptive linguistics that held that each language must be studied in its own terms, this research program may seem to be senseless or illegitimate, although one should note that this point of view was, in part, an ideology that was not observed in practice. If we are interested in discovering the real properties of the initial state of the language faculty and of its particular realizations as potential or actual I-languages, the ideology must be abandoned, and we must regard a theory of one language as subject to change on the basis of evidence concerning other languages (mediated through a theory of UG), or evidence of other sorts.

We observed that it is a task for the brain sciences to explain the properties and principles discovered in the study of mind. More accurately, the interdependency of the brain sciences and the study of mind is reciprocal. The theory of mind aims to determine the properties of the initial state S_0 and each attainable state S_L of the language faculty, and the brain sciences seek to discover the mechanisms of the brain that are the physical realizations of these states. There is a common enterprise: to discover the correct characterization of the language faculty in its initial and attained states, to discover the truth about the language faculty. This enterprise is conducted at several levels: an abstract characterization in the theory of mind, and an inquiry into mechanisms in the brain sciences. In principle, discoveries about the brain should influence the theory of mind, and at the same time the abstract study of states of the language faculty should formulate properties to be explained by the theory of the brain and is likely to be indispensable in the search for mechanisms. To the extent that such connections can be established, the study of the mind—in particular, of I-language—will be assimilated to the mainstream of the natural sciences.

So little is now known about the relevant aspects of the brain that we can barely even speculate about what the connections might be. We can, however, imagine how they might be established in principle, however remote the goal. Suppose that the study of I-language establishes certain general principles of binding theory that explain facts of the sort discussed in Chapter 1. Then a task of the brain sciences is to determine what mechanisms are responsible for the fact that these principles hold. Suppose that we have two grammars—two theories of the state of knowledge attained by a particular person—and suppose further that these theories are "extensionally equivalent" in the sense that they determine the same E-language in whatever sense we give to this derivative notion. It could in principle turn out that one of these grammars incorporates properties and principles that are readily explained in terms of brain mechanisms whereas the other does not. Similarly, two theories of UG that are equivalent in that they specify exactly the same set of attainable I-languages might be distinguishable in terms of properties of the brain. For example, one might contain certain principles and possibilities of variation that can be readily explained in terms of brain mechanisms, and the other not.

It is easy enough to imagine cases of this sort. Suppose that theory I contains the principles $P_1, \ldots, P_n$ and theory II contains the principles $Q_1, \ldots, Q_m$, and that the two theories are logically equivalent: The principles of each can be deduced from the principles of the other so that any description of behavior or potential behavior in terms of one of these theories can be reformulated in terms of the other. It could be that the brain sciences would show that each P_i corresponds to some determinate complex of neural mechanisms, whereas there is no such account of the Q_i's; some brain injury, for example, might selectively modify the P_i's but not the Q_i's. In such a case, facts about the brain would select among theories of the mind that might be empirically indistinguishable in other terms. Although results of this sort are remote in the current state of understanding, they are possible. The relation of brain and mind, so conceived, is a problem of the natural sciences.

2.4.3 Some Consequences of the Shift of Focus

To summarize, we may think of a person's knowledge of a particular language as a state of the mind, realized in some arrangement of physical mechanisms. We abstract the I-language as "what is known" by a person in this state of knowledge. This finite system, the I-language, is what the linguist's generative grammar attempts to characterize. If I say that this system has such-and-such properties, what I say is true or false. I am, in short, proposing a theoretical account of the properties of certain mechanisms, an account presented at a level of abstraction at which we believe that significant properties of these mechanisms can be expressed and principles governing these mechanisms and their functions elucidated. The study is in some ways similar to what Gunther Stent has called "cerebral hermeneutics," referring to the abstract investigation of the ways in which the visual system constructs and interprets visual experience (Stent, 1981). Similarly, UG is the study of one aspect of biological endowment, analogous to the study of the innate principles that determine that we will have a human rather than an insect visual system. The technical concept "knowledge of I-language" is a reasonably close approximation to what is informally called "knowledge of language," abstracting from several aspects of the commonsense notion as discussed earlier, although this consideration is a secondary one for reasons already mentioned.

The shift of point of view to a mentalist interpretation of the study of language was, as noted earlier, one factor in the development of the contemporary cognitive sciences, and constituted a step toward the incorporation of the study of language within the natural sciences, because it helps pave the way to an inquiry into the mechanisms with the properties exhibited in the study of rules and representations. This shift also led at once to a recasting of many of the traditional questions of language study. Many new and challenging problems arose, while a number of familiar problems dissolved when viewed from this perspective.

Consider the study of sound structure, the primary focus of attention in structural and descriptive linguistics. Taking E-language as the topic of inquiry, the problem is to discover the elements into which the stream of speech is subdivided and their properties and structural arrangements: phonemes and features, regarded as segments of an acoustic wave form or of a series of articulatory motions. Much of phonological theory consisted of analytic procedures for accomplishing this task. Focusing on the I-language, however, the problem is a rather different one: to find the mental representations that underlie the production and perception of speech and the rules that relate these representations to the physical events of speech. The problem is to find the best theory to account for a wide variety of facts, and we do not expect that analytic procedures exist to accomplish this task, just as there are no such procedures in other fields.

Consider, for example, the words listed below, where column I is the conventional orthography, column II appears

I	II	III
bet	bet	bet
bent	bent	bẽt
bend	bend	bend
knot	nat	nat
nod	nad	nAd
write	rayt	rayt
ride	rayd	rAyd
writer	rayt+r	rayDr
rider	rayd+r	rAyDr

to be the correct phonological representation, and column III, the approximate phonetic representations in one dialect of English, taking [a] to be a short vowel and [A] a corresponding long vowel (their exact phonetic character is irrelevant here), [ẽ] a nasalized counterpart to [e], and D a tongue flap rather like a trilled [r].

We may assume that the phonetic representations of column III correspond to actual speech events by universal principles of interpretation that essentially preserve linearity; that is, the sequence of phonetic symbols corresponds to the sequence of sounds (the matter is not this simple, as is well known). The phonological representations of the second column, not the phonetic representations of the third, correspond to the way that we intuitively "hear" these words. Although phonetic analysis reveals that *bet* and *bent* differ only in nasalization of the medial vowel, and that each has three phonetic segments as distinct from the four-segment word *bend,* this does not correspond to the intuitive perception; we hear *knot* and *nod* as differing only in one feature, voicing of the final consonant, not in both the vowel and the consonant (as, e.g., *knot* versus *Ned*). The representations of *writer* and *rider* that we intuitively perceive and that clearly relate to lexical and syntactic structure are as indicated in the second column (with + standing for the break between the lexical item and the agentive affix), not the third, although the latter expresses the phonetic fact that the words differ only in vowel quality. Examples such as these posed difficult problems for an approach to phonology that sought to determine phonological units by analytic procedures applying to actual speech events. The question is the status of the representations of column II, which were always recognized to be "correct" in some sense although their elements do not correspond point-by-point to the actual sounds of speech, the subparts of the actual specimens of E-language.

Shifting the focus of attention to I-language, the problems quickly dissolve. The representations of column II are essentially the mental representations of the lexicon, which enter into the syntax and semantics. The phonetic representations of column III derive from these by straightforward rules, most of them quite general: Vowels assume a particular quality before voiced and unvoiced consonants and become nasalized before nasal consonants, the nasal consonant drops before an unvoiced dental, and (in this dialect) the dental stops merge as [D] medially under this stress contour. Applying these rules, we derive the phonetic forms (III) from the lexical-phonological representations (II). The latter representations are not derived from the speech sounds by analytic procedures of segmentation, classification, extraction of physical features, and so forth, but are established and justified as part of the best theory for accounting ultimately for the general relation between sound and meaning of the I-language. Further syntactic and semantic rules apply to the representations of (II) in the expressions in which these words appear. The I-language, incorporating the rules that form the representations (II) and the rules that relate them to (III), is acquired by the child by applying the principles incorporated in the initial state S_0 to the presented facts; the problem for the grammarian is to discover these principles and show how they lead to the choice of the representations (II) (assuming these to be correct). The failure of taxonomic procedures is of no significance, because there is no reason to believe that such procedures play any role in language acquisition or have any standing as part of UG.

As these very simple examples illustrate, even at the level of sound structure, mental representations may be relatively abstract—i.e., not related in a simple way to actual specimens of linguistic behavior (in fact, this is even true of the phonetic representations, as a closer analysis would show). As we move to other levels of inquiry into the I-language, we find increasing evidence that mental representations are abstract in this sense. The systems of rules and principles that form and modify them are fairly simple and natural, although they interact to yield structures of considerable complexity and to determine their properties in quite a precise fashion. In short, the language faculty appears to be, at its core, a computational system that is rich and narrowly constrained in structure and rigid in its essential operations, nothing at all like a complex of dispositions or a system of habits and analogies. This conclusion seems reasonably well established and has been given considerable substance; there is no known alternative that even begins to deal with the actual facts of language, and empirically meaningful debate takes place largely within the framework of these assumptions.

Nevertheless, it should be observed that the conclusion is in many ways a rather surprising one. One might not have expected that a complex biological system such as the language faculty would have evolved in this fashion, and if indeed it has, that discovery is of no small significance.[26]

The scope of the shift to a mentalist or conceptualist interpretation, to internalized rather than externalized language, is broader than has been sometimes appreciated. Quite explicitly, it included the study of syntax, phonology, and morphology. I think it also includes much of what is misleadingly called "the semantics of natural language"—I say "misleadingly" because I think that much of this work is not semantics at all, if by "semantics" we mean the study of the relation between language and the world—in particular, the study of truth and reference. Rather, this work deals with certain postulated levels of mental representation, including representations of syntactic and lexical form and others called "models" or "pictures" or "discourse representations" or "situations," or the like. But the relation of these latter systems to the world of objects with properties and relations, or to the world as it is believed to be, is often intricate and remote, far more so than one might be led to believe on the basis of simple examples. The relation cannot, for example, be described as "incorporation" or element-by-element association.

Consider, for example, the principles of pronominal reference, which have been central to these quasisemantic investigations. If I say "John thinks that he is intelligent," *he* may refer to John, but not if I say "he thinks that John is intelligent."[27] We can account for such facts by a theory of the structural configurations in which a pronoun can acquire its "reference" from an associated name that binds it. The same principles, however, apply to such sentences as "the average man thinks that he is intelligent," "he thinks that the average man is intelligent" (or "John Doe thinks that he is intelligent," where "John Doe" is introduced as a designation for the average man). But no one assumes that there is an entity, the average man (or John Doe), to which the pronoun is permitted to refer in one but not the other case. If I say "John took a look at him, but it was too brief to permit a positive identification," *it* can refer to the look that John took; but the near synonym "John looked at him" cannot be extended in this way with the same interpretation, although no one believes that there are looks that a person can take, to one of which the pronoun *it* in the first sentence refers. Or, consider such widely discussed examples as "everyone who owns a donkey beats it," problematic because the pronoun *it* does not appear to be formally within the scope of the quantified noun phrase *a donkey* that binds it. One might try to approach the analysis of such sentences by constructing a representation with the property that for every pair (man, donkey), if *own* holds of the pair, then so does *beat*. Then we should say the same about "everyone who has a chance wastes it," without, however, committing ourselves to the belief that among the things in the world there are chances. Even if we restrict ourselves to the context "there are...," we can hardly assume that there are entities in the world, or in the world as we believe it to be, that correspond to the terms that appear ("there are looks that injure and others that charm," "there are chances that are too risky to take," "there are opportunities that should not be passed up," etc.).

One can think of many still more extreme examples. Although there has been much concern over the status of fictional and abstract objects, the problem, in fact, cuts far deeper. One can speak of "reference" or "coreference" with some intelligibility if one postulates a domain of mental objects associated with formal entities of language by a relation with many of the properties of reference, but all of this is internal to the theory of mental representations; it is a form of syntax. There seems no obvious sense in populating the extra-mental world with corresponding entities, nor any empirical consequence or gain in explanatory force in doing so. Insofar as this is true, the study of the relation of syntactic structures to models, "pictures," and the like, should be regarded as pure syntax, the study of various mental representations, to be supplemented by a theory of the relation these mental objects bear to the world or to the world as it is conceived or believed to be. Postulation of such mental representations is not innocuous but must be justified by empirical argument, just as in the case of phonological or other syntactic representations. Thus, the shift toward a computational theory of mind encompasses a substantial part of what has been called "semantics" as well, a conclusion that is only fortified if we consider more avowedly "conceptualist" approaches to these topics.

To proceed, we are now concerned with I-language and the initial state of the language faculty, with the linguist's grammars and UG. As a tentative empirical hypothesis, we might take the I-language to be a rule system of some sort, a specific realization of the options permitted by UG, fixed by presented experience. The rule system assigns to each expression a structure, which we may take to be a set of representations, one on each linguistic level, where a linguistic level is a particular system of mental representation. This structure must provide whatever information about an expression is available to the person who knows the language, insofar as this information derives from the language faculty; its representations must specify just what the language faculty contributes to determining how the expression is produced, used, and understood.

A linguistic level is a system consisting of a set of minimal elements (primes), an operation of concatenation that forms strings of primes, as much mathematical apparatus as is necessary to construct appropriate formal objects from these elements, the relevant relations that hold of these elements, and a class of designated formal objects (markers) that are assigned to expressions as their representations on this level. The rule system expresses the relations among the various levels in the language in question and determines the elements and properties of each level. At the level of phrase structure, for example, the primes are the minimal elements that enter into syntactic description (*John, run, past-tense,* N, V, S, etc.), the basic relation is *is-a* (*John* is an N, *John ran* is an S, etc.), and the phrase-markers will be certain formal objects constructed out of primes that express completely the relation *is-a*. The phrase-marker for the string *John ran* will indicate that the full string is an S (sentence), that *John* is an N (noun) and an NP (noun phrase), and that *ran* is a V (verb) and a VP (verb phrase); examples appear below.

The theory of linguistic structure (UG) will have the task of specifying these concepts precisely.[28] The theory must provide grammars for the I-languages that can, in principle, be attained by a human mind/brain, given appropriate experience,[29] and it must furthermore be so constrained that just the right I-language is determined, given the kind of evidence that suffices for language acquisition. We turn next to these questions.

NOTES

1. These observations, generally considered truisms, are rejected by Katz (1981, pp. 79–80) on the grounds that to recognize the fact that the concepts language and dialect of colloquial usage involve a sociopolitical dimension would be "like claiming that the concept of number is not a concept of mathematics but a sociopolitical one." There is no reason to accept this curious conclusion.

2. However, there were exceptions, for example, the theory of "overall patterns," of which each English dialect was held to be a subsystem. See Trager and Smith (1951). Note that the question of "variable rules," as discussed by some sociolinguists, is not relevant here.

3. We put aside here just what this term would mean in Bloomfieldian or any other variety of "behaviorist" linguistics. Pursuing such an approach, one would have to explain just what it means to say that people speak the very same language although they do not tend to say the same things in given circumstances. The same question arises if language is defined as a "complex of present dispositions to verbal behavior" (Quine, 1960), as do other problems that seem insoluble if the technical constructed concept "language" is to be a useful term for the investigation of language, or to have any relation to what we call "language." On this matter, see Chomsky (1975b, pp. 192–195).

4. One might also note some unintentionally comical objections, such as the charge by Oxford professor of linguistics Roy Harris (1983) that the standard idealization (which he ascribes to Saussure-Bloomfield-Chomsky) reflects "a fascist concept of language if ever there was one," because it takes the "ideal" speech community to be "totally homogeneous."

5. For some discussion, see Chomsky (1964) and Postal (1964). For comparison of transformational generative grammar with Harris's early theory of transformations, regarded as an analytic procedure applying beyond the sentence level of "structural grammar," see the introduction to Chomsky (1975a).

6. Lewis (1975). Lewis provides one of the clearest presentations of an "extensional" approach to language and also a critique of studies of "internalized language" in the sense described below. For critical discussion, see Chomsky (1980b).

7. Editorial comments in Joos (1957); Whitney (1872); Sapir (1921). Whitney, who exerted a major influence on Saussure and American linguistics, was criticizing Steinthal's Humboldtian approach, which I believe, falls naturally into the earlier tradition referred to

above. Humboldt, who is widely regarded (e.g., by Bloomfield) as an extreme relativist, in fact held that "all languages with regard to their grammar are very similar, if they are investigated not superficially, but deeply in their inner nature." See Chomsky (1966), p. 90, and references cited, for further discussion.

8.   This question, however, was surely not what Whitney had in mind.

9.   Jespersen (1924). On Jespersen's notions as compared to those of contemporary generative grammar, see Reynolds (1971); Chomsky (1977), Chapter 1.

10.   One might argue that the systems we are considering constitute only one element of the faculty of language, understood more broadly to encompass other capacities involved in the use and understanding of language, for example, what is sometimes called "communicative competence," or parts of the human conceptual system that are specifically related to language. See Chomsky (1980b). I will put such questions aside here, continuing to use the term "language faculty" in the narrower sense of the previous discussion.

11.   For a related but somewhat different way of viewing these questions, see Higginbotham (1983b).

12.   Those that tend to yield a false parse, such as Thomas Bever's example "the horse raced past the barn fell," where the first six words are generally taken to constitute a full clause, leaving no interpretation for the final word, although on reflection it is clear that the expression is a well-formed sentence stating that a certain horse fell, namely, the one that was raced past the barn.

13.   Obviously, the questions of innateness and species-specificity are distinct. It has been alleged that I and others have taken "innate" and "species-specific" to be "synonyms" (Cartmill, 1984). I am unaware of any examples of such confusion, although there are a number of articles refuting it.

14.   See Chomsky (1980b), pp. 134–139.

15.   On this matter, see Marr (1982). Note that the question of the legitimacy or sense of a realist interpretation of science in general is not at issue here; rather, nothing new in principle seems to arise in the case of the study of I-language and its origins. If one wants to consider the question of realism, psychology and linguistics seem poor choices; the question should be raised with regard to the more advanced sciences, where there is much better hope of gaining insight into the matter. See Chomsky (1980b) for further discussion.

16.   For some commentary on the general issue, see Enc (1983).

17.   On some misunderstandings, which are repeated in subsequent work that I will not discuss here, see Chomsky (1980b), pp.

123–128. As for the publishing history, the earliest publications on generative grammar were presented in a framework suggested by certain topics in automata theory (e.g., my *Syntactic Structures*, 1957—actually course notes for an undergraduate course at MIT and hence presented from a point of view related to interests of these students). Specifically linguistic work, such as Chomsky (1975a), was not publishable at the time. In the latter, considerations of weak generative capacity (i.e., characterizability of E-languages), finite automata and the like were completely absent, and emphasis was on I-language, although the term was not used.

18. For further discussion of this matter, see Chomsky (1980b).

19. See Katz (1981) and Bever (1983).

20. This would follow if the evidence stipulated to be relevant to identifying a certain Platonic language as P-English is distinct from the evidence that bears on the theory of the I-language actually represented in the mind/brains of speakers of English, or if some novel canons are adopted for interpreting evidence. By a similar procedure, we could establish "Platonistic biology," concerned, for example, with what Katz calls the "essential property" of a heart (that it is a pump) and thus abstracting from the physical laws that make it beat (a nonessential property). We might then find that the best biological theory is distinct from the best theory of Platonistic biology just as the best (ultimately, biological) theory of I-language might be distinct from the best theory of Platonistic language (however it is specified; for Katz, by analysis of "our concept of the abstract object natural language").

21. For some recent discussion of the matter in connection with historical linguistics, see Lightfoot (1979).

22. Katz insists that disciplines such as chemistry, biology, and so forth have inherent, conceptually determined boundaries. Indeed, he regards the claim as uncontroversial, the alternative being a form of "nihilism" that "would turn the spectrum of well-focused academic disciplines into chaos" (*op. cit.*).

23. Arguments that have been offered to the contrary seem to me question-begging or otherwise flawed. Thus, Katz argues against Hilary Putnam that if what we call "cats" were discovered to be robots controlled from outer space, then they would not be cats, because the meaning of "cat" in the Platonic entity P-English is "feline animal"; this would remain true even if it were determined that in the I-language of each speaker of English, "cat" is understood in accordance with Putnam's analysis, which takes cats to be of the same natural kind (a concept of science) as particular exemplars. The argument goes through, trivially, with regard to P-English as Katz stipulates its

properties. But Putnam was proposing a theory concerning human languages and conceptual systems, concerning English, not P-English as Katz defines it, and Katz offers no reason to believe that his Platonic object merits the name "English" any more than an equally legitimate abstract object that would incorporate Putnam's assumptions. Throughout, the arguments are of this sort. Katz also presents an account of the history of generative grammar and of documents he cites that is seriously inaccurate, as is often evident even on internal grounds. See also Chomsky (1981), pp. 314–315.

24.   For discussion of some common misunderstandings about these and related matters, see Newmeyer (1983).

25.   On the relevance of this material, see Bickerton (1984) and references cited, and discussion in the same issue of the journal.

26.   For some discussion, see Chomsky (1980b, 1981); and Chomsky, Huybregts, and van Riemsdijk (1982).

27.   The matter is more complex. See Evans (1980) and Higginbotham (1983a). But we can put aside the required sharpening of these notions here.

28.   For an early effort, see Chomsky (1975a), dating from 1955–56.

29.   A stronger requirement would be that UG specify *exactly* the I-languages attainable under normal conditions. It is not obvious, however, that UG meets this conditions. The attainable languages are those that fall in the intersection of those determined by UG and the humanly learnable systems, and conditions on learnability might exclude certain grammars permitted by UG. Similar remarks hold with regard to parsing. For background on these matters, see Wexler and Culicover (1980) and Berwick and Weinberg (1984).

3   Facing Plato's Problem

3.1.   A MODEL OF EXPLANATION

With the shift of focus from E-language to I-language, from the study of behavior and its products to the study of systems of mental representation and computation, a number of questions arise. Some relate to the legitimacy or the proper bounds of this move; these I will put aside until Chapter 4. Others arise internally to the research program that develops naturally from this shift of focus. These are substantive questions as to how the general ideas should be fleshed out. Let us now turn to these questions.

The central task is to find the basic elements of I-language—henceforth, language. One must, in the first place, show that the devices provided by the theory of UG are adequate to the descriptive task at hand—i.e., that they are rich enough to account for the attested variety of languages and, indeed, for their possible variety. A second task is to show that these devices are meager enough so that very few languages are made available to the language-learner, given data that, in fact, suffice for language acquisition. Unless this condition is satisfied by the theory of UG, it will be impossible to account for the fact that languages are learned. The transition from the initial state to the steady state takes place in a determinate fashion, with no conscious attention or choice. The transition is essentially uniform for individuals in a given speech community despite diverse experience. The state attained is highly articulated and very rich, providing a specific interpretation for a vast array of sentences lacking close models in our experience. These conditions of our variant of Plato's problem set the second task that the research program must address.

The two tasks just mentioned are in conflict. To achieve descriptive adequacy, it often seems necessary to enrich the system of available devices, whereas to solve our case of Plato's problem we must restrict the system of available devices so that only a few languages, or just one, are determined by the given data. It is the tension between the two tasks that makes the field an intellectually interesting one, in my view.

The earliest ideas were roughly as follows. Suppose that UG provides a certain format for languages, that is, a specification of permitted types of rules and permissible interactions among them. Any rule system satisfying the proposed format qualifies as a possible human language. We assume initially that there are infinitely many such rule systems; that is, there is no bound on the complexity of the rules that may enter into these systems. The mind employs certain primitive operations to interpret some of the data presented to it as linguistic experience, then selects among the languages consistent with this experience in accordance with an evaluation metric that assigns an abstract value to each language. The initial state of the language faculty, S_0, incorporates the primitive operations, the format for possible rule systems and the evaluation metric. Given experience, the language faculty in the state S_0 searches the class of possible languages, selecting the highest valued one consistent with the data and entering the state S_1, which incorporates the rules of this language. Given new data, the system enters S_2, and so forth, until it enters a state S_s in which the procedure terminates, either because of some property of S_s or because the system has reached a state of maturation that does not permit it to proceed. At each step, the learner's mind selects the highest valued ("simplest") language consistent with the newly presented evidence and its current state.[1]

We might further suggest, as an empirical hypothesis, that order of presentation of data is irrelevant, so that learning is "as if it were instantaneous," as if S_0 maps the data directly to S_s. More explicitly, consider the following empirical hypothesis:

Suppose we regard S_0 as a function mapping a collec- (1)
tion of data E to a state attained. If E is the totality of data
available to the language learner, then the steady state S_s
attained is $S_0(E)$, the result of applying the principles of
S_0 to E.

We then have a certain model of language acquisition and also a model of explanation. We explain the fact that so-and-so (e.g., that such sentences as (2)–(14) of Chapter 1 have the range of meanings they do have), and that the person H knows this, by showing that these facts are determined by the rules of the highest valued language consistent with the data presented to H.

Continuing to think of a grammar as a theory of a language, we may say that a grammar is *descriptively adequate* for a particular language to the extent that it correctly describes this language. A theory of UG meets the condition of *explanatory adequacy* to the extent that it provides descriptively adequate grammars under the boundary conditions set by experience. A theory of UG that meets this condition will, then, permit relevant facts about linguistic expressions to be derived from the grammars it selects, thus providing an explanation for the facts.

This is, in fact, the model of explanation generally used in linguistics, insofar as one or another approach is concerned with explanation at all. This model depends crucially on the legitimacy of the idealization to instantaneous learning, that is, on the correctness of the empirical assumption (1). Insofar as this move is empirically incorrect, there will be no explanations of the standard form; conversely, if such explanations can be produced, that counts as evidence that the empirical assumption, which is not at all an obvious one, is correct. One can imagine various intermediate positions, but as a working hypothesis, the assumption (1) so far seems rather credible, perhaps surprisingly.

It is important to be clear about what is and what is not implied by the idealization to instantaneous learning, that is, the empirical hypothesis (1). A wide range of empirical possibilities are consistent with this hypothesis. For example, it might be that some of the principles of S_0 are available to the language learner only at a late stage of language acquisition, that the language faculty matures through childhood making various principles available at particular stages of the process. Furthermore, it might be that because of memory restrictions or whatever, only "simpler" parts of the evidence E that leads to attainment of the steady state are available to the child at early stages of language acquisition. It may also be that an option permitted by UG is fixed in one manner at an early stage of acquisition, and the choice is reversed at a later stage on the basis of evidence not available or unused at the earlier stage.[2] These possibilities are not in themselves inconsistent with the empirical hypothesis that the steady state attained is, in fact, identical to the result of applying the principles of S_0 "instantaneously" to the available evidence E, taken as a set presented at an instant of time (or, perhaps more realistically, that this is true to a close approximation). What the empirical hypothesis asserts is that irrespective of questions of maturation, order of presentation, or selective availability of evidence, the result of language acquisition is as if it were instantaneous: In particular, intermediate states attained do not change the principles available for interpretation of data at later states in a way that affects the state attained.

If certain principles come into operation only at later stages of maturation, this does not show that they are not to be attributed to the initial state S_0. The course of maturation is genetically determined although influenced by the course of experience in various ways. The onset of puberty, for example, varies over a wide range depending on such factors as nutrition, but the processes are genetically determined; presumably death is determined by genetic factors, although its timing and manner reflect environmental factors. Genetically determined factors in development evidently are not to be identified with those operative at birth.

There is good reason to believe that the language faculty undergoes maturation—in fact, the order and timing of this maturation appear to be rather uniform despite considerable variation in experience and other cognitive faculties—but this does not bear on the correctness of the empirical assumption embodied in the idealization to instantaneous learning, which appears to be at least a very good first approximation to the facts and, as noted, is presupposed, explicitly or implicitly, in work that does attempt to offer explanations for what is known.[3]

The model of acquisition and explanation assumed in this early work is essentially that of Peircean abduction: Innate limitations (the "guessing instinct") yield a small class of admissible hypotheses that are submitted to "corrective action," a procedure that works because "Man's mind has a natural adaptation to imagining correct theories of some kind" (Peirce).[4] In light of the facts of language acquisition, the basic problem is to construct UG so that the class of admissible hypotheses is small, perhaps single-membered. If so, UG provides a significant part of the answer to question (1ii) of Chapter 1 and attains explanatory adequacy in significant respects; if not, it does not. Similar considerations apply in other cognitive domains as well, I believe; see Chomsky (1975b, 1980b).

As discussed earlier, the basic problem is that our knowledge is richly articulated and shared with others from the same speech community, whereas the data available are much too impoverished to determine it by any general procedure of induction, generalization, analogy, association, or whatever. There is good reason to believe that children learn language from positive evidence only (corrections not being required or relevant), and they appear to know the facts without relevant experience in a wide array of complex cases, such as those illustrated in Chapter 1. It must be, then, that the "guessing instinct" submits very few admissible hypotheses to the evaluation procedure.

The richness of the class of languages admitted by UG (its generative capacity) is a matter of no obvious empirical import. What is important is a requirement of "feasibility" that has no clear relation to scope of UG. What is required for feasibility is that given data, only a fairly small collection of languages be made available for inspection and evaluation (e.g., languages might be sufficiently "scattered" in value so that only few are so available). A theory of UG might fail to satisfy the feasibility requirement if its scope were finite and might satisfy it if it were to permit the maximum variety of rule systems in a sense that can be made precise. Other facts concerning the structure of UG are relevant at this point, not generative capacity.[5]

As noted, there is a tension between the demands of descriptive and explanatory adequacy. To achieve the latter, it is necessary to restrict available descriptive mechanisms so that few languages are accessible (many might be consistent with the evidence, but this would not matter if only few are highly valued). To achieve descriptive adequacy, however, the available devices must be rich and diverse enough to deal with the phenomena exhibited in the possible human languages. We therefore face conflicting requirements. We might identify the field of generative grammar, as an area of research, with the domain in which this tension remains unresolved.

The dilemma arose in a clear and sharp form as soon as the research program of generative grammar was formulated. As noted in Chapter 1, the earliest efforts to construct explicit grammars quickly uncovered an array of new phenomena previously unobserved in studies that relied on the intelligence of the reader, including quite simple ones. To deal with these facts it seemed necessary to enrich the class of descriptive devices; but this could not be the correct move, given the requirement of explanatory adequacy. Let us consider now how the problem has been addressed, and the recent conceptual shift to which these efforts have led.

3.2. RULE SYSTEMS

The format proposed in the earliest work allowed for two types of rules: phrase structure rules that form phrase-markers (see p. 46, above), namely, representations in which categorial structure (noun phrase, prepositional phrase, clause, etc.) is indicated; and transformational rules that convert phrase-markers into other phrase-makers. This proposed format for rules was adapted from traditional descriptive and historical grammar, recast in terms of ideas developed in the theory of computation (recursive function theory, the theory of algorithms).

Classical grammar recognized that words are organized into phrases. an idea that was clear in the seventeenth-century Port-Royal grammar and that has antecedents in classical rhetorical theory. Here "nonfigurative style" is characterized as "untransposed," that is, with "words that are connected placed next to one another," in the formulation of a Sophist handbook of the Aristotelian period, the first statement of this idea according to Richard Ogle (1980). It was a straightforward matter to formalize these ideas within the framework of rewriting systems in the sense of Post, one of the standard approaches to the theory of recursive functions, by imposing various constraints on the form of rules. The infinite class of structures generated by a finite system of such rules sufficed to represent phrase structure, at least for relatively simple sentences.

These phrase structure representations must then be associated with phonetic form. The natural device for this purpose was an adaptation of the approach of historical phonology, which derives the elements of a given language from a (sometimes abstract) historical antecedent by a succession of rules of sound change. Adapting this idea to the framework of synchronic description, lexical items can be given in an abstract form in phrase structure representation, then converted by a succession of phonological and phonetic rules to their actual phonetic form—the basic idea of contemporary generative phonology.

A simple system of phrase structure rules, in this sense, is the following:

$$\text{(i) S} \rightarrow \text{NP VP} \qquad\qquad\qquad (2)$$

(ii) VP → V NP

(iii) NP → DET N

(iv) NP → N

(v) V → *hit*

(vi) N → *boy*

(vii) N → *John*

(viii) DET → *the*

(ix) X → ...

Rules (i)–(iv) are syntactic rules. Rules (v)–(viii) are lexical rules, where *hit, boy,* and so forth are understood to be single symbols (as are NP, VP, and DET). Rule (ix) stands for a collection of lexical-phonological rules that associate each symbol X (*hit, boy,* etc.) with its phonological representation. Putting these rules aside and keeping to conventional orthography instead, the language containing the rules (2) generates, for example, the representation (3):

$$[_\text{S} [_\text{NP} [_\text{N} John]] [_\text{VP} [_\text{V} hit] [_\text{NP} [_\text{DET} the] [_\text{N} boy]]]] \qquad (3)$$

The representation (3) is the phrase-marker of the terminal string *John hit the boy,* in the sense of the earlier discussion. The phrase-marker (3) is generated by the system (2) in an obvious way. Suppose we want to determine whether a certain phrase-marker (for example, (3)) is generated by a certain rule system (for example, (2)). Assume the convention that a subpart of the phrase-marker of the form $[_X Y]$ is replaced by X if the rule system contains the rule $X \rightarrow Y$; then iterate this procedure, and if the final result is a single symbol, the phrase-marker is generated by the rule system; as a clause, if the single symbol is S. Applying to (3) the lexical rules (v)–(viii) of (2), we replace $[_N John]$ by N, $[_V hit]$ by V, and so forth, thus reducing (3) to:

$$[_S [_{NP} N] [_{VP} V [_{NP} DET N]]] \tag{4}$$

Applying rules (2iv) and (2iii) to (4), we derive:

$$[_S NP [_{VP} V NP]] \tag{5}$$

Applying rule (2ii) to (5) we derive $[_S NP VP]$, and applying rule (2i) to this, we reduce (3) finally to S, indicating that (3) is the phrase-marker of a well-formed clause, *John hit Bill.* We understand $[_X Y]$ as indicating that Y' is an expression of the category X, where Y' is the string of lexical elements derived from Y by removing all of its brackets. Thus, in the phrase-marker (3), *John* is of the category N and also NP; *the* is of the category DET (determiner); *boy* is of the category N; *the boy* is of the category NP; *hit the boy* is of the category VP, *John hit the boy* is of the category S (sentence).

The rule system (2) must be modified to exclude the possibility of generating well-formed phrase-markers for such sentences as *John hit*, with the transitive verb *hit* lacking an object. We, therefore, modify (2v) to the form:

$$V \rightarrow hit \; / \!\!-\!\! NP \tag{6}$$

We understand (6) to mean that V can replace *hit* in the procedure described only when *hit* is in the context—NP (i.e., preceding a noun phrase). In general, then, the phrase structure rules will be of the form:

$$X \rightarrow Y \; / \; Z\!\!-\!\!W \tag{7}$$

Rules of the form (7) with Z or W non-null—for example, (6)—are called "context-sensitive rules"; the rules of (2) are "context-free rules."

The grammatical function "subject-of" can be defined as "NP of S" (i.e., NP immediately contained in S), so that *John* is the subject of *John hit the boy* in (3); or in a different terminology, *John* is the subject of the verb *hit* or of the verb phrase *hit the boy*. The grammatical function "object-of" can be defined similarly as "NP of VP," so that *the boy* is the object of *hit the boy*, or of the verb *hit*. We call the verb *hit* the "head" of the VP *hit the boy* and the noun *boy* the head of the NP *the boy* (similarly, the noun *John* is the head of the NP *John*). These notions can be extended readily to other constructions.

Implicit in (2) is the assumption that there is an asymmetry present in the relation of subject and object to the transitive verb: The object is paired directly with the verb, whereas the subject is related to the verb only indirectly, being paired directly with the verb phrase consisting of the verb and its object. This assumption is empirical, therefore controversial, but it appears to be well supported by cross-linguistic evidence of varied types.

Certain syntactic and semantic properties of simple NP-V-NP sentences provide relatively direct evidence in support of this asymmetry. English, for example, permits the string V-NP to move as a unit, as in the sentence (8), where the symbol *e* fills the position from which the string V-NP is moved:

John wanted to win the race, and [win the race] he   (8)
did *e*

Such "transformational rules" move phrases, not strings that do not constitute a phrase, indicating that [*win the race*] is a phrase, a VP. In contrast, there are no rules that move the string NP-V of an NP-V-NP sentence.

Similarly, in NP-V-NP sentences it is not uncommon for the V-NP string to function as a semantic unit with a compositionally determined meaning, as in the following examples:

(i) John threw a party (threw a fit, threw the ball)   (9)
(ii) John broke his arm (broke the window)

In (i), semantic rules determine the meaning of *threw*-NP, and the semantic role of the subject may vary depending on the meaning assigned to this unit; thus, *John* is the agent in "John threw the ball" but not in "John threw a fit." Similarly in (ii), *John* is the agent with the object *the window* and also in one interpretation of "John broke his arm" (e.g., "John broke Bill's arm"). But there is a second interpretation of the latter with the sense "John's arm broke," in which case *John* is not the agent. Again, the V-NP string is assigned its meaning as a unit, and the semantic role of the subject is determined compositionally, depending on the meaning of the unit V-NP. This situation is not unusual, but one rarely if ever finds NP-V-NP structures in which the subject-verb combination is assigned a meaning that then determines the semantic role of the object. This makes sense on the assumption that the verb-object string is a phrase, a VP, which is given a meaning and the capacity to assign a semantic role as a unit (in most cases, as determined solely by the verbal head).[6]

There is also direct phonological evidence for this analysis; prosodic contours, for example, commonly apply to NP and to the unit V-NP. There is further evidence of a more abstract sort from considerations of binding theory. One principle of this theory is:

> A pronoun cannot take an element of its domain as (10)
> its antecedent

This principle has many consequences and as far as is known is invariant across languages; we will return to the question of its proper formulation and its status within binding theory.

The *domain* of an element is the minimal phrase containing it. Thus, consider the following sentences, where the domain of the pronoun *he* is indicated by brackets:

> (i) [he thinks John is intelligent] (11)
> (ii) John thinks [he is intelligent]
> (iii) the woman [he married] thinks John is intelligent
> (iv) [his mother] loves John

In cases (ii), (iii), and (iv), *John* is not in the domain of the pronoun, so that *John* can serve as its antecedent in accordance with (10); but in case (i), *John* is in the domain of the pronoun and so cannot be its antecedent.

But now consider the following example:

[John's mother] loves him (12)

Here, *him* may take *John* as its antecedent, so we know that *John* is not in the domain of *him*. If the sentence had the tripartite structure NP-V-NP, then the domain of *him* would be the entire clause and would include *John*. Therefore, it follows from (10) that there must be a phrase containing *him* but not *John*, as in the representation:

$[_{NP}$ John's mother] $[_{VP}$ loves him] (13)

With some complications that we may ignore, the counterparts of such sentences as (12) also generally permit the antecedent relation in languages with a word order that is more free, for example, Japanese, where objects may precede subjects (the order, then, is object-subject-verb, because Japanese is a verb-final language). We conclude, then, that at the level of representation where the binding principle (10) applies, Japanese too has a VP or similar phrase. The structure of an object-subject-verb sentence might, for example, be (14i), where *e* indicates the position from which the object was moved from the underlying structure (14ii) generated by the phrase structure rules of Japanese:[7]

(i) object $[_S$ subject $[_{VP} e$ V]] (14)
(ii) $[_S$ subject $[_{VP}$ object V]]

The conclusion that the VP-configuration with the asymmetry of subject-object relations it induces holds cross-linguistically is plausible, if it is found in some languages. It seems reasonable to assume that the same lexical concepts are expressible across languages, and that these are intimately associated with grammatical functions such as subject, object, complement, and so forth, where these concepts have a cross-linguistic sense. If this sense is formally expressed in terms of properties of phrase-markers as suggested here (a controversial assumption), then phrase-markers of the appropriate form, including VP to express the subject-object asymmetry, will be available cross-linguistically at a level of representation that is associated with interpretation of lexical items.

These structures again present a case of "Plato's problem." Of course, it would be possible to replace the phrase structure rules (2), which express the subject-object asymmetry, with rules that yield a tripartite structure NP-V-NP (or NP-NP-V for Japanese), or that associate the subject and the verb in the structure [NP-V]-NP instead of what appears to be the actual structure, NP-[V-NP]. The evidence that supports the VP-analysis over others is available to the linguist investigating the language but not to the language learner. That is, it is unreasonable to suppose that the language learner makes use of the kind of evidence illustrated above to determine the structure; rather, it must be that the structure is determined independently of such evidence, and that the language learner then knows, for example, that (12) permits an antecedent-pronoun relation by virtue of the structure that has been assigned to it. If so, then UG must restrict the rules of phrase structure so that only the VP analysis is available at the relevant level of representation.

This conclusion, of course, does not conflict with a semantic analysis of transitive verbs as two-termed relations, as in familiar versions of modern logic. If correct, that analysis would now be derived, one step removed from the syntax. The semantic properties can be described by either syntactic theory, although in slightly different ways.

The rule system (2) generates only a finite number of sentences (in fact, only four). It can be given infinite capacity by allowing rules that license a category α within the category α, for example, by replacing rules (2iii), and (2iv) by the syntactic rules (15), adding also the lexical rule (16):

(i) NP → Det N′   (15)
(ii) N′ → N
(iii) N′ → N S

$$N \rightarrow claim \qquad\qquad (16)$$

In accordance with (15), the representation (3) is slightly modified: The nouns [$_N$ *man*], [$_N$ *John*] now appear as [N' [$_N$ *man*]],
[N' [$_N$ *John*]], respectively. Noting that *claim* is also a verb and
adding some other lexical items, we extend the rule system to
generate such structures as (17), with a number of brackets
omitted and the status of *that* put to the side:

> (i) John [$_{VP}$ claimed [$_S$ that Bill hit the man]]   (17)
> (ii) the [N' claim [$_S$ that Bill hit the man]]

With the addition of appropriate lexical rules, among the
sentences generated will be "the claim that John hit the man
surprised Bill," "the assertion that the claim that John hit the
man surprised Bill astonished Tom," and so forth.

     The two structures of (17) are very similar; the VP of (i)
consists of a verbal head, *claim* (with an added inflection), and
a complement clause, *that Bill hit the man;* and the N' of (ii)
consists of a nominal head *claim* with the same complement
clause. In short, the word *claim*, whether used as a noun or a
verb, takes a clausal complement. The parallelism becomes
even clearer if we extend the rules to allow genitive "subjects"
of noun phrases, as in (18), which is parallel category by category
to (17i) and has essentially the same internal semantic properties:

> John's claim that Bill hit the man   (18)

Such examples indicate that one of the choices of DET in
English may be a full noun phrase, which is assigned a case-
marker, genitive. The same case-marker is assigned in gerunds,
as in (19):

> John's hitting the man   (19)

Here, *hitting the man* is an ordinary VP (with *hit* taking the
inflection *ing* instead of the tense-agreement inflection of a
clause), and the NP subject is again genitive, indicating that
the case-marker is assigned to the "subject" of an NP whether it

is paired with a VP (as in (19)) or an N' (as in (18)). Again, we see a parallelism between VP and N'. Note that we can readily generalize the notion "subject-of" to include this case as well as the familiar case of subject of a clause.

Considerations such as these suggest that we should rethink the nature of phrase structure rules in such a way as to bring out these parallels more clearly. This revision has some rather far-reaching effects, to which we will return.

Phrase structure rules can generate representations of syntactic structure quite successfully, along the lines indicated, for quite a range of expressions, and were introduced for this purpose in the earliest work on generative grammar. It was at once apparent, however, that phrase structure rules of the sort just illustrated are insufficient in themselves to account properly for the variety of sentence structures. The earliest approach to this problem, which has a number of subsequent and current variants, was to enrich the system of rules by introducing complex categories with features that can "percolate down" to the categories contained within them, expressing global dependencies not captured in a simple system of phrase structure rules. For example, to guarantee that singular and plural subjects will be associated with singular and plural verbs, respectively, one might add the features [singular] or [plural] to the symbol S, yielding the complex symbol [S, singular] or [S, plural], with a convention that the features percolate from S to its constituents NP, VP, then to the heads of these constituents. The rules introducing lexical items will then refer to the feature in question in the complex symbol [N, singular], [V, singular]. I adopted this approach in an undergraduate thesis of 1949, modifying ideas of Zellig Harris from a somewhat different framework. Such an approach can be enriched much further and has been in subsequent work that takes a rather different tack from the one I am discussing here.

An alternate approach, also adapting ideas of Harris to the framework of generative grammar, was to avoid this enrichment of phrase structure rules and to factor the full complexity of existing structures into two basic components: Phrase structure rules with only simple categories generate a class of abstract underlying structures (call them "D-structures"[8]); these D-structures are mapped by rules of a different type, transformational rules, into structures (call them "S-structures") that correspond more closely to the actually observed forms with their surface structures. The transformational rules express the "global" properties of phrase-markers, as in the case of number agreement, and also derive complex structures (passives, interrogatives, relative clause constructions, etc.) from the D-structures that correspond directly to simple sentences. The transformational rules, too, were an adaptation of informal devices of traditional grammar, which, of course, recognized systematic relations between active and passive forms, declaratives and interrogatives, relative and full clauses, and so on. The seventeenth-century Port-Royal grammar and logic, for example, incorporated devices similar to phrase structure and transformational rules in this sense and used them to explain the semantic properties of sentences and to develop a theory of inference.[9]

Each transformational rule is defined by a "structural description," identifying the class of phrase-markers to which it applies and specifying how they are analyzed for the purpose of the transformation in question, and a "structural change," indicating what is done to this phrase-marker to yield a new phrase-marker. The transformational rule for forming interrogatives, for example, applies to a phrase-marker of the form $(X, wh-, Y)$, where X and Y are any expressions and $wh-$ is a $wh-$ phrase such as *who* or *which books;* this rule moves the second term, $wh-$, to the front of the sentence. The structural description of the rule states that it applies to the sentence (20), with the analysis indicated, and the structural change states that the rule moves *who* to the front yielding (21):

you think—who—saw John   (20)

(X   *wh-*   Y   )

who—you think saw John   (21)

A subsequent transformation yields the surface form "who do you think saw John." This subsequent transformation is restricted to nonembedded clauses. It does not apply when the interrogative construction is embedded, as in "I wonder [who you think saw John]," or in the formation of relative clauses (e.g., "the man [who you think saw John]"), which uses the same rule that applies to form questions.

The transformational rule for formation of questions, then, might be expressed in the form (22), or the simplified form (23):

SD: (X, *wh-*, Y)   (22)
SC: (1, 2, 3) → (2, 3, 1)

(X, *wh-*, Y) → (2, 3, 1)   (23)

Later work postulated that when a category is moved by a transformation, it leaves behind an empty category, a "trace"; thus, the transformation just described yields not (21) but rather (24), with the trace [$_{NP}$ *e*] (where *e* is an empty element), a category of the type NP, the NP subject of *think*, but with no phonetic content:

who—you think [$_{NP}$ *e*] saw John   (24)

I have adopted this device in some of the examples cited above and will continue to do so—anachronistically—in discussing earlier work.

If S-structures contain traces, then grammatical relations are also represented at S-structure, although in an abstract way. Thus, assuming *who* and [$_{NP}$ *e*] to be associated (say, by co-indexing) in (24), we can say that *who* has the function "subject of *saw*"as mediated through its trace, or more perspicuously, that *who* is an operator binding the variable *e*, the actual subject of the verb, so that the representation is understood as:

for which person *x*, you think *x* saw John   (25)

In effect, this interpretation is assigned to the S-structure form (24) by assigning to *who* its meaning ("for which person") and interpreting co-indexing in the notation of variables. Hence, the assumption that S-structures contain traces makes it possible to provide the semantic interpretation in a simple and perspic-uous way, making use of operator-variable relations and of grammatical functions and relations carried over from their

D-structure representation. There is, in fact, substantial evidence of various sorts to support the hypothesis that empty categories do appear in representations at various syntactic levels. We will return to the question, which is of considerable interest and a topic of much current research.

The theories of phrase structure and transformational rules provide a rich class of devices to achieve descriptive adequacy while still restricting the class of possible languages consistent with presented data—or more precisely, scattering them in terms of a natural evaluation measure, the empirically significant requirement. Thus, they constituted a step toward the twin goals of the research program. Furthermore, the various representations determined by rules satisfying the postulated format for rule systems seemed in many respects appropriate for the semantic interpretation of sentences, a central motivating concern from the earliest work.[10] Specifically, the D-structures serve as an abstract representation of semantically relevant grammatical relations such as subject-verb, verb-object, and so on, one crucial element that enters into semantic interpretation of sentences (recall that these relations are also indirectly expressed at S-structure, assuming traces). It has, however, become clear that other features of semantic interpretation having to do with anaphora, scope, and the like are not represented at the level of D-structure but rather at some level closer to surface structure, perhaps S-structure or a level of representation derived directly from it—a level sometimes called "LF" to suggest "logical form," with familiar provisos to avoid possible misinterpretation.[11] The term is used because this level of representation has many of the properties of logical form in the sense of other usages. We return to the matter.

The resulting general picture of language structure, sometimes called "the Extended Standard Theory" (EST), assumes that the general organization of a rule system is as shown on the following page:

The arrows correspond to various subsystems of rules; their orientation expresses structural relations and entails nothing about temporal order of speech production or processing. Phrase structure rules (I) of a very simple kind generate an infinite class of D-structures that express semantically relevant grammatical functions and relations; transformational rules

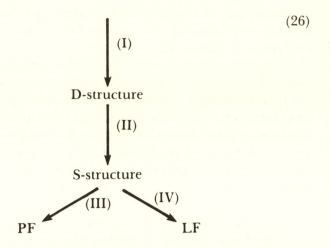

(26)

(II) convert these to S-structures in which the same relations (and others) are also represented through the medium of traces. Phonological and other rules (III) convert S-structures to phonetic representations with their surface phrasal categories (PF, or phonetic form; surface structure); and independently, rules of the LF component (IV) convert S-structures to representations in LF, where scope and other properties are directly represented. PF and LF constitute the "interface" between language and other cognitive systems, yielding direct representations of sound on the one hand and meaning on the other as language and other systems interact, including perceptual and production systems, conceptual systems and pragmatic systems. The levels of representation, in the sense of earlier discussion, are D-structure, S-structure, PF, and LF; the rules are the phrase structure and transformational rules generating D- and S-structure representations, and the rules of the PF and LF components.

3.3 RESTRICTING THE VARIETY OF RULE SYSTEMS

3.3.1 The Transformational Component

With this brief review of the proposed account of rule systems (which, in fact, amalgamates proposals extending over about 20 years), let us return to the dilemma faced at the outset: the tension between the requirements of descriptive and explanatory adequacy.

Once explicit proposals were made as to the character of rule systems, the immediate task was to show that these devices suffice for descriptive adequacy. To illustrate the kind of problem that arose, consider again the rule (23) that forms interrogative and relative clauses. We have such examples as (27), where an asterisk indicates an ungrammatical sentence,[12] and we continue to assume (anachronistically) the trace theory of movement rules:

> (i) the man [who John saw e] (27)
> (ii) I wonder [who John saw e]
> (iii) the man [John saw e]
> (iv) *I wonder [John saw e]
> (v) I wonder [what John found of yours]
> (vi) *I wonder [who John found of yours]
> (vii) *I wonder [who a picture of e is on the table]
> (viii) *the man [[to whom]$_2$ I wonder [what$_1$ John gave $e_1 e_2$]]
> (ix) *what$_2$ did you meet the man [who$_1 e_1$ saw e_2]

Examples (i) and (ii) are straightforward. We could describe them in the format provided as follows: Phrase structure rules generate declaratives with a noun phrase (NP) (or in other structures, a prepositional phrase PP = P NP) in the position of e. We may think of *wh-* as a feature that appears in the surface form within a word (a noun, in this case) but is abstractly associated with the NP of which this noun is the head (or the PP containing this NP). This is the "*wh*-phrase," designated "*wh-*" in (23), repeated here:

$$(\text{X}, wh\text{-}, \text{Y}) \rightarrow (2, 1, 3) \qquad (28)$$

The NP is spelled out as *who* or *what,* depending on the category of the noun. The *wh*-phrase is moved to the left of its clause by the transformation (28). This is a simple rule, covering both relatives and interrogatives. It can readily be extended to other syn   .ic categories. Let us refer to it as the rule: Front-*wh*.

Consider next (27iii). Evidently, the *wh*-phrase can be deleted, so there is a further transformation: Delete-*wh*. But (27iv) shows that this transformation must be replaced by a more complex one with an extended structural description (SD), that permits it to delete the *wh*-phrase in a relative but not an interrogative. Turning next to (v) and (vi), with such corresponding declaratives as "John found a book of yours" and "John found a friend of yours," we see that some further condition must be imposed on the rule Front-*wh* (the same is true of the corresponding relatives). Example (vii), with the corresponding declarative "a picture of John is on the table" for the embedded clause, shows that the SD of (28) (see (22)) must be complicated to rule out movement in this case. Examples (viii) and (ix) (with the corresponding declaratives "he gave the book to the man" and "the man saw the book" for the embedded clause) indicate that the SDs must be further complicated.

The descriptive mechanisms provided by the format of UG can be elaborated to provide mechanisms that sufficed for these purposes but at a serious cost. The problem can be put in various forms: (I) why does the child not just use the simple rules Front-*wh* and Delete-*wh* throughout, thus deriving the wrong answers in many cases, instead of the more complex rules required for descriptive adequacy?; (II) the richness of the mechanisms allows far too many possibilities to be readily described so that far too many languages are submitted to the evaluation metric for choice; (III) explanatory power is sacrificed, because we have no explanation for the facts as they are. Many problems of this sort arose as soon as the task of constructing explicit grammars was faced.

The obvious way to approach such problems is to seek general principles governing rule application that can be abstracted from individual rules and attributed to the initial state S_0, thus expressed in UG rather than particular grammars; if feasible, this approach would preserve the simple rules Front-*wh* and Delete-*wh*. The earliest proposals, motivated by the examples (27), appear in Chomsky (1964).[13] A principle of recoverability of deletion states that an element can be deleted only if it is fully determined by a structurally related phrase containing its lexical features or if it is a "designated element," where these notions have to be made precise. In (27i), the relative element *who* is determined by "the man" and can therefore be deleted, giving (27iii); but in (27ii) it is not determined so that (27iv) is ungrammatical. For the same reason, *to whom* could not be deleted in "the man to whom you spoke," because the preposition *to* is unrecoverable. Taking the designated representative of NP to be the singular indefinite *someone, something,* so that only these elements can be replaced by a *wh*-phrase, we reduce (v)–(vi) to the fact that "I found something of yours" is grammatical but "I found someone of yours" is not.[14] The A-over-A principle states that a phrase of the category A (A arbitrary) cannot be extracted from another phrase of the category A—thus barring (vii), which requires that the NP *who* be extracted from the NP "a picture of who." Turning to (viii) and (ix), a general principle of UG states that a particular rule (here, Front-*wh*) cannot apply twice to the same clause, thus barring these examples.

With these general principles attributed to UG (i.e., to the initial state S_0), we can keep to the simple rules Front-*wh* and Delete-*wh* for both relatives and interrogatives. What the child has to learn is that English moves a *wh*-phrase to clause-initial position and that this phrase can be deleted; other properties of the constructions then follow by principles of S_0, expressed in UG. On this assumption, the child will know that the facts are as in (27) once Front-*wh* and Delete-*wh* have been learned, and these rules can be learned from very simple data, for example, (27i) and (27iii).

Note that if the reduction to Front-*wh* can be sustained, we no longer have rules associated with particular constructions: There is no "rule of relativization" or "interrogative rule." Rather, there are general principles such as Front-*wh* which enter into the formation of various constructions, along with other principles. Later work led to the conclusion that this "modular" character of the system of language is quite general.

A major step forward in this direction was taken by John Ross (1967), who developed a catalogue of "island constraints," structural configurations that do not permit extraction by movement rules. Subsequent work attempted to explain a variety of such constraints in terms of deeper and more natural principles from which their effects could be deduced, for example, the "subjacency condition" of bounding theory, which states that a transformation cannot move a phrase "too far" in a well-defined sense, and from general conditions (such as those of binding theory) holding of the representations to which the rules apply and those that are formed by them. Important work by Joseph Emonds (1976) led to further reduction of the variety and freedom of application of possible rules on principled grounds. The apparent obligatoriness and optionality of various rules and their order of application were also shown to be reducible to independently motivated properties of representations over an interesting range,[15] and the first attempts were made to derive certain general principles of rule application, or their effects, from such properties (Freidin, 1978).

Such general principles as the principle of cyclic application of rules, the island constraints, the subjacency condition, conditions on representations, and so forth serve to restrict the class of permissible rules because it is no longer necessary to incorporate within the rule itself the conditions on its application; in effect, these conditions are factored out of many rules and attributed to the initial state S_0. Formulation of such principles, then, is a step toward explanatory adequacy— assuming that the variety of potential human languages is not improperly delimited, either as too narrow or too broad a set. Again, the problem reflects the tension noted earlier.

Other work showed that directionality need not be stipulated in the transformation Front-*wh,* so that the rule can be reduced further from Front-*wh* to Move-*wh.* Further investigations along these lines gave substantial support to the idea that a large variety of transformational rules can be reduced to a form similar to Move-*wh* once the general principles are correctly formulated.

Correspondingly, the study of NP movement led to the conclusion that the various cases reduce to Move-NP. In the earliest work, there was, for example, a "passive transformation" converting (29i) to (29ii) by a rule with the structural description and structural change indicated informally in (30), moving the third term to the position of the first, adding *be-en* to the second term *see* (which becomes *be see-en* = *be seen* by a later rule; we overlook here the placement of tense), to the third position where it is assigned *by:*

(i) John saw Bill   (29)
(ii) Bill was seen by John

(NP, V, NP) → (3, be-en 2, by 1)   (30)

Similarly, the rule of raising that converts (31i) to (31ii) was expressed as a transformation (32), moving the third term of the structural description to the position of the first, which is empty in the underlying D-structure generated by phrase structure rules:

(i) *e* seems [John to be happy]   (31)
(ii) John seems [*e* to be happy]

(NP, V, [NP, X]) → (3, 2, 4)   (32)

With appropriate formulation of general principles on rules and representations, both (30) and (32) reduce simply to Move-NP, so that there is no passive or raising rule but simply an interaction of principles of UG yielding various constructions, differing from language to language as a consequence of options that the languages allow. Furthermore, the differences between Move-*wh*, Move-NP, Move-PP, and so forth can be in large part (perhaps completely) explained in other terms, so that we are left with the rule Move-α, α being an arbitrary category. It would be too strong to claim that this conclusion has been demonstrated, but it is a reasonable hypothesis, and many particular cases appear well substantiated.

Notice that the rule of raising is obligatory: The form (31i) is not a possible S-structure form and must be converted to (31ii). The same will be true of the passive rule if we assume that the structure immediately underlying the S-structure form is not (29i) but rather (33):

e was *see-en* Bill (by John)   (33)

We can explain the obligatoriness of these rules in terms of another subsystem of grammar, Case theory, along lines suggested originally by Jean-Roger Vergnaud.[16] We return to details and the general motivation, noting now only that this theory includes the Case filter (34) (to be modified below):[17]

Every phonetically realized NP must be   (34)
assigned (abstract) Case

In some languages, Case is morphologically realized, in others not, but we assume that it is assigned in a uniform way whether morphologically realized or not. We assume that objective Case is assigned to the object of a verb and nominative Case to the subject of a finite clause, and that prepositions assign oblique case to their objects. Intransitive verbs generally assign no case, except under restricted conditions as in "he dreamt a dream." The verb *seem* is intransitive, and *John* in (31i) is subject of a nonfinite (infinitive) clause; thus, the NP *John* in (31i) receives no Case and the expression violates the Case filter. Application of the rule Move-NP places *John* in the subject position of the finite main clause so that it receives nominative Case, satisfying the Case Filter. The same principles will apply in (33) if we assume that the general defining property of passive morphology is that it "absorbs Case," so that *see-en* is intransitive. Then *Bill* must move to the subject position in (33), to satisfy the Case filter.[18]

Notice that movement to subject position is not a property of the "passive transformation" (in fact, there no longer is such a rule); rather, it is derivative from the Case filter and the fact that passive morphology absorbs (objective) Case. If a passive verb takes a complement that is not an NP, then there need be no movement, as in (35) where the complement is a clause:

it is widely believed that John is intelligent   (35)

If a language permits some other Case to be assigned to the complement NP, then there need be no movement at all, as in Spanish or Italian where we have the equivalent of (33) with no movement, because these null subject languages permit the empty subject of (33) to remain in place, associated with the object of the passivized verb to which it transmits its nominative Case in a way to which we will return.[19]

Insofar as such conclusions are accurate, the transformational component of the grammar can be reduced to the rule Move-α—i.e., move anything anywhere—or perhaps even Affect-α (do anything to anything: delete, insert, move), as suggested by Lasnik and Saito (1984). Structural descriptions and structural changes can be eliminated; there is no need to stipulate obligatoriness and optionality for transformational rules, or to stipulate meta-rules (what had been called "traffic rules") governing the order in which they apply.

Nevertheless, there is some variation among languages in the way these rules apply. Thus, whereas in English, *wh*-phrases are moved, in Chinese and Japanese they are left in place. English has the S-structure form (24), derived from the D-structure (20), repeated here as (36ii) and (36i), respectively; but in Chinese and Japanese, both D- and S-structure forms correspond to (36i):

(i) you think [$_{NP}$ who] saw John (36)

(ii) who—you think [$_{NP}$ *e*] saw John

We might assume, then, that the general principle Move-α has associated with it a parameter determining the choice of α; its value must be fixed by experience to the extent that it is not determined by other features of the language.[20]

The exact nature of this difference among languages has been the subject of much study since the important work of Huang (1982), who gave strong evidence, later extended by others, that even in Chinese-Japanese the *wh*-phrase is moved to the boundary of the clause, leaving an empty category as a variable, although this operation does not take place overtly, as in English, but rather in the mapping of S-structure to the level of LF, in which scope and other properties are indicated. Thus, at LF, Chinese-Japanese also has forms corresponding to the form (36ii) of English, interpreted as (37) (=(25)):

for which person *x*, you think *x* saw John (37)

In brief, Chinese-Japanese and English share D-structure and LF representations (apart from choice of lexical items and other properties such as word order) but differ at S-structure; in Chinese-Japanese S-structure is the same as D-structure, whereas in English S-structure is the same as LF. We thus have the following arrangement:

	Chinese-Japanese	**English**	(38)
D-Structure	(36i)	(36i)	
S-Structure	(36i)	(36ii)	
LF	(36ii)	(36ii)	

The LF representation (36ii), common in essentials to both language types, is interpreted uniformly as (37).

English too has instances of LF-movement of wh-phrases, as in multiple wh-questions such as (39), first studied in this general framework by Baker (1970):

I wonder who gave the book to whom   (39)

We may assume that the LF representation of (39) is (40i) with the interpretation (40ii):

(i) I wonder [whom$_j$, who$_i$ [e_i gave the book to e_j]]   (40)
(ii) I wonder [for which persons x, y, [y gave the book to x]]

Thus, the option of applying Move-wh- in the LF-component is used in both language types, although under different conditions; and the LF representations of English, Japanese, and Chinese will be very similar, although the S-structures differ. This is what we might expect, if it is LF representation that is the interface between syntax (in the broad sense) and the systems of language use. If these conclusions are correct, then the parameter in question will have to do not with choice of α in the rule Move-α, but rather with the level at which the rule Move-α applies for various choices of α.[21]

There are other complexities in the system just discussed. Thus, compare (27viii), repeated here as (41i), with (42ii–42iv):

(i) *the man to whom I wonder [what he gave e e]   (41)
(ii) *the man whom I wonder [what he gave e to e]
(iii) *the man to whom I wonder [what to give e e]
(iv) *the man whom I wonder [what to give e to e]

With regard to (i), there is variation in judgments, and few speakers find it as hopelessly bad as (ii). Similarly, (iii) and (iv) are somehow intermediate between full well-formedness and the completely unacceptable status of (ii), with (iii) more acceptable than (iv) and, for many speakers, fully acceptable. Hence, something is missed when we mark all these examples simply as ungrammatical (*); see note 12. One relevant difference seems to be the finiteness of the embedded clause; extraction from a finite clause is harder than from an infinitival. Another relevant difference is that in (ii) and (iv), the two empty categories are NPs, whereas in (i) and (iii), one is an NP and one a PP. We might reformulate the principle that blocks multiple application of a rule to a clause (see p. 71) as a "filter" on S-structure: a VP cannot immediately contain two NP traces. Then (i) violates the finiteness constraint but not the filter, (ii) violates both, (iii) violates neither, and (iv) violates the filter. All may violate conditions that are subject to lower-level parametric variation among languages. These considerations, which should be incorporated within bounding theory, rank the examples in approximately the right fashion.[22]

The trace-theoretic analysis of *wh*-movement has a rich variety of consequences, some of which we will discuss below. Let us now consider one, related to the binding principle (10), which states that a pronoun cannot take an element in its domain as its antecedent. The proper formulation of (10) is a question of binding theory, the subtheory of UG that is concerned with the principles that govern the relations between referential dependents such as reciprocals, reflexives, and pronouns on the one hand, and their possible antecedents on the other. Let us express the antecedent-pronoun relation by co-indexing.[23] Then, an element X *binds* an element Y in its domain if X and Y are co-indexed, where we assume that Y is not contained within the category X. The principle (10) can now be understood to state that a pronoun can bind a distinct element X only if X is its trace.[24]

Suppose that we construct *wh*-questions from (11i) and (11ii), repeated here, replacing *John* by *who* and fronting *who*, thus forming the corresponding S-structures (42):

    (i) [he thinks John is intelligent]   (11)
    (ii) John thinks [he is intelligent]

(i) who does he think *e* is intelligent   (42)
(ii) who *e* thinks he is intelligent

Again, these may be assumed to be the LF representations as well. Interpreting *e* as a variable bound by the quasi-quantifier *who,* and replacing the latter by its meaning, we derive the corresponding interpretations:

(i) for which person *x,* he thinks *x* is intelligent   (43)
(ii) for which person *x, x* thinks he is intelligent

Pronouns may, in general, be interpreted as referentially dependent or free in reference; thus, in (11ii), *he* may refer to John or to someone else. Suppose we take *he* to be referentially dependent on *e* in (42ii), thus taking *he* in (43ii) to be a bound variable identified with *x.* The interpretation, then, is:

for which person *x, x* thinks *x* is intelligent   (44)

Here we are asking for the identification of a person satisfying the condition: *x* thinks *x* is intelligent. In fact, (44) is a possible interpretation of (42ii).

Suppose now that we interpret *he* as referentially dependent on *e* in (42i), so that *he* in (43i) is a bound variable identified with *x.* Again this yields the interpretation (44), but in this case, the interpretation is unavailable: (42i) does not have the sense of (44). This phenomenon is known as "strong crossover"[25] — "crossover" because in the barred case the *wh*-phrase has crossed over the pronoun, "strong" because the effect is stronger than in crossover constructions of other kinds.

As before, we ask how the language learner knows these facts, which are not necessary properties of any imaginable language and are surely neither taught nor derivable by general principles of induction or analogy from direct experience. An answer is provided by the principle (10). In (42i) but not (42ii), *x* is in the domain of *he* and therefore cannot be bound by *he.* Thus, the phenomenon of strong crossover is reduced to a more general principle of binding theory.[26]

The binding principle (10) is stated as a property of pronouns: A pronoun cannot bind its antecedent. We might, alternatively, think of the principle as stating a condition on the expression that serves as antecedent. Then the import of (10) is that an expression such as *John, the man,* or a variable may not be bound by a pronoun. Let us refer to such expressions as *r-expressions,* where the term is intended to indicate that they function in a quasireferential fashion, not in the sense of true semantic reference but rather in that they may be taken to denote elements in an associated model (see p. 44–45, above; take "denotation" to be the relation between an r-expression and the element or elements of the model to which it "refers" or which satisfy it, in the case of a variable).

Now it seems that (10) can be generalized to:

An r-expression must be free   (45)

This revision overcomes the problem raised in note 24. Principle (10) is the special case of (45) where the r-expression is bound by a pronoun, hence not free. But (45) also rules out such sentences as (46) with the interpretation indicated by the indexing:

*John$_i$ didn't realize that [the fool]$_i$ had left the   (46)
headlights on

In contrast, this association of an epithet such as *the fool* with its antecedent is permissible when the epithet is free, as in (47), where brackets [$_d$ and] bound the domain of the potential antecedent:

(i) [$_d$ John$_i$ turned off the motor], but [the fool]$_i$ (47)
    had left the headlights on
(ii) [$_d$ John's$_i$ friends] didn't realize that [the fool]$_i$
     had left the headlights on

The point extends beyond epithets; consider (48i) and (48ii) as contrasted with (49):

(i) [$_d$ Reagan$_i$ was elected], although [the former   (48)
    actor]$_i$ is regarded by many with a good deal of
    skepticism

(ii) [d Reagan's$_i$ main problem] is that [the former
actor]$_i$ is regarded by many with a good deal of
skepticism

*[d Reagan$_i$ is aware that [the former actor]$_i$ is   (49)
regarded by many with a good deal of skepticism]

It seems reasonable, then, to extend (10) to the more general
binding principle (45) holding of r-expressions, although
questions arise in this connection that I will put aside here,
including the question of whether (45), unlike (10), may be
parametrized.[27]

Note that (45) cannot be correct as it stands because it rules
out variables entirely, these being operator-bound, hence, not
free. The principle evidently does not refer to "operator-
binding" but rather to binding in the sense relevant to
referential-dependence. We can express these facts by distinguishing two kinds of positions in which noun phrases can
appear.[28] The first class of positions contains those that are
assigned grammatical functions such as subject and object
(including the object of a preposition); let us call these "A-
positions," indicating that they may (although they need not)
be filled by arguments, the latter being quasireferential elements
that require a semantic role. The A-positions, then, are the
positions in which semantic roles such as agent, patient, and so
forth can in principle be assigned, although whether they are in
fact assigned depends on the choice of lexical items. Other
positions we will call "Ā-positions" in particular, the clause-
external position occupied by operators such as *who*. The
principle (45) is then restricted to "A-binding," that is, binding
from an A-position.[29] The principle states that r-expressions
must be A-free. Some further sharpening is required, as we will
see directly.

3.3.2   The Phrase Structure Component

We have so far been considering some of the steps that were
taken to restrict the descriptive power of the transformational
component of a rule system so that explanatory power is
increased and we progress toward a solution of our variant of

Plato's problem. Evidently, developments of the sort just outlined would constitute no progress at all if some other component of the rule system were enriched in descriptive power while the transformational component is restricted; in that case, the same problems would arise once again. A crucial element of this work, then, was that it did not lead to an increase in the variety of possible systems of phrase structure rules.

In fact, the phrase structure component poses essentially the same problems as those illustrated with regard to transformations: Far too many possible systems of the permitted format are available, so explanatory adequacy is sacrificed and our variant of Plato's problem is unresolved. The solution is the same: Find ways to reduce the variety of phrase structure systems by abstracting general properties, assigning them to S_0. This topic too was addressed from the early 1960s. For example, it was noticed that reference to context in phrase structure rules is restricted to rules such as (6) that assign lexical items to their syntactic categories. The obvious suggestion, then, is to separate the lexicon from the syntax, as a separate component; syntactic phrase structure rules are then context-free, so that their possible variety is sharply reduced.

Separation of the lexicon from the syntax permits still further reduction of the phrase structure component, which can be regarded as a kind of "projection" of lexical properties. As we have seen, phrases typically consist of a head (noun, verb, adjective, preposition, and possibly others) and an array of complements determined by lexical properties of the head. The category consisting of the head and its complements is a *projection* of the head (NP if the head is an N, VP if the head is a V, etc.). Consider again the examples (17) and (18), repeated here as (50) and (51):

(i) John [$_{VP}$ claimed [$_S$ that Bill hit the man]]   (50)
(ii) the [$_{N'}$ claim [$_S$ that Bill hit the man]]

John's [$_{N'}$ claim [$_S$ that Bill hit the man]]   (51)

As a lexical property, *claim* takes a clausal complement (as one option). If it is a verb, then it and its complement form a VP with *claim* as head, as in (50i); if it is a noun, then it and its complement form an N', with *claim* as head as in (50ii) and (51). Since these facts are expressed in the lexicon, they need not be duplicated in the syntax by phrase structure rules. We therefore need no phrase structure rules to determine that *claim* takes a clausal complement in the examples (50) and (51); selection of the lexical item *claim* (with this lexical option) determines these aspects of the syntactic representations with no recourse to phrase structure rules. In general, the phrase structure rules expressing head-complement structure can be eliminated apart from order by recourse to a projection principle, which requires that lexical properties be represented by categorial structure in syntactic representations: If *claim* takes a clausal complement as a lexical property, then in syntactic representations it must have a clausal complement.

Furthermore, it is a general property of language, not a specific property of English, that an N' takes a determiner, although it is a specific property of English that this determiner may be a full NP, as in (51). Hence, virtually no options concerning these examples need to be specified in the phrase structure rules for English.

These and other general properties of the system are formulated in a component of UG called "X-bar theory," with further reduction of the options for phrase structure rules. Subsequent work suggested that the order of complements can in large part be determined by other general principles of UG. For example, one principle of Case theory is a principle of Case adjacency requiring that where Case is not morphologically realized, a Case-marked element must be adjacent to its Case-assigner (with some variations), so that if a verb takes an NP and a PP complement, the former will be closer to the verb ("put [the book] [on the table]," *"put [on the table] [the book])."[30]

The end result of this work has been to suggest that the phrase structure component can be entirely eliminated, apart from certain parameters of X-bar theory: For example, does the head precede its complements, as in English-like languages, so that we have the constructions N-complement, V-complement, A-complement, and P-complement; or does it follow them, as in Japanese-like languages, so that we have the corresponding constructions complement-N, complement-V, complement-A, and complement-P? There are also more complex cases. The exact nature of these parameters is currently under investigation, but it seems now that rules of phrase structure are not among the elements learned in the transition to the steady state; rather, values are fixed for certain of the parameters of X-bar theory. In other words, insofar as these conclusions can be supported, it follows that there are no phrase structure rules—a highly desirable consequence for reasons already discussed.[31]

To summarize, we observed at the outset of Section 3.2 that the first attempts to answer the questions (1) of Chapter 1 postulated a format for rule systems that allowed for two types of rules: phrase structure rules and transformational rules. Each type was an adaptation of traditional notions to the framework of generative grammar. Concern for the problem of explanatory adequacy—our variant of Plato's problem—led to efforts to reduce the variety of possible rule systems allowed by this format. Both types of rules allow a wide range of options that are never realized and are presumably unrealizable, and the availability of these options makes it extremely difficult to account for the fact that a specific language is fixed by the available evidence. The device of phrase structure rules is particularly suspect, because these rules so closely reflect lexical properties. Statement of the lexical properties is ineliminable from the grammar: For example, the grammar cannot avoid stating that *claim* takes a propositional complement as part of its lexical entry. Therefore, it is to be expected that the phrase structure rules should be eliminable insofar as they merely restate, in another form, the essential content of lexical entries. In fact, it seems that such rules are eliminable more generally, that there are no rules of this type in language. In the case of transformational rules, we have no comparable reason for skepticism concerning their existence, but it seems that the variety of these rules can be significantly reduced, perhaps to Move-α or Affect-α, with some parametric variation. These steps sharply restrict the class of possible languages to be submitted to an evaluation metric, given linguistic evidence. In fact, it seems possible that this device too can be eliminated, and that the system of UG is so designed that given appropriate evidence, only a single candidate language is made available, this language being a specific realization of the principles of the initial state S_0 with certain options settled in one way or another by the presented evidence (e.g., the value for the head-parameter).

3.3.3   General Principles of UG

3.3.3.1   *The Projection Principle and Empty Categories.*
A number of general principles have been proposed concerning well-formed structures that reduce the recourse to rule systems. One is the projection principle, already mentioned, which states that lexical structure must be represented categorially at every syntactic level.[32] This principle is one of those that contribute to eliminating phrase structure rules—completely, apart from some language-specific idiosyncracies, if the order of various complements and adjuncts is also determined by general principles once the parameters such as head-first, head-last are fixed.

A consequence of the projection principle is, to put it informally, that if some element is "understood" in a particular position, then it is *there* in syntactic representation, either as an overt category that is phonetically realized or as an empty category assigned no phonetic form (although its presence may affect phonetic form; see pp. 162f. below). Thus, if *see* is lexically characterized as a transitive verb, it must have an object, syntactically represented as its complement in a Verb Phrase, at every syntactic level: that is, at D-structure, S-structure, and LF but, of course, not necessarily at surface structure (PF). If there is no overt element in this position, then there must be an empty category of the required type. The structural representation of "the man I saw," then, must be (52), where the empty category *e* is the NP object of *see*:

the man [I [$_{VP}$ saw *e*]]   (52)

Furthermore, the properties of empty categories, determined in a manner to which we will return, require that *e* in this case be a variable bound by an operator in clause-initial position, so that there is still another empty category in (52). The structure is then (53), where O is an empty category operator binding *e*:

the man [O [I [$_{VP}$ saw e]]]   (53)

This empty operator might be lexically realized as *who;* in either case, the operator moves to the Ā-position preceding the clause by the rule Move-α. We might assume, as before, that a *wh*-phrase was moved and then deleted under the recoverability condition (see p. 70), or that the empty element was itself base-generated at D-structure and fronted by Move-α.

In short, in such cases as these, properties of lexical structure and general principles of various subsystems of UG determine the form of syntactic representations without recourse to phrase structure rules at all. We turn directly to less transparent cases.

Notice that the variable in (53), although bound by the operator O, does not have its range specified by O, since the latter is an empty category. In fact, the semantic role of the variable is determined in another way here: Its value is fixed by the phrase, *the man*, that heads the relative clause. The interpretation of (52), in short, is:

the man x such that [I saw x]   (54)

We may assume that in this case the embedded relative clause is "predicated" of its head so that the index shared by O, e is identified with that of *man*. This property is quite general. A variable must not only be bound by an operator in the sense described earlier but must be bound in a still stronger sense: Either its range must be determined by its operator, or its value must be determined by an antecedent that binds it. Let us call this property *strong binding* as distinct from ordinary binding. Then, a further principle is:

A variable must be strongly bound   (55)

This requirement seems entirely natural; it has interesting empirical consequences, as we will see.

These considerations lead us to modify slightly the binding principle (45), which states that an r-expression, in particular a variable, must be free, meaning A-free (see pp. 79–80). In (53) the variable is not A-free because it is A-bound by *the man*.[33] The obvious extension of (45) is:

An r-expression must be A-free (in the domain of its   (56)
operator)

We understand (56) to stand for the two principles (57i) and
(57ii), applied disjunctively—i.e., the second applies only when
the first is inapplicable:

(i) An r-expression must be A-free in the domain   (57)
    of its operator
(ii) An r-expression must be A-free

The first applies to variables, the second to nonvariables. Further
reduction is, perhaps, possible, but I will not pursue the matter.[34]

3.3.3.2   *Some Properties of the Lexicon.*   Having virtually

eliminated phrase structure rules through recourse to certain
general principles and properties of the lexicon, we now consider
just what information the latter must contain. In the first place,
the lexicon presents, for each lexical item, its (abstract) phonological form and whatever semantic properties are associated
with it. Among these will be the "selectional properties" of
heads of constructions: nouns, verbs, adjectives, and particles
(prepositions or postpositions, depending on how the head-
complement parameters are set in the language). The entry for
the word *hit*, for example, will specify that it takes a complement
with the semantic role of recipient of action (patient), and that
its subject has the semantic role of agent (perhaps determined
compositionally; see pp. 59–60). For the word *persuade,* the
lexical entry will specify that it takes two complements, the
target of the action (let us say, with the general semantic role of
goal) and a proposition, and that the phrase of which *persuade*
is head assigns the role of agent to the subject. Let us call these
properties "semantic selection" (s-selection), putting aside their
further properties.

Is it also necessary to specify in the lexicon properties of
categorial selection (c-selection), for example, that *hit* takes an
NP complement (*hit John*)? The latter specification seems
redundant; if *hit* s-selects a patient, then this element will be an
NP. If c-selection is redundant, in general, then the lexicon can
be restricted to s-selection.[35]

Let us assume that if a verb (or other head) s-selects a semantic category C, then it c-selects a syntactic category that is the "canonical structural realization of C" (CSR(C)). Take CSR(patient) and CSR(goal) to be NP; then *hit* c-selects NP. Consider now the more complex case of the verb *persuade,* which appears in the following syntactic frames:

$$\begin{align}&\text{(i) } -[\text{John}]\,[\text{that he should go to college}]\\&\text{(ii) } -[\text{John}]\,[\text{to go to college}]\\&\text{(iii) } -[\text{John}]\,[\text{of the importance of going to college}]\end{align} \tag{58}$$

The lexical entry of *persuade* indicates that it s-selects a goal and a proposition. Can we derive the facts of (58) from this property alone, given the principles of UG?

Continuing to assume that CSR(goal) = NP, we can dispense with the stipulation that *persuade* c-selects NP. Suppose we assume that CSR(proposition) is either clause or NP, where the NP will then receive a propositional interpretation (and only NPs that permit such an interpretation will appear). Then, in addition to its object NP, *persuade* will c-select a second category that is either clause or NP. Furthermore, we need not stipulate that the object precedes the second complement; this follows from the Case adjacency principle.[36] Thus, the possible structures for a VP headed by *persuade* are (59), where NP_1 is the object:

$$\begin{align}&\text{(i) } -NP_1 \text{ clause}\\&\text{(ii) } -NP_1\ NP_2\end{align} \tag{59}$$

In case (ii), the second NP violates the Case filter as it stands; English deals with this problem, quite generally, by employing the semantically empty proposition *of* as a Case-marker, so that the actual form of (ii) is:

$$-NP_1\,[\text{of-}NP_2] \tag{60}$$

We return to the properties of this rule of *of*-insertion. Assuming it, we have the structures:

$$\begin{align}&\text{(i) } -NP_1 \text{ clause}\\&\text{(ii) } -NP_1\,[\text{of-}NP_2]\end{align} \tag{61}$$

Returning now to (58), we see that case (iii) is an instance of (61ii), where the NP "the importance of going to college" is interpreted as a proposition ("that is important to go to college"). The other two cases of (58) are instances of (61i), with the two options for a clause: finite and infinitival.

In short, the lexical entry for *persuade* need only indicate that it s-selects two complements, one a goal, the other a proposition. All other features of the VP headed by *persuade* are determined by general properties of UG. A child learning English must, of course, learn the meaning of the word *persuade* including its properties of s-selection and must also learn the value of the head-complement parameter for English (head-first) and the specific properties of Case assignment in English (the fact that the Case adjacency principle is invoked, presumably a reflex of the poverty of the morphological Case system). Nothing more must be learned to determine the forms of (58). In particular, no properties of c-selection and no rules of phrase structure are required in this case.

Consider the verbs *ask, wonder,* and *care,* each of which s-selects an interrogative proposition:

(i) I asked [what time it is]   (62)
(ii) I wondered [what time it is]
(iii) I (don't) care [what time it is]

Since these verbs s-select proposition, they should c-select CSR(proposition), either clause or NP. They do c-select clauses, as in (62), but only *ask* c-selects NP:

(i) I asked the time   (63)
(ii) *I wondered the time
(iii) *I cared the time

Thus, (63i) has the meaning of (62i), as we expect, but (63ii) does not mean (62ii), and (63iii) does not mean (62iii). What is the cause of these discrepancies?

Pesetsky suggests that the answer lies in Case theory. The verb *ask,* but not *wonder* or *care,* is transitive, assigning objective Case. Thus, (63ii) and (63iii) violate the Case filter. In fact, corresponding forms are possible if a preposition is inserted assigning Case:

> (i) I wondered about the time (of his arrival) (64)
> (ii) I cared about the time (of his arrival)

The same paradigm is found in the case of adjectives such as *uncertain:*

> (i) John is uncertain [what time it is] (65)
> (ii) John is uncertain [about the time]
> (iii) John is uncertain [of the time]
> (iv) *John is uncertain [the time]

As distinct from intransitive verbs, adjectives permit *of*-insertion (as in *proud of John,* etc.). Thus, we have (65iii) but no corresponding form for the intransitive verbs *wonder* and *care.*

Further evidence supporting Pesetsky's analysis, as he notes, is given by the paradigm:

> (i) it was asked what time it is (66)
> (ii) *it was wondered what time it is
> (iii) *it was cared what time it is

These results follow from the fact that passivization in English (but not some other languages, such as German) is generally limited to transitive verbs: hence, *ask* but not *wonder* or *care.*

A consequence of this analysis is that among the verbs that s-select propositions, some will c-select clause and NP (those that are transitive) and some will c-select only clause (those that are intransitive), but none will c-select only NP. This generalization, noted by Grimshaw, follows from Pesetsky's proposal. As he notes, some suggested counterexamples are only apparent, for example, *approve of:*

> (i) I don't approve of [rising employment] (67)
> (ii) *I don't approve of [that unemployment is rising]

But this clearly follows from the fact that for other reasons, preposition-clause structures are excluded in English so that we may assume that as expected, both cases of CSR(proposition) are, in principle, available.

If the argument can be generalized—by no means a trivial task—we may conclude that while lexical entries must specify s-selection (as part of the semantic characterization of an item) and transitivity, they need not specify c-selection. If so, then c-selection is eliminated not only from syntactic phrase structure rules but from the lexicon as well.

Again, these are all steps toward explanatory adequacy, toward overcoming the problem of "poverty of stimulus," Plato's problem.

If we succeed in eliminating recourse to c-selection as well as phrase structure rules, thus reducing syntactic representations at D-structure to projections of semantic properties of lexical items, it will follow that the complement of any head in a syntactic representation must be s-selected by it, because there is no other way for the position to exist. For example, there cannot be such sentences as (68), where V is a verb that does not s-select an object and *there* is a pleonastic element (an "expletive," in traditional terminology) lacking any semantic role, as in (69):

$$John \; [_{VP} \; V \; there] \tag{68}$$

$$there \; is \; a \; man \; in \; the \; room \tag{69}$$

Example (68) would not be semantically anomalous, since no semantic role is assigned to the object, and the expletive object, not being an argument, requires no such role; but the structure cannot exist as a projection of the lexicon, hence, cannot exist at all if other modes of forming syntactic structures have been eliminated. Similarly, we cannot have "raising to object" to yield (70ii) (with *e* the trace of *Bill*) from the D-structure (70i):

(i) John [$_{VP}$ believes *e* [$_S$ Bill to be intelligent]]   (70)
(ii) John $_{VP}$ believes Bill [$_S$ *e* to be intelligent]]

The verb *believe* s-selects only a proposition. Therefore, in (70i) the position occupied by *e* cannot exist at D-structure, because it is not s-selected by *believe*. The sentence "John believes Bill to be intelligent" must have (71) as its D- and S-structure:

John [$_{VP}$ believes [$_S$ Bill to be intelligent]]   (71)

These conclusions are controversial, and there is consider-able literature and extensive work in progress bearing on their general validity, which I will not review here. They follow on principled grounds, if the argument just outlined can be sus-tained. I will assume here that they are correct, noting, however, that there are important empirical consequences in many lan-guages and a number of problems to be resolved.

There may be more complex modes of s-selection. Consider, for example, such "small clause" structures as:

(i) we held [$_\alpha$ John responsible]   (72)
(ii) we made [$_\alpha$ John leave]
(iii) we consider [$_\alpha$ John intelligent]

Over the years there have been various proposals for the analysis of such structures as these. The main verbs appear to s-select a proposition so that α should be some clauselike element. The verbs do not s-select the subject of α (John is not held, made, considered, in these examples), and pleonastic elements such as nonreferential *it* may appear as the subject in some such cases, for example:

we consider it obvious that John is intelligent   (73)

There also appears to be a close relation between the main verb and the predicate of the phrase α.

The earliest proposals within the framework of generative grammar analyzed *held-responsible, made-leave,* and *consider-intelligent* as complex verbs (constructed in a manner that we need not review) taking *John* as object (see Chomsky, 1975a, 1962). There are considerations that suggest that something of the sort may be the case. In certain interesting respects, the subject of α does behave like a main clause object although it is not s-selected by the verb. These facts might be accommodated by assuming that the main verb s-selects proposition and that the main verb and the predicate of α jointly s-select the subject of α.

It would follow, then, that the subject of α cannot be an expletive, because it is s-selected by the "complex verb." Thus, such forms as (74) are barred:

(i) we consider [$_\alpha$ there a man in the room] (74)
(ii) we made [$_\alpha$ it seem that John is intelligent]

The result is correct for (i), dubious for (ii), incorrect for (73). Similar questions arise in connection with (71); consider

(i) John believes [it to be obvious that S] (75)
(ii) *John believes [it to seem that S]

The distinction between *seem* and *is obvious* shows up elsewhere as well; compare (76) with (77):

(i) its being obvious that John is intelligent (76)
(ii) that John is intelligent is obvious
(iii) it is true that John is intelligent without being obvious that he is

(i) *its seeming that John is intelligent (77)
(ii) *that John is intelligent seems
(iii) *it is true that John is intelligent without seeming that he is

The example (ii) indicates that the pleonastic subject of *is obvious* but not *seem* is in a position to which a semantic role is assigned; the same is true of (i), for reasons to which we return, and also of (iii) (noted by Luigi Burzio), if we assume that the "understood subject" of the adjunct phrase is necessarily an element bearing a semantic role.

These constructions raise a variety of questions that we will not pursue here. They might be addressed in terms of the assumption that there is compositional s-selection in these cases along the lines just indicated, although many problems remain.

3.3.3.3 Conditions on Representation.

3.3.3.3.1 *Licensing, Theta Theory, and Visibility.*
Considerations of the sort reviewed above lead to a conception of UG as a virtually rule-free system. The representations that appear at the various levels are those that can be projected from semantic properties of lexical items in such a way as to accord with the various principles of UG with their parameters set.[37] Every element that appears in a well-formed structure must be *licensed* in one of a small number of available ways. The licensing options will include, among others, the following. An operator is licensed by binding a variable, from which it is not "too distant," in a certain well-defined abstract sense. A variable must be strongly bound (see (55)). Referential dependency must meet the conditions of binding theory. Every complement of a head must be s-selected by it. An element that assigns semantic roles must have recipients in appropriate syntactic positions: For example, the verb *hit* must have an (s-selected) object to receive the role of patient. A predicate (in particular, a VP) must have a subject, where the notions are syntactically defined (see Williams, 1980, and subsequent work). An element that requires a semantic role must be assigned such a role, where this assignment is determined by its grammatical function (subject, object, etc.) and by lexical properties of heads, the grammatical functions being expressed in syntactic configuration.

We call the semantic properties assigned by heads *thematic roles* (θ-roles). We refer to the conditions on proper assignment of θ-roles as the "theta criterion." Noun phrases that require θ-roles (e.g., *John, the man*) are *arguments;* nonarguments include such expletive elements as *there* in (69). Note that θ-roles are assigned only to elements in A-positions (see p. 80); we refer to those A-positions that are assigned θ-roles (that are θ-marked) as "θ-positions." Complements of a head always occupy θ-positions, but the subject may be an A-position that is not a θ position, as in (69).

In (69), we assume that *a man* is linked at D-structure to the position occupied by the expletive element *there,* this linking (say, co-indexing) being maintained through the derivation. Note that *there* takes the same number as the noun phrase linked to it, as we can see from such sentences as:

(i) there seems to be a man in the room   (78)

(ii) there seem to be men in the room

The S-structure of these raising constructions, as we have seen, is (79), where *there* has been moved from its D-structure position leaving the trace *e:*

there seem(s) [$_S$ *e* to be men (a man) in the room]   (79)

The verb of the main clause agrees with its subject *there,* which in turn agrees with the phrase *a man* to which it is linked. In (69) and (78), the nonargument subject *there* is an NP in an A-position but not a θ-position.

In (69), the noun phrase *a man* is not in a Case-marked position and, therefore, appears to violate the Case filter (34). We may assume, however, that it receives Case derivatively from the expletive element with which it is linked. Case is "transferred" from *there* to *the man* in (69); similarly, in (78).

The Case filter (34) can be sharpened and to a certain extent motivated by relating it to considerations of theta theory. Following Joseph Aoun, let us assume that an element is *visible* for θ-marking only if it is assigned Case. According to this visibility condition, a noun phrase can receive a θ-role only if it is in a position to which Case is assigned or is linked to such a position as in (69). Much of the content of the Case filter is now derivable from the visibility condition. The Case filter requires that phonetically realized NP must have Case. The visibility condition yields the same consequence for lexical arguments such as *John,* and *the man:* A lexical argument must have Case, or it will not receive a θ-role and will not be licensed. Similarly, it follows from the visibility condition that an expletive element linked to a non–Case-marked argument must have Case. The argument must have Case transferred to it by the linked expletive if it is to receive a θ-role, so that the expletive element must be in a Case-marked position. Hence, we must have raising in (78) from the non–Case-marked embedded subject position to the Case-marked main clause subject position. And we cannot have such sentences as "there to be a man in the room is unlikely"; rather, we must have "for there to be...," where *there* receives Case from *for,* transmitting it to the argument *a man*, which is now visible for θ-marking. In fact, *there* is linked only to non–Case-marked argument NP for reasons to which we turn directly, so the effects of the Case filter follow in full for this expletive element under this analysis.

But the visibility condition diverges from (34) in a number of other cases. In the first place, it requires that empty categories must have Case if they are arguments. The result is correct for variables; thus, we cannot derive such sentences as (80i) by *wh*-movement from the underlying structure (80ii):

> (i) *who does it seem [*e* to be intelligent]   (80)
> (ii) it seems [who to be intelligent]

The reason is that the variable *e* bound by *who* in (i) requires a θ-role, and, therefore, must receive Case, but in (i) no Case is assigned, as we have seen.

Second, the visibility condition does not require Case assignment to an NP that is not θ-marked (unless this NP must "transfer" Case to an argument, as in (69)). In (81), for example, the Case filter in the form (34) requires that Case be assigned to the bracketed NPs, but the visibility condition arguably does not:[38]

> (i) John is [a fine mathematician]   (81)
> (ii) [John], I consider [a fine mathematician]
> (iii) John did it [himself]

Let us assume this to be accurate and consider the Case filter to be eliminated as an independent principle, valid insofar as it follows from the visibility condition.[39]

3.3.3.3.2. *Full Interpretation.* The notions just discussed and other related to them can be formulated perspicuously in terms of the concept *chain*, where a chain is the S-structure reflection of a "history of movement," consisting of the positions through which an element has moved from the A-position it occupied at D-structure; we include here the vacuous case of the single-membered chain of an element that remains in its D-structure A-position. Thus, in (82i), we have the chain (*John, e*), indicating that movement has been from the position occupied by e to the position occupied by *John* (the *head* of the chain); in (82ii), we have the chain (*John*, e_1, e_2), indicating that movement has been from the position of e_2 to that of e_1 and then to the head position occupied by *John*:[40]

    (i) John was hit e by a car   (82)
    (ii) John seems [e_1 to have been hit e_2 by a car]

Example (i) is formed by one application of Move-NP; example (ii) by two applications (passive followed by raising). We will refer to the pair of successive elements in a chain as a *link* of the chain; thus, the chain (*John*, e_1, e_2) has two links; (*John*, e_1) and (e_1, e_2).

We may think of a chain as an abstract representation of the phrase that is its head and assume that θ-roles and Case are assigned to chains. The chains of (82i, 82ii) are abstract representations of *John*. The elements e in (82i) and e_2 in (82ii) are in θ-positions, and although the positions are not Case-marked, they are visible for θ-role assignment because the head of the chain is in a Case-marked position. This situation is typical: The chain is headed by a Case-marked position and terminates in a θ-position; Case is "transferred" from the head to the terminal position of the chain making the latter visible to receive the θ-role that it, in turn, "transfers" to the argument that heads the chain.

We now have two structures of "Case transfer": chains, and pairing of argument and expletive as in (69), repeated here:

there is a man in the room   (69)

We restrict attention here to the case of argument-headed chains, where the argument head is in a Case-marked position, returning to the more general case and to a closer consideration of the properties of chains and expletive-argument pairs in Section 3.4.3.

The theta criterion (see p. 93) can now be formulated as a property of chains, recalling that a position P is visible in a chain if the chain contains a Case-marked position, which we may take to be the head.

Each argument α appears in a chain containing a   (83)
unique visible θ-position P, and each θ-position P is
visible in a chain containing a unique argument α

The argument α then assumes the θ-role assigned in P.

This is one way of stating the intuitive idea that each argument is uniquely assigned its semantic role, and each available semantic role is uniquely assigned to an argument.[41] We will return to a direct counterexample to the visibility requirement in Section 3.4.1.

Note that this formulation of the theta criterion permits a θ-position to receive multiple θ-roles, as in (84):

John left the room angry   (84)

Here the position occupied by *John* receives one θ-role from the VP *left the room* and a second from *angry*, which is predicated of *John*.[42] That predication assigns θ-roles follows from the theta criterion because of such small clause structures as "John considers Bill intelligent" (see (72)). Here the argument *Bill* is in a D-structure A-position, which requires a θ-role that can be assigned only by predication by *intelligent,* unless, in accord with the suggestion on pp. 91–92., Bill is θ-marked by the compound verb *consider-intelligent.*

A further condition is required to block such structures as (85), where *angry* assigns a θ-role to *John,* although the sentence is still plainly a violation of theta theory:

*John seems [that it is raining] angry   (85)

What is required is the condition that D-structures are "uniform" with respect to θ-marking: Either they are θ-marked by every potential θ-marker or by none, where the potential θ-markers are heads and predicates. Suppose we say that α T-governs β if β is the complement of the head α or the subject of the predicate α; thus, T-government is the configuration of potential θ-marking, a special case of the concept of government to which we will return. Then D-structure meets the condition:

> If a position X is T-governed by α, then X is occupied   (86)
> by an argument if and only if X is θ-marked by α

The example (85) is now barred by the fact that the main clause subject is an argument although not θ-marked by one of its T-governors, namely, the VP.

We have been tacitly assuming throughout that D-structure is a "pure" representation of theta structure, where all and only the θ-positions are filled by arguments. Let us now make this assumption explicit as expressed in (86), which strengthens it slightly by the addition of the uniformity requirement.

We have so far been considering chains headed by an element in an A-position (A-chains), but the same ideas extend directly to Ā-chains headed by an element in an Ā-position. In terms of these notions, we can make a slight modification of binding principle (56), which required that an r-expression be A-free in the domain of its operator if it has one, otherwise A-free. Let us replace this with (87), understood as a pair of disjunctively ordered principles as before:[43]

> An r-expression is A-free (in the domain of the head   (87)
> of its maximal chain)

This gives the same results as before in the cases discussed but differs in a crucial case to which we will turn directly.

We might express many of these ideas by saying that there is a principle of full interpretation (FI) that requires that every element of PF and LF, taken to be the interface of syntax (in the broad sense) with systems of language use, must receive an appropriate interpretation—must be licensed in the sense indicated. None can simply be disregarded. At the level of PF, each phonetic element must be licensed by some physical interpretation. The word *book*, for example, has the phonetic representation [buk]. It could not be represented [fburk], where we simply disregard [f] and [r]; that would be possible only if there were particular rules or general principles deleting these elements. Similarly, we cannot have sentences of the form (88), interpreted respectively as "I was in England last year," "John was here yesterday," "John saw Bill," and "everyone was here," simply disregarding the unlicensed bracketed elements *the man, walked, who,* and *every:*

    (i) I was in England last year [the man]   (88)
    (ii) John was here yesterday [walked]
    (iii) [who] John saw Bill
    (iv) [every] everyone was here

This is not a logically necessary property of all possible languages; for example, FI is not observed in standard notations for quantification theory that permit vacuous quantifiers in well-formed expressions, as in (89i), which is assigned the same interpretation as (89ii):

    (i) (Ax) $(2+2 = 4)$ (for all x, $2+2 = 4$)   (89)
    (ii) $2+2 = 4$

But FI is a property of natural language.

Given the very general property FI and an appropriate theory of licensing, it would be redundant—i.e., flat wrong—to include in a grammar of English rules that specifically bar examples of the sort just illustrated—for example, rules that bar (88iii) by requiring that *who* be followed by a sentence with a gap of a certain sort: a missing position, an empty category, or in some languages, a resumptive pronoun (as in such marginal English examples as "who did you think that if he gets married, then everyone will be happy"; this device is typically used in English to overcome violation of conditions on gaps but is used more freely in many other languages). It is, then, a mistake to construct a rule system that bars (88iii) or (90) while permitting (91i), (91ii), and in some languages (91iii) or (more commonly) (91iv), where the pronoun is necessarily understood as bound by the operator *who* or an empty operator:

    (i) who did John see Bill   (90)
    (ii) the man (who, that) John saw Bill

    (i) who did John see *e*   (91)
    (ii) the man (who, that) John saw *e*

(iii) who did John see him
(iv) the man that John saw him

Such rules would simply restate in some complex way facts that follow from quite general syntactic properties of human languages. There is, then, no justification on the basis of these constructions for enriching the class of available descriptive devices to permit these facts to be stated directly in a rule system—an undesirable move in any event for reasons already discussed.

Recall that the language assigns to each expression a structure $\Sigma = (D, S, P, L)$, these being the representations at the levels of D-structure, S-structure, PF and LF, respectively. The elements of Σ must be appropriately related: Thus, S must be formed from D by successive applications of Move-α (or perhaps, more broadly, Affect-α) with its specific properties, P must be the result of applying to S the rules of morphology and phonology, and L, the result of applying to S the rules of the LF component, which may be invariant. We have now discussed a number of conditions that must be satisfied by D, P, and L. D satisfies one general formal condition and one general semantic condition. The formal condition is that it conform to the principles of X-bar theory (in general, representations at other levels do not conform to these principles; for example, if a VP is fronted in a clause yielding a structure $[VP [s...]]$, the resulting structure does not conform to X-bar theory); the semantic condition is that it be a "pure" representation of theta structure in the sense indicated, which we extend slightly below. P and L must satisfy the general principle FI, which requires that each element be licensed in an appropriate fashion.

The levels P and L constitute the interface of the language faculty with other cognitive systems, and correspondingly, the licensing conditions at P and L are, in a sense, "external." At PF, the general requirement is that each phonetic segment receive a phonetic interpretation by some invariant principle, external to the particular language and grammar. At LF, we have mentioned a number of licensing conditions, but we might look forward to the possibility of expressing them in a more organized manner relating to some broader theory of semantic interpretation. We may, first of all, distinguish the licensing conditions for maximal and nonmaximal projections. The latter are licensed relative to the maximal projections in which they appear, by X-bar theory. For maximal projections, we might expect that each phrase α must be licensed "externally" as either an argument or the trace of an argument, a predicate, or an operator. If an argument, α must be assigned a θ-role; if a predicate, α must assign a θ role; and if an operator, α must bind a variable (which, furthermore, is an argument and must be strongly bound). Then the licensing conditions on LF representations are analogous to those on PF representations, except that the elements of the former are more complex: maximal projections with internal structure rather than phonetic segments.

A requirement this strong on LF would have numerous consequences. For example, it would require that in such sentences as "John left town at noon," *at noon* be predicated of some element of LF (perhaps, an element of INFL, as suggested by Rothstein (1983)), and that all pleonastic elements be eliminated at LF. The latter conclusion, to which we return, has certain specific empirical consequences under plausible assumptions as to how this elimination of pleonastics may be carried out.

These conditions refer to the elements D, P, and L of the structure $\Sigma = (D, S, P, L)$ assigned to an expression. Are there independent conditions that hold of S, or are the properties of S fully determined by the requirement that S be properly related to D, P, and L? We have assumed that the projection principle holds independently of S, and we will discuss a series of chain conditions on the S-structure representation as well. However, these properties of S-structure may be reducible to the independent conditions of FI holding of PF and LF representation and the conditions on D-structure, given an appropriate account of the ways in which the elements of a structure $\Sigma = (D, S, P, L)$ may be related.

3.4. EXPLANATION IN A PRINCIPLES-AND-PARAMETERS THEORY OF UG

3.4.1 Some Sample Cases

In Section 3.1 of this chapter we considered the model of explanation that underlies the study of generative grammar. In

Section 3.2, we reviewed the first attempts to deal with the problems that arise, based on the assumption that a language is an elaborate rule system. Section 3.3 was concerned with various attempts to resolve the tension between explanatory and descriptive adequacy and to overcome serious difficulties in a rule-system model. This work has led finally to a rather different picture of language structure, as sketched in Section 3.3.3. This is the second of the two major conceptual shifts we have discussed, the first being the shift to the framework of generative grammar.

I will return to some further remarks about these ideas, but without further elaboration we can see how they will apply. UG consists of various subsystems—X-bar theory, binding theory, Case theory, theta theory, bounding theory (dealing with locality conditions on movement that account for such cases as (27vii–ix)), and so forth—each containing certain principles with a limited degree of parametric variation. In addition, there are certain overriding principles such as the projection principle, FI (full interpretation), and the principles of licensing. Certain concepts, such as the concept of domain discussed earlier and the related technical notions c-command and government, to which we return, play a central role throughout these subsystems. The interaction of the principles of these various "modules" determines the structure of each possible string—its representations on each level (see note 5). There are no rules for particular constructions such as interrogative, relative, passive, raising, and so on. Indeed, there are no rules at all, in the conventional sense, in the central areas of syntax. In particular, phrase structure rules can be largely eliminated, perhaps completely so.

To illustrate how such a system works, consider the sentence:

who was John persuaded to visit (92)

Let us ask what specific knowledge the child must acquire in order to be able to assign to the sentence (92) the structure that underlies its semantic interpretation and use. In other words, what specific knowledge must we have beyond that incorporated in the initial state S_0 in order to understand this sentence, insofar as the language faculty (in our sense) contributes to this end?

We must, first of all, know the lexical properties of the words; otherwise we cannot understand the sentence. We must know, then, that *visit* is a transitive verb that s-selects a category canonically realized as an NP object. By X-bar theory, *visit* must head a VP and, by the projection principle, its NP object must appear in the syntactic representation. The object must be an empty category, because no overt NP is present. One of the values of the X-bar theory parameters for English is that English is a "head-first" language, so that the object is to the right of *visit*. Furthermore, to be licensed, the predicate [*visit e*] must have a subject, the two forming a clause (S); since the subject is not overt, it must be another empty category.

Turning to *persuade*, we know that it is a verb that takes an object and a clausal complement, their order determined by the Case adjacency principle as we have seen. Continuing in this way, we conclude that the structure of (92) must be (93), where I omit a number of categories and category labels, for simplicity:

who was [John [$_{VP}$ persuaded e_i [e_j to [$_{VP}$ visit e_k]]]]   (93)

This much of the structure is determined simply on the basis of lexical properties and the value of the head-complement parameter, given principles of UG.

For the structure (93) to be well formed, each element must be licensed. The *wh*-phrase must bind a variable, and each argument must be assigned a θ-role. For reasons determined by UG, only e_k may be a variable (the other empty categories are not in Case-marked positions and, therefore, are not visible for θ-role assignment). Therefore, *who* must bind e_k. *John* is the subject of a passive, a position to which no θ-role is assigned (a non-θ-position), as we can see from the fact that nondenoting expressions appear there ("it is alleged that...," "advantage was taken of Bill," etc.).[44] Therefore, *John* must bind some element in a θ-position that can transfer its θ-role to *John* by the general convention regarding chains. Unless bound by *John*, e_i will not be licensed. Therefore, *John* must bind e_i, which, although not in a Case-marked position, is nevertheless visible for θ-marking by *persuade* because it is in a chain headed by the Case-marked element *John.*

This leaves e_j, *an element* that we will refer to as **PRO**, an empty category with a restricted distribution to which we will return; in particular, it appears in non–Case-marked subject position, as in (93). Like a pronoun, this element may be either bound, as in (94i) where **PRO** is bound by *Bill* (the meaning is that John persuaded Bill that he, Bill, is to leave), or free, in which case it is generally understood in the sense of an "arbitrary pronoun" such as English *one,* as in (94ii):

> (i) John persuaded Bill [PRO to leave]   (94)
> (ii) it is time [PRO to leave]

Note that the element **PRO**, which is always an argument, is visible for θ-marking even though not Case-marked, and the same is true of a trace that it binds, as in (95), where a θ-role is assigned to e and transferred to the head **PRO** of the chain (**PRO**, e):

> it is time [PRO to be introduced e to the visitors]   (95)

This is the direct counterexample to the theta criterion mentioned earlier (p. 97). The principles formulated so far and others that we will discuss below extend to this case without modification if we assume that **PRO** has an inherent Case.[45] We will, therefore, assume this, noting, however, that this decision conceals a problem rather than solving it.

Returning to (93), we know that *persuade* requires that its object control **PRO**, as we see in (94i). So in (93), **PRO** (namely, e_j) is controlled by e_i, the object of *persuade*. In (93), then, $i = j$, e_i is bound by *John,* and e_k is bound by *who.*

All these connections are uniquely determined by general principles. Spelling them out, we interpret (92) roughly as "for which person x, someone persuaded John that John should visit x." To achieve this interpretation, the only information required specifically about English is knowledge of the lexical items. This, of course, must be learned, although there undoubtedly are very heavy universal constraints in this system as well, as is clear from the remarkable speed and precision of lexical acquisition, which pose another variant of Plato's problem in quite a sharp form. The remainder is deduced from general principles.

Let us return now to the examples (2)–(7) introduced in Chapter 1 to illustrate the problem of poverty of stimulus, repeated here as (I-2),...,(I-7):

I wonder who [the men expected to see them]	(I-2)
[the men expected to see them]	(I-3)
John ate an apple	(I-4)
John ate	(I-5)
John is too stubborn to talk to Bill	(I-6)
John is too stubborn to talk to	(I-7)

The problem posed by examples (I-2) and (I-3) is that the bracketed phrase has a different range of interpretation in the two cases: In (I-2), the pronoun may be referentially dependent on the antecedent *the men,* but in (I-3) it may not. The problem posed by (I-4)–(I-7), is that the natural inductive procedure that (partially) accounts for (I-5) fails utterly for (I-7), because the (missing) object in (I-7) is understood to be *John* rather than some arbitrary person, while the subject of *talk to* is understood to be some arbitrary person, not *John* as in (I-6).

How do we know these facts? They must be largely or completely deducible from general principles, because relevant information is unavailable to the language learner. What, then, do we know about the structure of (I-2)–(I-7), given just UG and specific information about English concerning the lexical entries and the parameters of the various modules?

Consider first (I-2) and (I-3). The verb *expect* s-selects a proposition, hence, c-selects a clause S. The latter may be finite or infinitival—in this case, it is infinitival with the predicate "to [$_{VP}$ see them]." The predicate requires a subject, which in this case is an empty category. The structure of (I-2) and (I-3), then, is:

I wonder [who the men expected [$_S e_1$ to see them]]	(I-2')
the men expected [e_2 to see them]	(I-3')

For general reasons that we have already discussed, e_1 must be the variable bound by *who* and e_2 must be PRO, bound by *the men.*

The interpretation of the pronoun *them* in (I-2) and (I-3) should, therefore, be determined by the principles that apply in (96), where we have an overt rather than an empty category in the embedded subject position:

$$\text{the men expected } [_S \text{ the boys to see them}] \tag{96}$$

In (96), *them* cannot be bound by *the boys,* but it may be bound by *the men* (or it may be free, always an option for a pronoun). The sentence, therefore, means that the men expected the boys to see either the men or some entities otherwise identified. The property of binding theory illustrated by this example is that a pronoun must be free in the domain of the nearest subject—one case of the specified subject condition (SSC), a principle of binding theory.

Turning now to (2′), we see that it is exactly like (96) except that it has *e* instead of *the boys.* By SSC, the pronoun in (2′) must be free in the domain of the embedded subject *e* and may be bound by the more remote subject *the men.* The sentence (I-2) thus means that I wonder for which person(s) x, the men expected that x would see them (the men, or entities otherwise identified).

Consider next (3′). By SSC the pronoun cannot be bound by the embedded subject PRO. But PRO is bound by the main clause subject *the men,* so the pronoun cannot be bound by this remote subject for that would entail that it is bound by PRO (assuming, throughout, that binding is expressed by co-indexing). Therefore, in (I-3), the pronoun must be free, not referentially dependent on *the men.*

The binding theory principle SSC is motivated independently of examples of the type (I-2) and (I-3). Presumably, it is a principle of UG, or a consequence derived from principles of UG, perhaps with some parameters set. Knowing SSC and the principles of UG that yield the structures (2′) and (3′), the speaker of English need learn nothing more to know that the pronoun in (I-2) can be bound by the subject of the clause in brackets, whereas in (I-3) it cannot be bound by that element.

The principle SSC requires that a pronoun must be free in the domain of its nearest subject, and that an anaphor such as *each other* must be bound in this domain. The judgments thus reverse if we replace *them* in (2′) and (3′) by *each other:*

<blockquote>

(i) I wonder [who the men expected   (97)

    [s e_1 to see each other]]

(ii) the men expected [e_2 to see each other]

</blockquote>

Here *each other* takes the trace e_1 of *who* as its antecedent in (i) and takes e_2 (= PRO bound by *the men*) as its antecedent in (ii). Thus, (i) means that I wonder for which persons, the men expected each of these persons to see the other persons; and (ii) means that the men expected that they (the men) would see each other.

These examples involve the trace of *wh*-movement in the position of the object of a verb or the subject of an embedded infinitive. The same argument motivates the presence of a trace in the position of the subject of a tensed verb:

<blockquote>

who do you think [e left]   (98)

</blockquote>

Consider, for example, the sentence (99i) with the S-structure representation (99ii) after *wh*-movement:

<blockquote>

(i) *which boy do they think likes each other   (99)

(ii) [which boy]$_i$ do they$_j$ think [e_i likes each other$_j$]

</blockquote>

The anaphor *each other* cannot take *they* as antecedent because of SSC, the "closest subject" being the trace e_i of [*which boy*]; it cannot take the trace as antecedent because it is singular. If the trace were missing, then *they* would be the appropriate antecedent, and the sentence would be grammatical with the meaning: For which boy x, each of them thinks that x likes the others. In contrast, in (100i) with the S-structure (100ii), *them* can take *they* as antecedent, by virtue of SSC and the presence of the trace of *which boy:*

<blockquote>

(i) which boy do they think likes them   (100)

(ii) [which boy]$_i$ do they$_j$ think [e_i likes them$_j$]

</blockquote>

Ample evidence of other sorts supports the same conclusions. Thus, in certain structures, anaphors are "subject-oriented" in the sense that only a subject can be antecedent, and the antecedent must be the "nearest subject," as illustrated in (101):[46]

(i) they told me that pictures of each other would   (101)
be on sale
(ii) *I told them that pictures of each other would
be on sale
(iii) *they thought I said that pictures of each other
would be on sale

But now consider (102):

(i) they saw the men, who (we think) [e believe   (102)
that pictures of each other are on sale]
(ii) they wonder who (we think) [e believe that
pictures of each other are on sale]

Here, *each other* is again in a configuration in which it must take the nearest subject as its antecedent. As the sense makes clear, the antecedent is the trace left by *wh*-movement in both cases, not *we* or *they*. The examples fall under the general principle that the nearest subject is the antecedent only if the trace of *wh*-movement is present.

Consider finally the example (I-7), and the question why it is not understood "on the analogy" of (I-6) in the manner of (I-5) and (I-4). As in the case of (92), we know that *talk to* has an empty category object with which it forms a VP, and an empty category subject forming a clause with VP as predicate. Thus, the structure is, to begin with something like:

John$_i$ is too stubborn [$_S$ e$_j$ to [$_{VP}$ talk to e$_k$]]   (103)

Because *John*, e$_j$, and e$_k$ are each θ-positions, each must be in a separate chain or the theta criterion will be violated. Therefore, neither empty category can be the trace of *John*, and e$_k$ cannot be the trace of e$_j$. Since e$_j$ is not in a Case-marked position, it cannot be a variable and must be PRO.

Turning to e_k, the distributional requirements of PRO exclude it from this position for reasons to which we return, so that e_k must be a variable, this being the only option left. The embedded clause, then, must have an empty operator binding e_k. The structure, then, must be (104), where O is an empty operator and e_k the variable that it binds:

John$_i$ is too stubborn [O$_k$ [PRO$_j$ to talk to e_k]]   (104)

But to be licensed, the variable e_k must be strongly bound in the sense defined earlier (see (55)). Since its operator, being empty, does not specify a range, the variable must be associated with an antecedent in a structurally appropriate position that assigns it a value. Only *John* is available as an antecedent, and it is in an appropriate position, as the subject of the predicate "too stubborn to talk to e_k," for general reasons. Therefore, e_k takes John as value. It follows, then, that $i = k$.

Recall that the binding principle (87) requires that a variable be A-free in the domain of the head of its chain. This condition is satisfied by (104); the variable is A-bound by *John*, but the latter is not in the domain of its operator O, which is the head of the chain formed by movement of O from its D-structure position to the position it occupies in (104).

Consider now the interpretation of PRO. Recall that this element is pronounlike in that it can either be bound or free. Suppose that PRO were bound by *John* so that $j = i$. But $i = k$ so it follows that $j = k$. This, however, is a violation of the principle of strong cross-over, analogous to (42) (p. 78). In other words, it is a violation of the more general binding theory principle (87). Therefore, PRO cannot be bound by *John*. But there is no other binder. Therefore, PRO must be free, hence, arbitrary in interpretation, as in such sentences as (94ii) or (95).

The interpretation of the sentence (I-7), then, must be:

John is so stubborn that no one will talk to him   (105)
(John)

In contrast, (I-6) has the interpretation:

John is so stubborn that he (John) will not talk to   (106)
Bill

The pair (I-6) and (I-7) does not follow the analogy of (I-4) and (I-5).[47] For a mind initially equipped with the principles of UG, the interpretation of (I-7) requires only knowledge of the meaning of the words. The rest is determined by a computational process of the sort just outlined, so it appears.[48]

The same principles explain the interpretation of the more complex examples (9) and (10) of Chapter 1, repeated here as (I-9) and (I-10):

John is too clever to expect us to catch Bill	(I-9)
John is too clever to expect us to catch	(I-10)

By an argument analogous to the one just given, in (I-10) the "understood" object of *catch* is identified with *John* and the subject of *expect* is arbitrary, so that the meaning of (I-10) is "John is so clever that no one will expect us to catch him (John)," whereas the meaning of (I-9) is "John is so clever that he (John) will not expect us to catch Bill." Again, the structure and interpretation are deducible from general principles, given knowledge of the lexical items. As noted, something of the sort must be the case, given the empirical conditions of Plato's problem.

The analysis of (I-7) and (I-10) entailed by the principles of UG has many other verifiable consequences. If e_k in (104) is, indeed, a variable bound by an empty operator, it must observe a variety of conditions on movement to clause-initial position, such as those illustrated in (27) above. Indeed, these structures do observe these general conditions on movement. Consider, for example, the sets of expressions of (107) and (108):

(i) John is too stubborn to expect anyone to talk to (Bill)   (107)

(ii) John is too stubborn to visit anyone who talked to (Bill)

(iii) John is too stubborn to ask why Tom wondered who talked to (Bill)

(i) who do you expect anyone to talk to *e*   (108)

(ii) *who did you visit anyone who talked to *e*

(iii) *who did you ask why Tom wondered who talked to *e*

The examples of (107) are grammatical with *Bill* in place, but only (i) remains grammatical if *Bill* is deleted. Again, these facts are known without instruction or relevant experience. The results follow at once from the assumption that if *Bill* is missing, then there is an operator-variable structure analogous to (108) with an overt operator and the same pattern of grammatical and ungrammatical structures. The principles of bounding theory that account for (108) will therefore apply to (107), yielding the judgments just reviewed. Sentence (107ii), with *Bill* missing, is example (14) of Chapter 1, which, as noted there, is not understood on the analogy of (107ii) with *Bill* present or with the inversion strategy applied in (107i) with *Bill* missing; rather, it is assigned no interpretation at all. The facts are determined by UG, along the lines just indicated.

Further evidence for the operator-gap representation and the principles from which it follows is provided by so-called "parasitic gap" constructions such as:

which book did you file e_i [without reading e_j] (109)

Here the operator *which book* appears to bind both the variables e_i and e_j, so that the meaning is: "for which book x, you filed x without reading x." Only variables, not other empty categories, license such parasitic gaps, as we can see by comparing (109) with (110); in the latter, e_i is not a variable, and the sentence does not mean that someone can file the book without reading it:

*the book can be filed e_i [without reading e_j] (110)

We now observe that constructions such as (104) do license parasitic gaps:

John is too charming to talk to e_i [without liking e_j] (111)

Hence, (111) must have a structure similar to that of (109), not (110). It cannot be that *John* binds the trace e_i, or the structure would be as in (110), and the parasitic gap would not be licensed. Therefore, e_i must be bound by an empty operator, thus licensing the parasitic gap as in (109). We therefore have further evidence that the embedded clause is an operator-variable construction.

The distribution of possible gaps in the embedded clause is also explained on the assumption that e_j is a variable bound by an empty operator, although it is easier to see this point by considering other constructions of the same sort such as the purposive constructions of (112), where (i) is analogous to (113):

(i) it is time [for us to give a present to Bill]   (112)
(ii) it is time [—to give a present to Bill]
(iii) I bought a book [for us to give—to Bill]
(iv) I met someone [for us to give a book to—]
(v) I bought a book [—to give—to Bill]
(vi) I met someone [—to give a book to—]
(vii) *I bought someone a present [for you to give—to—]
(viii) *I bought someone a present [—to give—to—]

John is too angry [for us to give presents to his   (113) friends]

The embedded clause appears in full in (112i) and (113). The examples (ii)–(iv) of (112) illustrate that any one of the three NPs in this clause can be missing, with an appropriate choice of main clause context. We would, therefore, expect ("by analogy") that any pair of these may be missing and that all three may be missing. The expectation is, in part, confirmed, as illustrated by (v)–(vi), but not completely, as shown by (vii)–(viii).

Exactly this array of facts is predicted by the principles we have so far been led to assume: The subject can always be missing (hence = PRO), and exactly one other phrase can be missing by an application of the rule Move-α, which may place one (but no more than one) operator in the preclausal position. The embedded clauses of (112) have the same structure as the embedded clause complements of the "too stubborn S" structures, although more options are realized because the main clause can be richer.

Although not exhaustive, this discussion suffices to show that there is substantial empirical evidence in support of the analysis just outlined with its specific assumptions about the principles of UG. In particular, the interpretation of (I-7), (I-10), and (107)—as that of (I-2), (I-3), and other examples we have discussed—is completely determined by principles of UG, given knowledge of the lexical items. We can explain how children know these facts without instruction or relevant evidence on the assumption that the initial state S_0 of the language faculty includes the principles of the various subsystems of UG, and that the mind is capable of carrying out computations of the sort indicated here, in effect deducing the facts from these principles once the lexical items and their properties are given. We therefore have evidence of a nontrivial sort for the existence of the mental representations and principles that enter into these computations and for the truth of the principles of UG and their language-specific realizations with parameters fixed, in whatever sense one can be said to have evidence for the truth of theoretical statements and for the existence of the entities they deal with.[49]

Compare the representation (104), repeated here as (114), with (115i), derived from the D-structure (115ii) that underlies the well-formed structure (115iii):

$$\text{John}_i \text{ is too stubborn } [O_k \text{ } [PRO_j \text{ to talk to } e_k]] \qquad (114)$$

$$\text{(i) *John is illegal } [e' \text{ } [PRO \text{ to talk to } e]] \qquad (115)$$
(ii) e is illegal [PRO to talk to John]
(iii) it is illegal to talk to John

We can derive (i) from (ii) by two applications of Move-α: First, move *John* to the front of the embedded clause, as in forming (114), leaving the trace e; then move *John* from this "operator position" to the position of e in (115ii), leaving the trace e'. Now e is a variable bound by the operator e'. Recall that in (114), $k = i$. Furthermore, e' is identical to O of (114). Therefore, both (114) and (115i) have the S-structure form:

$$\text{John}_i \text{ is AP } [e_i \text{ } [PRO \text{ to talk to } e_i]] \qquad (116)$$

Nevertheless, (114) is well formed and (115i) is not.

The "improper movement" that yields (115i) is not barred by the theta criterion, because in both cases of movement, *John* moves to a non-θ-position. But it is barred by the binding condition (87), which requires that an r-expression must be A-free in the domain of the head of its chain. In (115i), *John* is the head of the chain (*John, e', e*), and the variable *e* is A-bound by *John* and, therefore, not A-free in the domain of the head of its chain (namely, *John*). The difference between (114) and (115i) has to do with the chain structure, where a chain, as before, is the S-structure reflection of a "history of movement" from D-structure. In (114), we have two chains, (*John*) and (O, *e*), whereas in (115i), we have only the single chain (*John, e', e*). A range of examples similar to (115i) motivate the modification of (56) to (87).

Notice that (114) could not be derived in the manner of (115i) by double application of Move-α because the main clause subject position is a θ-position, so that movement to this position would violate the theta criterion, yielding a chain with two θ-positions.

This analysis of improper movement crucially requires that we regard Move-α as an operation converting D-structure to S-structure. A possible alternative interpretation that regards Move-α as in effect a property of S-structure, so that D-structures is "abstracted" from S-structure, would require a somewhat different analysis of the phenomenon.[50]

3.4.2 Further Considerations on Empty Categories

One crucial feature of this discussion is the assumption that empty categories appear in mental representations in a manner determined by the trace theory of movement rules, the projection principle, and the various licensing principles. Examples such as (I-2) and (I-3) of p. 105 provide fairly direct evidence for these assumptions, which enable us to explain the interpretation of these sentences as a consequence of the principles required independently to account for such expressions as (96). Examples (I-4)–(I-7) of p. 105 and others discussed provide further evidence on the basis of more complex and, therefore, still more persuasive argument. If movement did not leave an empty category (trace), then these facts would remain a mystery. The hypothesis that movement leaves trace, then, is an empirical one, which is supported by evidence of the sort just illustrated. As in other cases discussed, this is by no means a necessary property of arbitrary languages, although it appears to be a property of human languages. Certain theories of UG assume that there is no trace in such structures—for example, earlier theories of transformational grammar, or some of the theories that complicate and extend the variety of phrase structure grammars instead of attempting to reduce or eliminate them.[51] Evidence of the sort just mentioned indicates that these theories are mistaken.

There is comparable evidence concerning other empty categories required by the UG principles discussed. Consider the empty category that we have called PRO, which appears as something like a free variable in (117i) and (117ii) and a bound pronoun in (117iii), and (117iv):

   (i) it is illegal [PRO to vote twice]   (117)
   (ii) John is too stubborn [PRO to talk to]
   (iii) John decided [PRO to vote twice]
   (iv) John is too stubborn [PRO to talk to Bill]

In examples (i) and (iii), the D-structure, S-structure, and LF representations are identical (with an indication of referential dependency in (iii), at least at LF), and the PF representation is the same except that the empty category is missing. Is it correct to assume that the "syntactic" representations are as in (117), or should PRO be missing here too, as it is at the PF level? Again, the question is an empirical one, concerning the form and properties of certain mental representations. There is considerable indirect evidence supporting (117). We have reviewed such evidence in the cases of (ii) and (iv). Let us now restrict attention to the simpler cases (i) and (iii).

The licensing principle that requires predicates to have subjects, and, hence, entails the presence of PRO in these cases, is supported by the fact that it accounts for the distribution of the semantically empty elements that appear in such sentences as (118):[52]

   (i) it [is raining]   (118)
   (ii) I expect there [to be rain tomorrow]
   (iii) its [having rained] surprised me
   (iv) it [seems that there will be rain tomorrow]

If the bracketed phrases in such constructions did not require subjects for some general reason, it is not clear why the semantically empty elements *it* and *there* should appear at all.[53] The assumption is supported further by evidence drawn from null subject languages such as Spanish or Italian, which allow the subject to be missing at PF but require it, whether as an argument or an expletive, as an empty category at the other levels, for reasons that would carry us beyond the bounds of this discussion.[54] But there is also more direct evidence.

The projection principle requires that complements of heads must be represented at each syntactic level (D-structure, S-structure, LF), so that, in particular, objects must be represented, but it says nothing about subjects. Thus, it distinguishes between what Edwin Williams calls "internal" and "external" arguments, specifically, object and subject. The projection principle requires that the former be syntactically realized, but not the latter, although they are required as subjects of predication (either arguments or expletives). The two principles—the projection principle and the requirement that clauses have subjects—constitute what is called the extended projection principle (EPP) in Chomsky (1981). Rothstein (1983) proposes that the two clauses of the EPP are in fact closely related. We may think of a lexical head as a "lexical function" that is "unsaturated" (in roughly the Fregean sense) if it is not provided with appropriate arguments fulfilling the θ-roles it assigns, and we may correspondingly regard a maximal projection (apart from those that are quasireferential: NP and clause) as a "syntactic function" that is unsaturated if not provided with a subject of which it is predicated. Then, the EPP is a particular way of expressing the general principle that all functions must be saturated.[55]

External arguments are required as subjects of VP in clauses, as in (119), but not as subjects in corresponding nominalizations such as (120i) with a subject, and (120ii) without one:

they destroyed the town   (119)

   (i) their destruction of the town   (120)
   (ii) the destruction of the town

The reason is that the clause contains a VP predicate, but the nominalization does not contain a predicate. The structure of the NP is [Det N']; because N' is not the maximal projection of the head N, it requires no licensing principle (apart from X-bar theory) and, in particular, is not required to be licensed as a predicate. Furthermore, subjects may be expletive, whereas objects may not if the discussion on p. 90 is correct.[56]

For reasons to which we return deriving from binding theory (or, some have argued, Case theory), the element PRO is restricted to subject position—in fact, the position of subject of infinitive or gerund—where its presence is required by the licensing principle for predicates assumed earlier. Notice that some of the properties of PRO are shared by pronouns with arbitrary reference such as *one* in English, or more narrowly, *man* in German or *on* in French. Thus, in English we have the following configuration of data, for *one* taken in the relevant sense:

> (i) one shouldn't do such things   (121)
> (ii) one's friends shouldn't do such things
> (iii) we would scarcely believe [one to be capable of such actions]
> (iv) we would scarcely believe [one capable of such actions]
> (v) *one was here yesterday
> (vi) *they ought to meet one

The property of modal interpretation illustrated in these examples holds also for arbitrary PRO, and like PRO, *one* is restricted generally to subject position (subject of a clause as in (i) or of a noun phrase as in (ii)), though the latter constraint is much weaker for *one* than for PRO, as (vi) illustrates.[57] These properties are unexplained, and raise questions about the correctness of an explanation of properties of PRO in terms of government or Case. I will put these questions aside, merely noting a potential problem, and will continue with the assumption that the explanation for the distribution of PRO is internal to the considerations developed here.

The question we are now asking is whether it is correct to assume the presence of PRO in subject position, or whether the

S-structure, D-structure, and LF representations have no element at all in these positions, like the PF representation. Note that, in principle, there are three ways in which a subject may fail to appear overtly in some clausal structure: (i) it may be syntactically realized as an empty category; (ii) it may be realized as a constituent of the V head of the VP predicate, which assigns it a θ-role; (iii) it may be missing in both syntactic and lexical representations. In fact, all three conditions are realized, and they have distinctively different properties.[58]

The three possible cases are illustrated in (122), where in (ii), *e* is the trace of *the boat*:

(i) I decided [PRO to sink the boat]   (122)
(ii) the boat was sunk *e*
(iii) the boat sank

Take these to be both S-structure and LF representations.

A number of properties distinguish these cases. Consider first the possibility of "spelling out" the missing agent of *sink* in an overt *by*-phrase. This is impossible in case (i), possible in case (ii), and impossible in case (iii):

(i) *I decided [to sink the boat by John]   (123)
(ii) the boat was sunk by John
(iii) *the boat sank by John

There is no semantic reason for the status of (i) and (iii); thus, (i) could mean "I decided that John should sink the boat" (analogous to "I wanted John to sink the boat"), but it does not. Rather, only a subject that is present lexically but not syntactically, as in (ii), can be overtly realized in a *by*-phrase.

This property distinguishes (ii) from (i) and (iii). Structures (i) and (ii) are distinguished from (iii) by the possibility of adding "agent-oriented" adverbs such as "voluntarily":

(i) I decided [PRO to leave voluntarily]   (124)
(ii) the boat was sunk voluntarily
(iii) *the boat sank voluntarily

These adverbs require an agent, which may be expressed syntactically as in (i) or lexically as in (ii). Notice that in (i), *voluntarily* is associated with **PRO**, not its binder *I*, as it would be in "I decided [PRO to leave] voluntarily." In the latter, it is my decision that is voluntary, whereas in (i) it is my leaving.

Thus, the three possible cases exist and are distinguished from one another. In particular, there is evidence for the syntactic presence of **PRO** and the lexical presence of a "missing argument."

A variety of further properties distinguish these cases. Consider the question of control (binding) of the formally missing understood subject:

> (i) they expected [PRO to give damaging testi-   (125)
>   mony]
> (ii) *they expected [damaging testimony to be
>   given]
> (iii) *they expected [the boat to sink]

The asterisk in (ii) and (iii) refers to the interpretation analogous to (i), with the subject of the main clause controlling the "understood subject" of the embedded clause—impossible in (ii)–(iii), required in (i).[59] Thus, only a syntactically present element can be controlled by an antecedent.

Consider control *by* the understood subject:

> (i) it is time [PRO to sink the boat [PRO to collect   (126)
>   the insurance]]
> (ii) the boat was sunk [PRO to collect the insurance]
> (iii) *the boat sank [PRO to collect the insurance]

An element present at the syntactic or lexical level can serve as a controller. In (iii) the sentence can be given only the senseless interpretation with *the boat* understood as the subject of *collect*.

Consider the binding of an anaphor by the understood subject:

> (i) they decided (that it was about time) [PRO to   (127)
>   hit each other]
> (ii) *damaging testimony is sometimes given about
>   each other
> (iii) *the boats sank for each other
> (iv) damaging testimony is sometimes given about
>   oneself

Examples (ii) and (iii) do not mean "some people give damaging testimony about each other," "some people sank the boats for each other," respectively. An anaphor requires an antecedent, either syntactic or lexical, and the reciprocal requires an antecedent more specific than the lexically incorporated subject of passive.

Note that in (127i) the anaphor is linked to PRO, not *they*, for its interpretation, as indicated by the meaning: "they decided that it was about time for each to hit the other," not "each decided that it was about time to hit the other." Correspondingly, *they* can be replaced by *they all:* "they all decided (last week) that it was about time [PRO to hit each other]." Similarly in (128), *each* is associated with PRO, not the main clause subject *they:*

they decided [PRO to read a book each]   (128)

The sentence does not mean that they each decided to read a book, but rather that they decided that each of them should read a book. Again, these facts support the assumption that there is a subject PRO distinct from the antecedent that binds it.

Certain adjuncts require explicit arguments, for example, *together* or *without reading them* (at S-structure: *without* [PRO *reading them*]). These can be predicated of PRO but not of a lexically represented understood subject:

    (i)(a) it is impossible [PRO to visit together]   (129)
       (b) it is impossible [PRO to be visited together]
       (c) it is impossible [PRO to file the articles [without reading them]]
    (ii)(a) *it is impossible [for me to be visited together]
       (b) *it is impossible [for the articles to be filed [without reading them]]
    (iii)(a) *the boat sank together
       (b) *the boat sank [without seeing it]

The examples of (i) are well formed, because an explicit formal subject, PRO, serves as the subject of the predication. Note that in case (ib), the adjunct is predicated of the explicit formal subject PRO, not the understood subject of *visit*. The example (iia) is excluded because the understood subject of *visit*, being only lexically represented, cannot serve as the subject of the adjunct; and *me* cannot be the subject of the adjunct *together*. The examples of (iii) are impossible, because there is no subject for the predication.[60]

Consider next the question of what the subject of adjectival predication can be:

(i) they expected [PRO to leave the room angry]   (130)
(ii) *the room was left angry
(iii) *the boat sank angry

The adjective phrase *angry* is predicated of PRO, not *they*, and only a syntactically present element can be its subject.[61]

Montalbetti (1984) provides a different kind of evidence for the existence of PRO. In the null subject languages such as Spanish and Italian there is a distinction between PRO, with the properties we have been considering, and an empty "pure pronominal," call it *pro*, which is the null counterpart of the lexical pronouns and appears as the subject of a tensed clause with specific reference or as an expletive. There are, however, certain differences in interpretation between the null pronominal *pro* and its lexical counterpart, as illustrated, in such Spanish examples as (131i, 131ii), which translate the English (132):

(i) muchos estudiantes piensan que ellos son   (131)
    inteligentes
(ii) muchos estudiantes piensan que *pro* son inte-
    ligentes

many students think that they are intelligent   (132)

The English sentence (132) may have the interpretation (133), with *they* interpreted as a bound variable, in which case it entails that if John is one of the many students in question, then John thinks that he (John) is intelligent; or (132) may be interpreted with *they* referring to some set S of people (perhaps the set of students), so that if John is one of the many students, then John thinks that the members of the set S are intelligent:

for many students x, x thinks that x is intelligent   (133)

But the Spanish counterpart (131i) is unambiguous, lacking the bound variable interpretation as in (133).[62]

This restriction is relaxed, however, if a bound pronominal intervenes between the quantifier expression and the overt pronoun, as in (134i) with the interpretation (134ii):

> (i) muchos estudiantes dijeron que *pro* piensan   (134)
>   que ellos son inteligentes
> (ii) for many students x, x said that x thinks that x
>   is intelligent

Here the quantifier expression does not bind the overt pronoun locally, because *pro* intervenes, and *ellos* can be treated as a bound variable as in (133). Crucially, the same is true if PRO intervenes, as in (135):

> (i) muchos estudiantes quieren [PRO creer [que   (135)
>   ellos son inteligentes]]
> (ii) many students want [PRO to believe [that they
>   are intelligent]]

The sentence (135i) can mean (136), as the English counterpart can:

> for many students, x, x wants to believe that x is   (136)
> intelligent

This fact provides quite direct evidence for the presence of PRO in these constructions, for if PRO were absent, then (135i) should be interpreted analogously to (131i) rather than (134i).

The evidence reviewed indicates that passives have an implicit unrealized subject position that is assigned the usual θ-role of a subject, a θ-role that may be "transferred" to an associated *by*-phrase; such "transfer" of θ-role is impossible with the PRO subject, as in (123i), or we would be left with a chain, namely, (PRO) lacking θ-role. We might ask whether the same is true of other derived forms such as nominalizations. The evidence supports a positive answer:

> (i) the destruction of the city by the barbarians   (137)

(ii) the destruction of the city [PRO to prove a
    point]

These and other examples indicate that an implicit subject is
present but, as distinct from the case of passives, it is possible
that it is present not in the nominal but in the DET position, as
a PRO-like element. Roeper (1984) provides evidence in support
of this conclusion. He notes that control is lost if the subject
position is filled by NP-movement, as in (138i) derived from
(138ii), where *e* is the trace left by movement of *the city,* and
(138ii) may surface directly with *of*-insertion to assign Case:

(i) muchos estudiantes quieren [PRO creer [que   (135)
    ellos son inteligentes]]
(ii) many students want [PRO to believe [that they
     are intelligent]]

In (ii), PRO is controlled by the understood agent of *destruction,*
but not in (i). Hence, it seems that the nominalized form does
not assign the subject θ-role unless the subject appears, either as
a lexical element (as in "their destruction of the city...") or as a
PRO-like element in the specifier position. Many other questions arise that bear on this conclusion, including considerations
of lexical structure that we have not touched on here. We will
return to the matter in the next section.

Further properties are exhibited when we consider other
constructions, such as causative and perception verb constructions in the Romance languages. Without going into these
rather complex matters, it seems clear from the above that all
three possible cases of (122) exist, and that they are differentiated
in their properties. In part, these properties are predictable on
general grounds, but, in part, it is not entirely obvious why they
distribute among the several types of understood elements as
they do.

As this discussion illustrates, there is considerable empirical
evidence to support the conclusion that empty categories appear
where they are predicted by the principles of UG discussed, and
that they have quite definite and distinctive properties. A
genuine explanatory theory of language that addresses the

problems raised in (1) of Chapter 1 has to come to terms with these facts. Although many questions can be raised about the specific principles proposed, they are clearly genuine empirical hypotheses with considerable explanatory import, bearing on the nature of I-language and the innate structures from which it arises, the mental representations that enter into the use and understanding of language, the computations into which they enter, and the principles that apply to them.

We have seen that the element PRO is similar to a pronoun in that it may be either free or bound, as in (117), with cases (i) and (iii) repeated here as (139), or (140):[63]

(i) it is illegal [PRO to vote twice]   (139)
(ii) John decided [PRO to vote twice]

(i) it was decided [PRO to vote twice]   (140)
(ii) the decision [PRO to vote twice]
(iii) John's decision [PRO to vote twice]

The question of when PRO may or must be bound or free falls under control theory, another module of UG.[64] We restrict ourselves here to a review of some of the cases that such a theory must deal with, noting that the status of these cases and judgments is often not entirely clear.

One central case is illustrated in (140) and (139ii). Here, PRO is the subject of a declarative clause C that is the complement of the head *decide, decision*. These examples are of the form (141), with the NP object of α missing in this case:

$$[_{\alpha'} \alpha \text{ (NP)} [_{C} \text{ PRO to VP}]] \qquad (141)$$

In this configuration, if there is a potential binder appropriately related to the head α, then PRO must be bound by this binder. The concept "appropriately related" includes subject and object, as illustrated in (139ii), (140iii), and (142):

(i) John persuaded Bill [PRO to vote twice]   (142)
(ii) the students asked the teacher [PRO to leave the room]

The examples (139ii) and (140iii) illustrate subject control, whereas (142i) is a case of object control (*Bill* controls **PRO**). Example (142ii) is ambiguous; subject control is, in fact, strongly preferred if we replace "to leave" by "to be allowed to leave." Evidently, lexical and perhaps other factors are involved in the choice of controller.

   In these cases, **PRO** behaves much in the manner of an anaphor; its structural relation to its controller is essentially the same as that of an antecedent-anaphor pair, and its interpretation is very much like that of a reflexive (in fact, in earlier work **PRO** was considered to be a variant of reflexive for such reasons).[65] **PRO** is also anaphor-like in that it (typically) lacks independent specific reference, being either bound or interpreted as arbitrary. Similarly, **PRO** in these configurations cannot take a split antecedent, just as a reflexive cannot, in contrast to pronouns that can take a split antecedent:

   (i) *Bill wanted [Tom to decide [**PRO** to swim   (143)
        across the pond together]]
   (ii) *Bill wanted [Tom to feed themselves]
   (iii) Bill wanted [Tom to decide [that they would
        swim across the pond together]]

   In the very same structural configuration (141), however, **PRO** may be unbound as in (139i), (140i), and (140ii), where there is no antecedent appropriately related to the head α of (141). In this case, **PRO** behaves in the manner of a pronoun, either free with the arbitrary interpretation, as in (139i) or (140i) and (140ii), or bound by a more remote antecedent as in (144i–144iii):

   (i) John announced the decision [**PRO** to feed   (144)
        himself]
   (ii) John thinks it is illegal [**PRO** to feed himself]
   (iii) John thought Mary said that the decision
        [**PRO** to feed himself] was foolish
   (iv) *John's friends think it is illegal [**PRO** to feed
        himself]
   (v) John's friends think it is illegal [for him to
        feed himself]

As (iv) illustrates, PRO is still anaphorlike in that it must be in the domain of its antecedent (if any), as distinct from a pronoun; thus, *he* in (v) may take *John* as antecedent. Examples (i) and (ii), in fact, may also reflect anaphorlike properties.[66] PRO is like a pronoun rather than an anaphor in that it may take a split antecedent when not locally bound:

> (i) Bill wanted [Tom to approve the decision (145)
>   [PRO to swim across the pond together]]
> (ii) Bill wanted [Tom to agree that it was time
>   [PRO to swim across the pond together]]
> (iii) Bill's mother wanted [Tom to agree that it was
>   time [PRO to swim across the pond together]]

But even here, it seems, each of the antecedents must c-command as in the case of anaphors, so that in (iii) the split antecedents cannot be (*Bill, Tom*) (as noted by Joseph Aoun).

We have seen that anaphors are subject-oriented—in fact, bound by the nearest subject—if not locally controlled, as illustrated in (101), repeated here:

> (i) they told me that pictures of each other would (146)
>   be on sale
> (ii) *I told them that pictures of each other
>   would be on sale
> (iii) *they thought I said that pictures of each other
>   would be on sale

This property does not hold of PRO, however:

> (i) they told me that the decision [PRO to feed (147)
>   themselves] was foolish
> (ii) they told me that the decision [PRO to feed
>   myself] was foolish
> (iii) they thought I said that the decision [PRO to
>   feed each other] was foolish
> (iv) they told Bill that everyone said that [PRO to
>   feed himself] would be foolish

Examples (147ii) and (147iv) illustrate a pronounlike property of bound PRO when it is not locally bound: It need not be subject-oriented, unlike an anaphor, and it may have split subject antecedents (see (145)).[67] It is not very clear whether there is a real contrast between (147iii), (144iii), and (146ii); that is, whether the nearest subject must be the controller.

These examples illustrate that PRO is anaphorlike in some respects, pronounlike in others. They also illustrate the fact that PRO may have the full range of properties when it is the subject of a clause C that is a declarative complement of a head α, that is, in the construction (141), repeated here:

$$[_{\alpha'}, \alpha \text{ (NP)} [_C \text{ PRO to VP}]] \qquad\qquad (148)$$

In this construction, PRO must be bound if α has a potential binder as its subject or object. If there is no such potential binder, then PRO may be free with arbitrary interpretation or may be bound remotely under a range of other conditions.

This situation is slightly different if the clause C with PRO subject is the interrogative complement of a head α:

(i) they asked me [how PRO to rig the boat]   (149)
(ii) they asked me [how PRO to feed β]
(iii) I thought they wondered [how PRO to feed β]
(iv) John's mother asked me [how PRO to feed β]

In (i), PRO may be free or bound. The options are illustrated clearly in (ii). Here β may be *oneself, themselves*, and with *told* replacing *ask* it may be *oneself, myself*. In (iii), however, β can only be *themselves* or *oneself*, not *myself*, although there would be no semantic impropriety with the latter choice ("I thought they wondered how I should feed myself"). In case (iv), β may be *herself* or *oneself*, not *himself*, again illustrating anaphorlike properties. An interrogative complement is somewhat more free than a declarative complement in its control properties, but not entirely so. It exhibits some properties of pronouns and some properties of anaphors.

Adjunct clauses such as purposives (see (112)) are rather similar to declarative complements in the obligatoriness of local binding where possible. Thus, in (150), β must be *myself*, not *themselves* or *oneself*, despite the unnaturalness of the interpretation (to suppose that I bought presents for them to amuse themselves or for one to amuse oneself would make more sense):

they thought I bought the presents [PRO to   (150)
amuse β]

Here, PRO can be replaced by "for NP," permitting any interpretation (see (112)). We have also seen that in the adjunct
phrase of (151), PRO will be either bound or free, depending on
the choice of β (as *Bill* or trace, respectively):

John is too stubborn [PRO to talk to β]   (151)

If β is *him*, then PRO is bound by *John* if β is free and is
necessarily free if β is bound by *John* (otherwise, *him* would be
bound by PRO, which would violate binding theory, as in
"John talked to him" with *him* bound by *John*).
    Consider the following sentences:

   (i) we told them that John is too stubborn   (152)
      [PRO to bother β about]
  (ii) I thought you said that John is too stubborn
      [PRO to bother β about]

PRO may not be bound by *John* for reasons we have discussed.
In (i), β may be *ourselves, themselves, oneself*, and in (ii), β may
be *ourselves, myself, yourself*, or *oneself*. That is, PRO may be
free or bound by *we, them, I*, or *you*, and it may take a split
antecedent. In these respects, PRO is pronounlike, although it
is anaphorlike in its interpretation when bound and—perhaps,
although the facts are not entirely clear—in that it must be in
the domain of its binder (if any); thus, consider (152i) with *we*
replaced by *our friends* and β = *ourselves*.
    If the construction C with PRO as subject is itself a subject
rather than a complement or adjunct, other complications
arise, some already illustrated, and some illustrated in (153),
where β is some reflexive form:

   (i) [PRO to have to feed β] would be a nuisance   (153)
      for John
  (ii) [PRO to have to feed β] would annoy John
 (iii) [PRO to have to feed β] would annoy John's
      friends

    (iv) [PRO to have to feed β] would assist John's
        development
    (v) [PRO to have to feed β] would cause John to be
       annoyed

Choice of β = *oneself* is excluded throughout, meaning that PRO cannot have arbitrary interpretation and must be bound. Again, it is not the configuration but the presence of a potential binder in (153) that bars arbitrary interpretation, as (154) illustrates:

    [PRO to have to feed β] is a nuisance   (154)

Apart from case (iii), β in (153) is *himself*, with *John* the binder. This choice, however, is excluded in (iii), where β = *themselves*, bound by *John's friends*. Throughout, PRO is not in the domain of its binder, contrary to our general assumptions. The binder is, in an intuitive sense, the most prominent element within the complement that makes sense as a binder—thus, *John* in (iv) but *John's friends* in (iii). The binder may be in a PP-complement (as in (i)), or it may be the complement of the main verb (as in (ii) and (iii)). Or the binder may be the subject of the complement of the main verb (as in (iv) and (v); in the latter, the complement of *cause* is the infinitival phrase *John to be annoyed* at D-structure at least, and perhaps throughout). The binder cannot, however, be too deeply embedded:

    (i) [PRO to have to feed β] would result in John's   (155)
      being annoyed
    (ii) [PRO to be able to feed β] would imply that
       John is competent
    (iii) [PRO to be able to feed β] would cause us to
       conclude that John is competent

Choice of *himself* for β ranges from dubious to impossible.
    Further complexity is illustrated by embedding (153ii) in a higher clause, as in (156i) or the similar configuration (156ii):

    (i) we expected that [$_S$ [PRO to have to feed β] (156)
      would annoy John]

(ii) we expected that [$_S$ [PRO shaving β]
would annoy John]

In (i), S = (153ii). If S is not embedded, as in (153ii), then β must
be *himself* controlled by *John;* it cannot be *oneself* with arbitrary
interpretation of PRO. In (156), β once again cannot be *oneself,*
indicating that arbitrary PRO is excluded; but it can be either
himself or *ourselves,* indicating that either choice of controller
is possible; *John* or *we.* In these and a number of other cases
mentioned, it is unclear whether we are dealing with strong
preferences or sharp grammatical distinctions, although in
some of them, at least, the latter seems to be the case.

Occasionally, it has been suggested that PRO with arbitrary
interpretation may be controlled PRO with an "implicit
argument" not syntactically represented; thus, in (157) we might
assume an underlying implicit benefactive "for γ," not syntactically represented, where γ controls PRO as in (153i):

(i) [PRO to have to feed β] would be a nuisance   (157)
(for γ)
(ii) [PRO voting for β] is bad form (for γ)

If γ is understood as *one,* then PRO, now controlled by γ, is
arbitrary and β is *oneself.* If the context permits γ to be understood as referring to some specific person, say John, then β
would be *himself,* a marginally available possibility in such
cases.[68] An approach of this sort, if feasible, would leave free
PRO only in such cases as (158) or (159), where there is no
obvious location for the implicit controller:[69]

the crowd was too angry [PRO to hold the meeting]   (158)

(i) John is too stubborn [PRO to talk to]   (159)
(ii) it is time [PRO to leave]
(iii) it is common [PRO to sleep late on Sunday]
(iv) John asked Bill [how [PRO to entertain
oneself]]

These and many similar examples indicate that factors of a
rather complex kind enter into control theory, not all of them
well understood. PRO is anaphorlike in its interpretation and
in that it is in a certain structural relation to its binder: either in

its domain or with the binder sufficiently prominent in the construction K where PRO is the subject of the subject of K. PRO is pronounlike in that it can take a split antecedent, a "remote" controller, and an object controller when it is not locally bound and, we will continue to assume, in that it can be free as well as bound. Of the potential binders, the most prominent is the obligatory binder in certain constructions. Questions remain open about how to make these notions precise and how to explain the range of observed phenomena.

3.4.3. On the Abstract Representation of Arguments

In Section 3.3.3.3.2, we introduced the notion chain and some of its properties, illustrating them in Section 3.4.1. We put aside a second structure of "Case transfer," namely, expletive-argument pairs as illustrated in (69), repeated here:

there is a man in the room   (159)

The expletive-argument pair (*there, a man*) is similar to a chain in that the initial member of the pair is in a Case-marked position and the final member is in a θ-position. The Case on the initial element is transferred to the final element, which is now visible for θ-marking, as in the case of a chain. In this section we will consider these properties of chains and expletive-argument pairs, inquiring into their origins in terms of other principles and asking how they should be formulated more precisely. The discussion below is exploratory. In part, it is based on assumptions that are rather controversial, and, in part, on assumptions about possible structures deriving from X-bar theory and other modules of grammar, not all of which have been made explicit. Thus, these are really sketches of arguments, not complete in every detail. We will consider primarily *A-chains* headed by an element in an A-position, although many of the observations below hold for Ā-chains headed by an element in an Ā-position as well.

The two types of Case transfer just illustrated—in chains and in expletive-argument pairs—can co-occur:

    (i) there seems [e to be [a unicorn] in the garden] (160)
    (ii) there $_i$ seems [e_i to have been [a unicorn $_j$ killed
       e_j in the garden]] (where $i = j$))

In (i), we have the chain (*there, e*) and the expletive-argument pair (*e*, [*a unicorn*]), the latter analogous to the pair in (69); and in (ii) we have two chains (*there$_i$, e$_i$*) and ([*a unicorn*]$_j$, *e$_j$*), and the expletive-argument pair (*e$_i$*, [*a unicorn*]$_j$). The expletive moves to a position in which it receives Case, which is then transferred to the linked element "a unicorn" to void a Case filter violation. If the expletive is in a non-Case-marked position, then the violation remains, as in (161i) as contrasted with (161ii), where Case is assigned by *for:*

(i) *it is unimaginable [there to be a unicorn in   (161)
    the garden]

(ii) it is unimaginable [for there to be a unicorn in
    the garden]

The linked elements of an expletive-argument pair do not constitute a chain, but they behave in the manner of a chain with regard to the visibility condition and in other respects as well. Thus, *there* binds *a man* in (69), *e$_i$* binds [*a unicorn*] in (160i), and so forth; and, in fact, the properties of links of a chain are quite generally carried over to such pairs.[70] We will now simply stipulate that expletive-argument pairs have the properties of chain-links, returning in Section 3.5.2.3 to the question of why this should be so.

Suppose that we define a CHAIN to include both cases: A chain is a CHAIN and an expletive-argument pair is a CHAIN. We also generalize the second case to the pair consisting of the D-structure position of an expletive element EX and the argument α with which it forms an expletive-argument pair (EX, α) at D-structure. Thus, a pair (β, α) is a CHAIN if β is the terminal element of a chain (EX, ..., β) headed by the expletive EX, which is linked at D-structure to α in the expletive-argument pair (EX, α). The pair (*there, a man*) in (69) is a CHAIN; and the pair (*e*, [*a unicorn*]) in (160i) is a CHAIN, where *e* is the terminal element of the chain (*there, e*), *there* being linked to [*a unicorn*] at D-structure. Furthermore, if (α_1, ..., α_n), (α_n, ..., β_1), and (β_1, ..., β_m), are CHAINs, then (α_1, ..., α_n, β_1, ..., β_m) is a CHAIN (where n or m may be equal to 1). In this case we will say that the CHAINs (α_1, ... α_n) and (β_1, ..., β_m) are linked by the CHAIN (α_n, β_1). Typically, α_n is an expletive or its trace, and β_1 an argument bound by it, and the other two CHAINs are chains. Thus, in (160i), the sequence (*there, e,* [*a unicorn*]) is a CHAIN consisting of the chains (*there, e*) and ([*a unicorn*]) linked by the CHAIN (*e,* [*a unicorn*]); and in (160ii), the sequence (*there$_i$, e$_i$,* [*a unicorn*]$_j$, *e$_j$*) is a CHAIN consisting of the chains (*there$_i$, e$_i$*) and ([*a unicorn*]$_j$, *e$_j$*), linked by the CHAIN (*e$_i$,* [*a unicorn*]$_j$) (where $i = j$).

We now take θ-role and Case to be properties of CHAINs, and regard every member of a properly Case-marked CHAIN as visible for θ-marking.

In the previous examples, each CHAIN $C = (\alpha_1, \ldots, \alpha_n)$ has the property that for each i, α_{i+1} is in the domain of α_i; chains are formed by rules that "advance" an element to a less-embedded position (passive and raising), and the argument in an expletive-argument pair is in the domain of the expletive. We restrict ourselves to such cases now, returning briefly to a more general case in Section 3.5.2.3. We also assume that, as in the examples given so far, an expletive (or its trace) must be linked to an argument. Thus, if the CHAIN C is maximal, it contains an argument that originated in a D-structure θ-position. This argument heads its maximal chain C', a subCHAIN of C, and either heads C itself if C' = C, or is linked to the final element of a chain C_{EX} (which may be single- or multimembered) headed by an expletive, so that $C = (C_{EX}, C')$.

We assume that these notions are extended to include the pleonastic-argument link between nonargument *it* and the clausal complement of *believe* in (162i), so that we have the CHAIN (*it,* S) in (i) and the CHAIN (*it, e,* S) in (ii):

(i) it is believed [$_S$ that John is intelligent]   (162)
(ii) it seems [*e* to be believed [$_S$ that John is intelligent]]

Our general assumption, then, is:

Every maximal CHAIN contains a θ-position   (163)

We should expect this to follow from other conditions insofar as it is true. Some cases clearly do. Thus, if the maximal CHAIN C contains an argument α, then (163) holds of C because C contains the D-structure position of α, a θ-position by definition. The condition (163) would be violated by an example such as (68), repeated here, because *there* constitutes a maximal chain (hence, a maximal CHAIN) without a θ-position:

*John [$_{VP}$ V there]   (164)

But such examples are accounted for independently on grounds already discussed.

The only remaining possibility for a violation of (163) would be a structure in which an expletive element appears unlinked in a subject position or heads a chain terminating in an unlinked subject position:

   (i) *there hit John   (165)
   (ii) *there's fear of John
   (iii) *there seems [*e* to have hit John]

This possible violation of (163) would be excluded by our assumption that an expletive cannot appear unlinked. This assumption is arguably too strong, because one of its cases, namely, the case of constructions such as (164), is already excluded on independent grounds. The other cases would follow from the condition that an expletive element such as *there* cannot be inserted in the course of a derivation, along with a slight relaxation of the definition of D-structure as a pure representation of thematic structure. We now allow a non-θ-position in D-structure to be filled by an expletive linked to an argument.[71] Assuming that any element is linked to itself, we have the D-structure condition:

   A D-structure A-position is occupied by α, α non-   (166)
   empty, if and only if α is linked to an argument

Now (165i), (165ii), and (165iii) are underivable as S-structures with *there* unlinked: In D-structure *there* cannot appear unlinked and it cannot be inserted in the course of a derivation.

Notice that we still have to exclude (165) with *there* linked to *John* in an expletive-argument pair, but this problem does not bear on the independence of (163). This condition, then, can be derived on the basis of fairly plausible independent assumptions.

One consequence of (163) is that every verb must assign at least one θ-role; thus, *seem,* which assigns no θ-role to subject, must assign the θ-role proposition to its complement as in "it seems that John is intelligent," *"it seems." This follows for any verb V from (163) and the requirement that to be licensed, the VP projection of V requires a subject. By (163), this subject must head a CHAIN with a θ-position P. If P is the subject of V or in a complement of V, then V assigns a θ-role (namely, to the subject or the complement containing P; recall that complements must be s-selected and, hence, must have a θ-role assigned by V). But these are the only possibilities, because independently of this question, other principles exclude the possibility of a CHAIN-link (α, β), where α is the subject of V and β is not in the complement of V; there cannot, for example, be NP-movement from an adjunct of a clause to its subject.[72]

If θ-role and Case are, indeed, properties of CHAINS, then we require that each be uniquely assigned to a CHAIN, although some leeway remains as to exactly how this requirement is to be understood. A plausible requirement would be that a CHAIN can contain only one θ-position and only one Case-marked position; the former determines the θ-role of the CHAIN, the latter its Case. Let us examine these properties a bit more closely.

With regard to Case, we now have the following definitions:

A CHAIN is Case-marked if it contains exactly one   (167)
Case-marked position; a position in a Case-marked
CHAIN is visible for θ-marking

In these terms, we can reformulate the theta criterion (see p. 93) as follows:

A CHAIN has at most one θ-position; a θ-position   (168)
is visible in its maximal CHAIN

We assume that (168) holds of representations at the LF level.

If an argument α is in an A-position P in D-structure, then P must be a θ-position by definition, D-structure being a pure representation of theta structure (with the proviso (166)). By (168) P is visible at LF in its maximal CHAIN and is the only θ-position in this CHAIN. Then α receives the θ-role assigned in P; it receives its θ-role (or roles; see p. 97) in one and only one way from the maximal CHAIN containing P. If α is not in an A-position, then it must be licensed in some other manner (see (81)). Furthermore, since a maximal CHAIN contains a θ-position (see (163)), it must contain an argument, namely, the argument that occupies this θ-position at D-structure.[73]

Since the D-structure position of an argument is a θ-position by definition, it follows that an argument cannot be moved to a θ-position or the chain so formed will have two θ-positions, violating (168). Similarly, a nonargument cannot be moved to a θ-position or (168) will be violated.[74] Thus, movement is always to a non-θ-position (we will return to some questions about this conclusion in Section 3.5.2.4). We cannot, for example, have a derivation of (169i) from (169ii), yielding a chain (*John, e*) with two θ-positions:

(i) John hit *e* (169)
(ii) *e* hit John

Consider now a maximal CHAIN $C = (\alpha_1, \ldots, \alpha_n)$. From (163) and (168) it follows that C has exactly one θ-position. Since this must be visible, by (168), C must furthermore be Case-marked, which means it must have exactly one Case-marked position (see (167)). Then, given this formulation of the theta criterion and the assumptions from which (163) followed, we conclude that C must have exactly one θ-position and exactly one Case-marked position.

Furthermore, the θ-position in C must be the position occupied by α_n, its final term. This follows at once if α_1 is an argument and C is a chain, because α_n occupies a θ-position by the definition of D-structure. Suppose that α_1 is an argument and C is not a chain. This case is excluded on our earlier assumption that in an expletive-argument pair the expletive binds the argument, not conversely—a special case of the assumption that expletive-argument pairs share the properties of chain links. Suppose, then, that α_1 is a nonargument. Then, C terminates in a chain $(\alpha_i, \ldots \alpha_n)$ headed by the argument α_i, and again α_n must occupy its unique θ-position.

Suppose we now add the further condition that the head of C is Case-marked, thus:

If C = $(\alpha_1,\ldots,\alpha_n)$ is a maximal CHAIN, then α_1 is in (170)
a Case-marked position

We then have the general condition:

If C = $(\alpha_1,\ldots,\alpha_n)$ is a maximal CHAIN, then α_n (171)
occupies its unique θ-position and α_1 its unique
Case-marked position

This condition seems generally valid; it holds of well-
formed CHAINS and is violated in ungrammatical structures.
One expects the condition to follow from independent properties
of UG, and it does follow from plausible assumptions, as we
have seen, apart from (170). It remains an open problem to
derive (170), hence, (171) in full, from independent properties
of UG. See below, p. 144, for one possible direction. Recall that
a generalization is required for idiom chunks (see note 71),
along with other possible modifications if unlinked expletives
are permitted.

The condition (171) is violated in such ill-formed structures
as (165i) and (165ii), repeated here as (172) and (173):

    (i) *there hit John   (172)
    (ii) *there's fear of John

  *[there to hit John] is forbidden   (173)

We have suggested a basis for barring such examples with
there unlinked. Suppose now that *there* is linked to John. In
these examples, *John* is assigned Case by *hit, of;* and in (172),
there receives nominative Case in (i) and genitive Case in (ii).
John is in an s-selected θ-position throughout. Both cases of
(172) are barred straightforwardly by the theta criterion with no
recourse to (171); *John* is not visible in its maximal CHAIN
because the latter has two Case-marked positions and is, therefore, not Case-marked (see (167)). Example (173) is ruled out by
(171), requiring recourse to (170). We return in Section 3.5.2.5
to a different perspective on (172).

Consider the potential principle:

> If a lexical category α has a Case-marked object and (174)
> a subject, then the subject must be θ-marked by α (or
> its projection).

We are close to establishing this principle, which is relevant only to a verb or noun α because prepositions and adjectives do not have subjects. The subject cannot be an expletive as we have just seen. The subject can fail to be θ-marked, then, only if some element β is inserted in this position by Move-α. This element must move from a non–Case-marked position by (170); therefore, it cannot be the sole object of α. A remaining possibility is raising to main clause subject from the propositional complement of α, the latter a transitive verb; thus, from the D-structure (175), with β raised to the position occupied by *e:*

$$[e \ V \ NP \ [_s \ \beta \ to \ VP]] \qquad (175)$$

Whether this case should be excluded in principle is not clear. This construction is perhaps illustrated by such forms as "John struck me as stupid," which might be regarded as the analogue under raising of "it struck me that John is stupid." Also not barred by the analysis so far is a D-structure such as (175) with *e* replaced by an expletive linked to β, as in *"there struck me [a man as stupid]" (or "...[as a man stupid]," depending on assumptions about the embedded structure), again violating (174), in this case incorrectly. This is an instance of the problem mentioned in note 70. While a number of questions thus remain open, it appears that (174) is at least quite close to correct.

Some consequences of (174) are illustrated below:

> (i) John's offer of a loan (176)
> (ii) the offer of a loan
> (iii) *there's offer of a loan

> (i) John offered a loan (177)
> (ii) *offered a loan
> (iii) *there offered a loan

All these cases have a Case-marked object. Therefore, by (174), if a subject is present, it must be θ-marked by *offer* as its agent as in examples (i) of (176) and (177). In the examples (ii), no subject is present and no θ-role is assigned; (177ii) is barred because the VP predicate requires a subject, a consideration that does not arise in (176ii) because the N' "offer of a loan" is not a maximal projection and, hence, is licensed simply by X-bar theory. In examples (iii), there is a subject but no θ-role assigned, so the examples are barred by (174).[75] Hence, it appears that subject θ-role is assigned by the head α of (174) when a subject is present to receive it, obligatorily in the case of a VP, which must have a subject to be licensed at D-structure.

Consider the nominalized form of an intransitive verb such as *depart:*

    (i) the departure   (178)
    (ii) John's departure

In (i), there is no subject so no θ-role is assigned (but see the discussion of (137), (138), and Section 3.5.2.3). In (ii) the subject is present, and it must receive the θ-role assigned by *depart* to its subject as in "John departs." It seems, then, that a subject θ-role is assigned by a verb or noun α if the subject is present and α has a θ-role to assign. We have already seen that this is true for verbs lacking complements; see pp. 134–5.

Let us investigate more closely the factors that determine the assignment of θ-role. Consider first verbs. Recall that a verb heads a maximal projection VP, and for VP to be licensed (as a predicate) it must have a subject. By (174), if the verb is transitive, the subject must be θ-marked by the verb. More generally, the following proposition, known as "Burzio's generalization" (see Burzio, forthcoming), appears to be valid for verbs with objects, apart from a few questionable cases such as those just discussed:[76]

    A verb (with an object) Case-marks its object if and   (179)
    only if it θ-marks its subject

The preceding discussion gives an indication of how (179) might be derived from left to right. The earlier discussion of passive and raising suggests a derivation of (179) from right to left. Suppose that a verb θ-marks its subject but does not Case-mark its object. The object cannot receive Case in a CHAIN headed by an expletive subject, because the subject position is θ-marked. Therefore, there is a case filter violation unless the object moves to a Case-marked position. By the theta criterion, it can only move to a non-θ-position, hence, a subject. Properties of binding theory to which we return require that it move to the position of the "nearest" subject, the subject of the clause in which it is the object, but this is excluded because the position is θ-marked. Therefore, we have a Case filter violation; ultimately, a violation of the theta criterion.

If a verb α has a Case-marked object, then its subject, which must appear, is θ-marked by α. Suppose that α has no complement. As a consequence of (163), it must assign a θ-role (see pp. 134–5) Therefore, it must θ-mark its subject. Suppose that V has a non-NP complement:

(i) it seems that he had won   (180)
(ii) John believed that he had won
(iii) it believed that he had won

The verb necessarily θ-marks its s-selected complement in each case. In (i), the verb does not θ-mark its subject, which is pleonastic *it* linked to the complement clause as in (162), as required by (163).[77] In (ii) and (iii), however, the verb θ-marks its subject; thus, (iii) cannot be understood with *it* pleonastic, as in (i) or (162). We can include this case under (179) by assuming that in fact *believe,* as distinct from *seem,* Case-marks its clausal complement. Then the preceding argument applies: The expletive-argument CHAIN (*it, clause*) is barred by (170) as before, as is movement of the clause leaving a Case-marked trace. Thus, we avoid the necessity of stipulating the obligatoriness of θ-marking in some manner.

This suggestion is plausible in the case in question; thus, *believe,* but not *seem,* can take a Case-marked object as in (181), and can even Case-mark the subject of an embedded clause instead of the clausal complement as in (182), which must have the structure indicated on our assumptions (see p. 91):

John believed the claim that he had won   (181)

John believes [$_S$ Bill to be intelligent]   (182)

In (182), *Bill* must be Case-marked by the main clause verb *believe,* which does not s-select and θ-mark it, because there is no other mechanism of avoiding the Case filter violation. In the analogous structure (183i), however, Case cannot be assigned to the embedded subject by intransitive *seem* so that it must raise to the subject of the main clause yielding the S-structure (183ii), as we have seen:

$$\text{(i) } e \text{ seems } [_S \text{ Bill to be intelligent}] \qquad (183)$$
$$\text{(ii) Bill seems } [_S e \text{ to be intelligent}]$$

Further evidence that this line of argument may be correct is given by such examples as:

$$\text{(i) John believed that Bill is intelligent} \qquad (184)$$
$$\text{(ii) what did John believe } e?$$
$$\text{(iii) it seems that Bill is intelligent}$$
$$\text{(iv) *what does it seem } e?$$

Quite generally, verbs that take clausal complements permit the complement to be questioned if and only if they θ-mark their subjects—hence, *believe* but not *seem.* But as we have seen, the variable e in (ii) must be Case-marked. Hence, it seems quite reasonable to explain the optionality and obligatoriness of θ-marking in such paradigms as (180) along the lines just sketched.[78]

Notice that the argument that led to (174) applies not only to (180) but also to (182), where *believe* Case-marks the subject *Bill* of its complement. If *believe* does not θ-mark its subject then the latter must be an expletive linked to *Bill,* which is impossible by (168) and (170), or some non–Case-marked element must move to the subject position, which is impossible as in cases already discussed. Thus, (179) can be generalized:

A verb with a complement assigns Case if and only   (185)
if it θ-marks its subject

Apart from the questions already noted (see (175)), this will be valid insofar as expletives must be linked (i.e., insofar as (163) holds).[79]

A number of other cases remain to be considered, but it is plausible to suppose that for verbs, there is no need to stipulate the general property of obligatoriness of θ-marking. The subject must be θ-marked if the verb has the capacity to θ-mark the subject—hence, in the case of the verbs *believe, say,* and so forth, but not *seem*.

Consider now noun heads. Again, we need consider only θ-marking of subjects, because complements appear only if s-selected, hence, θ-marked. Recall that θ-role may be but need not be assigned to the position occupied by *there* in (172ii), repeated here, as we can see in (186):

*there's fear of John   (172ii)

(i) Bill's fear of John   (186)
(ii) the fear of John

In (186i), *Bill* receives the same θ-role (experiencer) that it receives in the corresponding clause "Bill fears John," but in (186ii), the corresponding θ-role is not assigned.[80]

Thus, whereas in clauses a transitive verb that may θ-mark the subject must do so, the same is not true of nominal heads of noun phrases. The reason for the difference, as we have seen, is that the subject of a clause must be present or the predicate VP will not be licensed, whereas *fear of John* in (172ii) and (186) is an N', not a maximal projection, and, therefore, need not be licensed by predication. It is licensed simply as an X-bar projection of its head *fear*. Therefore, no subject is required, as we see in (186ii), although if a subject is present, it must be θ-marked, barring (172ii); the subject cannot be an expletive. These facts follow from the theta criterion and (171). Therefore, we need not stipulate the property that the noun head must θ-mark its subject if the latter is present.

This argument appealed to (171), hence, to the assumption that the noun Case-marked its complement—indirectly, we have assumed—through insertion of the semantically empty preposition *of*, since nouns do not assign Case directly; we return to this topic. Putting aside a variety of other cases, consider a noun lacking a complement, such as *book, expectations,* and so forth:

(i) John's book (expectations,...)   (187)
(ii) the book (expectations,...)
(iii) *there's book (expectations,...)

Example (iii) does not suffice to show that *book* must θ-mark its subject, because this case is eliminated in any event by the requirement that expletives be linked (see (163) and (166)). The subject may or may not be present, because *book* is not a maximal projection, hence, not a predicate. The question of θ-marking of the subject thus remains open in this case. In fact, there is quite a range of relations possible between the subject and the noun phrase.[81]

Although some problems remain unresolved, it seems reasonable to suppose that θ-marking can be left entirely optional, applying freely, with apparent obligatoriness a consequence of other principles. This may be a property of grammatical processes in general.[82]

One consequence of (170) is that an NP-trace cannot have Case. Since an operator-bound trace (a variable) must have Case as we have seen, it follows that a trace is a variable (operator-bound) if and only if it is Case-marked. The conclusion that an NP-trace lacks Case has often been suggested as an independent principle,[83] and has consequences to which we will return. Its intuitive content is that movement is a kind of "last resort." An NP is moved only when this is required, either because it is a *wh*-phrase that must appear in an operator position (at least an LF), or in order to escape a violation of some principle: the Case filter, as in the case of passive and raising, or a principle to which we return requiring nongovernment of the empty category PRO. In the latter case, (171) requires that the position from which PRO moves not be Case-marked.

Constructions with *there* such as (69) violate the Binding Theory principle (87), since in this case *a man* is A-bound by *there*. Various proposals have appeared as to how to draw the required distinction. Let us simply stipulate (188) (following essentially Rizzi, 1982a):

Binding of an argument by a nonargument is not   (188)
subject to binding theory

The intuitive content of (188) is that binding theory is essentially a theory of referential dependency, and there is no such dependency in the case of binding of an argument by a nonargument.

We might consider generalizing the latter principle to

A binding relation between an argument and a (189)
nonargument is not subject to binding theory

Again, this makes intuitive sense, given the core sense of binding
in terms of referential dependence.

As it stands, (189) rules out application of binding theory
to NP-movement: The trace is a nonargument bound by the
head of the chain, typically an argument. There is reason to
suppose that binding theory does apply to NP-movement; see
Section 3.5.2.3. We can overcome this problem, if it is one, by
keeping to Case-marked nonarguments, rephrasing (189) as
(190):

A binding relation between an argument and a (190)
Case-marked nonargument is not subject to binding
theory

From (190) it follows that the trace of an argument NP must not
be Case-marked, on the assumption that an NP-trace is licensed
only if bound, hence, necessarily subject to the principle of
binding theory that requires it to be bound (in a certain domain).
It also follows that in an expletive-argument pair, the expletive
must be Case-marked, or binding theory will apply and (87)
will be violated. We therefore have virtually derived the
assumption (170), hence all of the basic condition (171) on
CHAINs.[84] This result is desirable, since the stipulation (170)
did not seem well-motivated apart from its consequences. The
principle (190), however, has questionable consequences, as we
shall see below, and we therefore do not adopt it, keeping to
(170), which basically stipulates the facts.

Summarizing, we have formulated the theta criterion as
(168) and the condition (171) on chains, the latter being derivable
from theta theory and other plausible assumptions apart from
the condition (170), tentatively assumed to be independent
apart from the possibilities just discussed. We have imposed the
condition (188) on binding and have modified the notion D-
structure slightly, incorporating the condition (166). The
observations reviewed then follow.

3.5. UG AS A SYSTEM OF PRINCIPLES AND PARAMETERS

3.5.1 Some Problems Reconsidered

We have been discussing two major conceptual shifts in recent study of language within the framework of generative grammar. The first reformulated a number of traditional questions in these terms, and the second developed in the course of efforts to come to grips with some cases of Plato's problem that arise in a rather striking form in the study of language. It would carry us far beyond the scope of this discussion to attempt a comprehensive or precise formulation of the ideas that have been proposed or the wide range of questions that are now being investigated. I will conclude the discussion with a brief review of the general picture of language and grammar that emerges and some remarks on a few selected further questions among the many that arise, in this section, and with some further development of modules of grammar, in the next section.

The discussion in Sections 3.3 and 3.4 illustrates a characteristic and important feature of the shift from the earlier conception of UG in terms of rule systems to a principles-and-parameters model. Argument is much more complex, the reason being that the theory is much simpler; it is based on a fairly small number of general principles that must suffice to derive the consequences of elaborate and language-specific rule systems. This striking change in the character of recent work reflects quite significant advances towards explanatory adequacy. I have kept largely to examples from English, but, in fact, this increase in depth of explanation has been accompanied by a considerable expansion in the range of linguistic materials subjected to an analysis in these terms. Many of the most important and far-reaching studies concern other languages, particularly the Romance languages, much of it based on the pioneering work of Richard Kayne.[85]

Although the specific ideas that have been proposed and developed are naturally open to question, there seems little doubt that the qualitative change in depth and complexity of argument revealed in much current work is the right kind of development. That is, the correct theory of UG, whatever it turns out to be, is very likely to have the properties manifested in this work: specifically, fairly complex derivation of operative principles and of properties of particular languages from a restricted and unified basis of fundamental principles of language. As has been observed several times, a conclusion of this sort is implicit in the very nature of Plato's problem.

In terms of the second conceptual shift, we no longer consider UG as providing a format for rule systems and an evaluation metric. Rather, UG consists of various subsystems of principles; it has the modular structure that we regularly discover in investigation of cognitive systems. Many of these principles are associated with parameters that must be fixed by experience. The parameters must have the property that they can be fixed by quite simple evidence, because this is what is available to the child; the value of the head parameter, for example, can be determined from such sentences as *John saw Bill* (versus *John Bill saw*).[86] Once the values of the parameters are set, the whole system is operative. Borrowing an image suggested by James Higginbotham, we may think of UG as an intricately structured system, but one that is only partially "wired up." The system is associated with a finite set of switches, each of which has a finite number of positions (perhaps two). Experience is required to set the switches. When they are set, the system functions.

The transition from the initial state S_0 to the steady state S_s is a matter of setting the switches. There may be general principles that determine how the switches are set, for example, the subset principle discussed by Berwick (1982), which states that if a parameter has two values $+$ and $-$, and the value $-$ generates a proper subset of the grammatical sentences generated with the choice of value $+$, then $-$ is the "unmarked value" selected in the absence of evidence; this is a necessary and sufficient condition for learning from positive evidence only, insofar as parameters are independent. There may also be specific principles of markedness relating various parameters, which need not and may not be fully independent.[87] When a particular language is determined by fixing the values of the parameters, the structure of each linguistic expression is determined, sometimes, by a rather complex computational process as in several of the examples that have been discussed—which are, it will be observed, relatively simple constructions.

The previous discussion has assumed the familiar Saussurean-Bloomfieldian idealization to a homogeneous speech community, but a further sharpening of these ideas is in order. The systems called "languages" in common sense usage tolerate exceptions: irregular morphology, idioms, and so forth. These exceptions do not fall naturally under the principles-and-parameters conception of UG. Suppose we distinguish *core language* from *periphery,* where a core language is a system determined by fixing values for the parameters of UG, and the periphery is whatever is added on in the system actually represented in the mind/brain of a speaker-hearer. This distinction is a theory-internal one; it depends crucially on a formulation of UG. It goes beyond the earlier idealization, because even under the assumption of homogeneity a core-periphery distinction can be maintained.

The idealization to a homogeneous speech community isolates for investigation a real property of the mind/brain, namely, the property that would account for language acquisition under the conditions of the idealization and that surely underlies real-world language acquisition. The same is true of the idealization to core language. What a particular person has in the mind/brain is a kind of artifact resulting from the interplay of accidental factors, as contrasted with the more significant reality of S_0 and core language (with its core grammar), a specific selection among the options permitted in the initial state.

The distinction between core and periphery leaves us with three notions of markedness: core versus periphery, internal to the core, and internal to the periphery. The second has to do with the way parameters are set in the absence of evidence. As for the third, there are, no doubt, significant regularities even in departures from the core principles (for example, in irregular verb morphology in English), and it may be that peripheral constructions are related to the core in systematic ways, say, by relaxing certain conditions of core grammar. The problem of formulating these notions precisely is an empirical one throughout, although not a simple one, and many kinds of evidence might be relevant to determining them. For example, we would expect phenomena that belong to the periphery to be supported by specific evidence of sufficient "density," to be variable among languages and dialects, and so forth.

The problem of constructing rule systems that achieve a degree of descriptive adequacy is difficult enough. The problem we now face with the shift of perspective to a system of principles and parameters constitutes a far more severe empirical challenge, however. Unless some phenomenon is consigned to the periphery, we must account for it by a computational (essentially deductive) process, which may be complex as in some of the cases already discussed, from invariant principles with parameters fixed. Furthermore, the system of UG is an intricate and highly constrained structure; small changes in the characterization of the principles and concepts have wide-ranging and complex consequences for some particular language under investigation and for others as well. Any proposal concerning these principles and concepts is answerable to a substantial range of evidence that is now fairly well understood, not to speak of wide and constantly expanding domains that still resist any persuasive analysis. As every researcher knows, the field is qualitatively different in these respects from what it was only a few years ago; it is far more difficult and far more interesting. These problems and challenges are clear enough in such attempts as Chomsky and Lasnik (1977), prior to the clear shift of perspective to a principles and parameters theory, and since then have become much more evident and compelling.

For reasons already discussed, the phenomena of particular interest are those for which direct evidence is lacking and which therefore pose the problem of poverty of stimulus in the sharpest form. One would expect the same to be true of constructions that are somewhat marginal, for example, the parasitic gap constructions (109). The properties of these constructions are quite curious, and, precisely because of their marginality, it is highly unlikely that these are learned or that UG has a specific component concerned with them.[88] We therefore expect that their properties must follow from UG, so that these properties pose a severe empirical challenge for UG. It would also follow that they must be the same in all languages. We find, however, that languages appear to differ quite widely in how they treat these constructions or whether they permit them at all. The *prima facie* contradiction can be resolved only by showing how these differences follow from the setting of parameters for other properties of the languages in question. The task to be faced is therefore intricate and complex, and the empirical conditions are quite heavy. There has been much discussion of "indeterminacies" that allegedly plague the study of language—of the alleged problem posed by the fact that there are, in principle, infinitely many grammars consistent with whatever evidence we may find. Although the observation is correct in linguistics as in every other empirical domain, the real problem lies elsewhere: namely to find even one theory of UG that is plausible over some interesting range of evidence.

If we limit our goals to rough coverage of major constructions, then there are indeed many alternatives and many ways to proceed. The same is true if we keep to description and do not undertake the challenge posed by Plato's problem. We cannot expect that the phenomena that are easily and commonly observed will prove to be of much significance in determining the nature of the operative principles. Quite often, the study of exotic phenomena that are difficult to discover and identify is much more revealing, as is true in the sciences generally. This is particularly likely when our inquiry is guided by the considerations of Plato's problem, which directs our attention precisely to facts that are known on the basis of meager and unspecific evidence, these being the facts that are likely to provide the greatest insight concerning the principles of UG.

As conceived in earlier work, UG permits an infinite number of languages. The conception just outlined, however, permits only a finite number of core languages (apart from the lexicon): There are finitely many parameters and each has a finite number of values. This is, of course, a qualitative change. Some recent work in formal learning theory by Osherson, Stob, and Weinstein suggests from an entirely independent point of view that this change may be in order. They formulate the thesis of "strong nativism," which asserts that there are only finitely many *essentially different* languages. According to this thesis, then, S_0 only permits finitely many essentially different realizations. They then show that the thesis of strong nativism follows from some plausible assumptions concerning the properties of a learning function.[89] Two languages are regarded as essentially the same if they differ only in finitely many sentences (e.g., English with n sentences of French added on) or if they differ in lexical items that do not change the syntax (thus, if L has the names *John, Bill,* and *Tom,* and L' is identical except that it has the names *John, Bill,* and *Mary,* then L and L' are essentially the same; but if L has the verb *persuade* and L' lacks any word with its selectional properties, then L and L' are essentially different). The thesis of strong nativism then follows from the assumption that the learning function f is not disturbed by a limited amount of noise (i.e., a finite number of intrusions not from the language being learned, each of which can occur indefinitely often), that it has a certain locality property (i.e., the next conjecture is based on the current conjecture and memory of only recent sentences), and the requirement that the space of accessible hypotheses is ordered in "increasing complexity" in such a way that the learning procedure never has to take too large a leap in forming its next conjecture (i.e., if there is a hypothesis much more complicated that will work, then there is also one that will work that is not more than some fixed distance from the current conjecture). These are natural conditions. Thus, there is some independent reason to believe that the thesis of strong nativism, which is close to the conclusions we have reached on entirely different grounds, is correct.

Osherson, Stob, and Weinstein point out that if the thesis of strong nativism is correct, then the language faculty must be a distinct component of the mind; that is, language acquisition is not a matter of applying general learning mechanisms (if such exist) to the particular case of language. Certainly, we cannot assume that "epistemic boundedness" is, in general, subject to this thesis. Quite apart from the thesis of strong nativism, the same conclusion seems in order, at least if the preceding discussion is at all on the right track. It is hardly conceivable that principles of the sort we have been considering have any general applicability beyond the language faculty, and no general mechanisms or principles have been proposed that shed any light on the questions we have been addressing, to my knowledge.

Returning to the questions (1) of Chapter 1, what we "know innately" are the principles of the various subsystems of S_0 and the manner of their interaction, and the parameters associated with these principles. What we learn are the values of the parameters and the elements of the periphery (along with the lexicon, to which similar considerations apply). The language that we then know is a system of principles with parameters fixed, along with a periphery of marked exceptions. What we know is not a rule system in the conventional sense. In fact, it might be that the notion of rule in this sense, like the notion of E-language (so it seems), has no status in linguistic theory. One can formulate algorithms that project rule systems from a choice of values for the parameters of UG, but it is not obvious that this is a significant move or that it matters how it is done.

This conceptual revision suggests a change in the way we view problem (1ii), of Chapter 1, the problem of language acquisition: not as a problem of acquiring rules but one of fixing parameters in a largely determined system. It also suggests a rethinking of the parsing problem, one aspect of the problem (1iii). Parsing programs are typically rule-based; the parser, in effect, mirrors a rule system and asks how these rules can assign a structure to a string that is analyzed word-by-word. The examples discussed above, and many others, suggest that a different approach might be in order. Given a lexicon, structures can be projected from heads by virtue of the projection principle, X-bar theory, and other subsystems of UG that are involved in licensing elements, which are associated with one another by these principles in the manner already illustrated. Perhaps, parsers should not be based on rules at all but should rather be based on lexical properties and principles of UG that determine structures from them. Rule-based parsers are in some respects implausible. For one thing, complexity of parsing increases rapidly as rules proliferate; for another, since languages appear to differ substantially if viewed from the perspective of rule systems, they will require quite different parsers if the latter are rule-based—an unlikely consequence. The entire question merits substantial rethinking, so it appears.

The conceptual shift to a principles-and-parameters theory also opens some new empirical questions for investigation and suggests a reformulation of others. Consider a few examples.

Note that a change in the value of a single parameter may have complex consequences, as its effects filter through the system. A single change of value may lead to a collection of consequences that appear, on the surface, to be unrelated. Thus, even languages that have separated only recently may differ in a cluster of properties, something that has been observed in comparative studies. We can use information of this sort to help determine the structure of principles and parameters of UG. Some new and intriguing questions of comparative linguistics and universal grammar are thus opened up for investigation, and quite suggestive work on these questions has been done in several language areas, notably the Romance languages.[91] We also expect to find, and apparently do find, that a few changes in parameters yield typologically different languages, another topic now being subjected to extensive investigation. These conclusions should be qualitatively correct, given the fact that typologically different languages can be acquired with equal ease and limited data on the basis of a fixed S_0.

Investigation of the empirical effects of slight changes in parameters can have broad implications concerning UG in other ways. One new line of inquiry of this sort is opened up by Huang's work on the parameters of Move-α, noted above. Recall that *wh*-movement can take place either in the syntax, affecting S-structure, or in the LF component, affecting LF representation but not S-structure. English is a language of the first type, Chinese-Japanese are of the second type (although English also has LF *wh*-movement, as noted). We thus find the array of data shown in (36) and (38), repeated here:

> (i) you think [$_{NP}$ who] saw John   (36)
> (ii) who—you think [$_{NP}$ *e*] saw John

	Chinese-Japanese	**English**	(38)
D-Structure	(36i)	(36i)	
S-Structure	(36i)	(36ii)	
LF	(36ii)	(36ii)	

Suppose that the range of interpretation of certain interrogatives is the same in Chinese-Japanese and in English. It is reasonable to conclude that these interpretations are determined by LF conditions, because it is at this level that the languages are alike. Suppose that the range of interpretation differs in Chinese-Japanese and English. Then, these interpretations are presumably determined by S-structure conditions, because it is here that the languages differ. Thus, we have a research tool for determining the exact point in the system at which various conditions of UG apply.

To illustrate, consider:

> (i) *who does John believe [the claim that   (191)
> [Bill saw e]]
> (ii) *what$_i$ does John know to whom$_j$
> [Bill gave e_i e_j]
> (iii) *to whom$_j$ does John know what$_i$
> [Bill gave e_i e_j]

> (i) what$_i$ did you wonder how$_j$ [to do e_i e_j]   (192)
> (ii) *how$_j$ did you wonder what$_i$ [to do e_i e_j]

The examples of (191) violate bounding theory: the wh-phrase has moved "too far" (see pp. 71–2, 76–7). But the corresponding sentences in Chinese-Japanese, Huang observes, are well-formed, with the wh-phrases in place. We therefore conclude that the conditions of bounding theory apply to the syntax proper, to S-structure representations or the rules forming them, not to LF representations or the rules converting S-structure to LF. The reason is that English differs from Chinese-Japanese at S-structure but not (in relevant respects) at LF.

Further support for this conclusion comes from the LF rule of wh-movement in English. Consider the multiple wh-constructions that are counterparts to (191), with who as the subject of the main clause in place of *John*:

> (i) who believes [the claim that [Bill saw whom]] (193)
> (ii) who knows to whom$_i$ [Bill gave what e_i]
> (iii) who knows what$_i$ [Bill gave e_i to whom]

In contrast to (191), these sentences are well-formed, and (ii) and (iii) permit the wide-scope interpretation for the embedded wh-phrase that is required in (i); (ii), for example, has as one option the interpretation: "for what person x and what thing y, x knows to whom Bill gave y." The same is true of such sentences as (194i), which may have either the interpretation (194ii) or (194iii):

> (i) who remembers where John read what   (194)
> (ii) for which person x and which thing y, x
> remembers in which place z, John read y in z

> (iii) for which person x, x remembers for which
> thing y and which place z, John read y in z

The answer to (ii) might be "Tom remembers where John read *Moby Dick* and Bill remembers where John read *Bleak House*," and the answer to (iii) might be "Tom remembers where John read what" (a construction that is perhaps more natural with "doesn't remember" in place of "remember"). In (ii), the embedded *wh*-phrase *what* of 193ii) has wide scope, violating bounding theory conditions that apply to *wh*-movement in the syntax proper, as we see in:

> *what do you remember where John read   (195)

It follows, then, that LF-movement of the *wh*-phrase is not constrained by the principles of bounding theory that bar (191) and (195).

Turning now to (192), both examples derive from the D-structure (196), common to English and Chinese-Japanese:

> you wondered [to do what how]   (196)

In Chinese-Japanese, this is also the S-structure while in English either (i) or (ii) of (192) is the S-structure, depending on how the rule Move-α is applied in the syntax.

But, Huang observes, the LF representation (192ii) is not well-formed either in Chinese-Japanese or in English. In Chinese-Japanese, the sentence (196) must be interpreted as in (192i), and in English the sentence "how did you wonder what to do" cannot be given the interpretation (192ii). Rather, the sentence has a rather anomalous interpretation, with *how* associated with *wonder*, not *do*, so that it does not derive from the D-structure (196) but from:

> you wondered [to do what] how   (197)

This interpretation is unavailable for the Chinese-Japanese sentence (196), because *how* is within the embedded phrase (as is clear from the actual word order, disregarded here).

Since Chinese-Japanese and English are alike in this respect, despite the difference in the surface and S-structure form of questions, we conclude that some property of LF bars the LF representation (192ii). The results follow from the empty category principle (ECP), which imposes certain narrow "identification conditions" on empty categories and has many and varied consequences.[92]

If this is the correct account of UG, then the range of similarities and differences between English-type and Chinese-Japanese–type languages follow from the choice of value for a parameter associated with the rule Move-α: α may include wh-phrases in the syntax proper, so that wh-clauses are constrained by bounding theory at S-structure and by the ECP at LF; or α may include wh-phrases only in the LF component, so that wh-clauses are constrained only by the ECP at LF. Again, the similarities and differences among language types are not expressed by alternative rule systems but by the choice of value for a certain parameter in an otherwise invariant system of principles. Many interesting questions arise: among others, the distinction between S-structure and LF and the properties of representations at each level, the point of application of various principles of UG, the ways in which the interaction of principles and parameters yields typological differences among languages, and the status of empty categories and operator-variable constructions.

In the course of this discussion, we have considered some general principles such as the projection principle and the principle of full interpretation (FI) with its various licensing conditions, and properties of such modules of grammar as X-bar theory, theta theory, binding theory, Case theory, control theory, and bounding theory. We have also considered the levels of representation determined by the interaction of their principles: D-structure, S-structure, LF and PF (phonetic form or "surface structure"). We have kept to the general framework of the extended standard theory (EST), while virtually eliminating the rule systems it presupposed. D-structure may now be defined as a "pure" representation of θ-structure: Each argument is in a θ-position and each θ-position is occupied by an argument, where an argument is a phrase that must be assigned a θ-role to satisfy the licensing conditions.

It then becomes an empirical hypothesis that D-structure is related to S-structure by Move-α, a rule that has definite properties involving the two positions related by movement (in particular, they cannot be "too far apart" in a structurally determined sense). We have been thinking of S-structure as derived from D-structure by application of Move-α. One might, alternatively, think of Move-α as in effect a relation on S-structure, so that D-structure is abstracted from S-structure by this rule. There may be empirical differences between these approaches; we have, in fact, come across a few differences, although they are rather subtle and hardly decisive. For most purposes—ultimately, perhaps, for all purposes—we may consider these as two equivalent formulations.[93]

The level of PF representation is derived from S-structure by the rules of morphology and phonology; at this level, sentences are represented in phonetic form with constituency marked. The level of LF representation is derived from S-structure by Move-α, assigning scope, but apparently not subject to the conditions of bounding theory. It is difficult to imagine that rules of the LF component are subject to parametric variation, because it is unclear what evidence to fix their character might be available to the language learner. Insofar as languages differ in their properties at this level, one would imagine that this is a reflex of overt features of the languages as determined by some principles of UG. Little is known in this area, and the limited evidence available poses many serious problems.[94] It is hardly necessary to stress that much the same is true generally. Indeed, the quite substantial progress of the past few years has exposed many more problems than it has solved—a healthy and encouraging phenomenon, to be expected in an area of inquiry that is worth pursuing.

On these assumptions, then, the modules of UG with values of parameters fixed assign to each expression a structure (D, S, P, L), where D is its D-structure, S its S-structure, P its surface structure, and L its "logical form."

Recall that the properties of LF are a matter of empirical fact, so that it may not coincide with what is called "logical form" in the tradition of philosophical logic. The term LF has been used, with explicit provisos, because it seems that LF does in fact have many of the notational properties of familiar logical form, including the use of quantifier-variable notation. Of course, this is by no means an *a priori* necessity, but there are empirical reasons to believe that the assumption is correct.[95]

More generally, the choice of levels of representation and their properties is an empirical matter, to be verified by their role in explanation. The matter has been discussed above primarily in connection with properties of S-structure, in particular, the properties determined by the projection principle and the licensing principles that require empty categories to appear in certain positions. The question of the existence and properties of empty categories lacking phonetic form is a particularly interesting one, because the language learner is presented with no direct evidence concerning them.

We may assume that the levels of PF and LF are the "interface" between formal structure and other components of the mind/brain which interact with the language faculty (in the sense of this discussion) in the use of language in thought, interpretation, and expression.

If D-structure is to be regarded as a pure representation of theta structure, it would be reasonable to suppose that lexical items appear at this level in a "reduced" form lacking inflectional elements that do not affect θ-marking and do not enter into s-selection. Thus, the derived form *destruction* would appear at this level as an N, because it heads such NPs as "the destruction of the city" which are the canonical structural realizations of s-selected elements (and furthermore, such derived forms often have semantic properties not strictly determined compositionally), but such verbal inflections as agreement, passive, and so forth would not appear because they do not enter into determining theta structure. The D-structure underlying *John was killed,* then, might be:

$$[_{NP} \, e] \; \text{INFL be} \; [_{VP} \, [_V \text{kill}] \, [_{NP} \text{John}]] \tag{198}$$

An affixation rule would then add the passive morpheme to *kill,* forming *kill-en* (which assumes its phonetic form in the PF component). The passive morpheme has the property of absorbing Case, so that this rule must be followed by an application of Move-α or (198) will violate the Case filter.[96] Then, an agreement rule will ensure that the AGR element of INFL matches the features of the derived subject, and a subsequent syntactic rule will assign these features to the verb.

In a language as poor in morphological structure as English, there is little evidence one way or another about these matters, but languages that are richer in this domain do provide suggestive evidence, as Mark Baker has observed.[97] In a survey of a variety of languages, Baker found general adherence to what he calls the "mirror principle," which asserts that the hierarchy of morphological structure mirrors syntactic structure in a definite sense. For example, if a language has a morphological structure indicating both subject-verb agreement and passive, and the morphological structure of a verb is (199i), then it follows that passivization applies before agreement so that a passive verb will agree with its surface subject (as in "the books were read"), the normal situation in languages with the relevant morphological features:[98]

(i) [[[verb] passive] agreement]   (199)

(ii) [[[verb] agreement] passive]

We will not find verbs with the structure (ii) where the verbs agree with the surface subject.

Suppose that a language has in addition to passive and agreement an "applicative" construction that converts a D-structure benefactive to an object, making the original object a "second object," a process that we might describe informally as follows:

$$NP_1 \ V \ NP_2 \ NP_3 \quad \rightarrow \quad NP_1 \quad V \quad NP_3 \ NP_2 \qquad (200)$$

subj   obj   ben   subj   obj obj2

This would convert a structure of the form "John bought a book for the children" into "John bought the children a book." In some languages (although not in English) there are productive syntactic processes of this type. Suppose now that the result of the applicative process (the right-hand side of (200)) undergoes passivization followed by agreement, so that the full derivation is as in (201), where (i) is the D-structure and (iv) the S-structure, and the verb forms V_i are those formed by affixation in the course of the derivation. Thus, V_2 includes the applicative affix *App*, V_3 includes both *App* and the passive affix *P*, and V_4 contains the agreement affix *Agr* in addition to these:

$$\text{(i)} \ e \ \text{V}_1 \ \text{NP}_2 \ \text{NP}_3 \ (\text{by NP}_1) \tag{201}$$
$$\text{(ii)} \ e \ \text{V}_2 \ \text{NP}_3 \ \text{NP}_2 \ (\text{by NP}_1) \ (\text{by applicative})$$
$$\text{(iii)} \ \text{NP}_3 \ \text{V}_3 \ e \ \text{NP}_2 \ (\text{by NP}_1) \ (\text{by passive})$$
$$\text{(iv)} \ \text{NP}_3 \ \text{V}_4 \ e \ \text{NP}_2 \ (\text{by NP}_1) \ (\text{by agreement})$$

This derivation would form a structure corresponding to "the children were bought a book (by John)" at S-structure. Then, according to the mirror principle, the actual hierarchic form of V_4 will be:

$$[[[\text{V} \ App] \ P] \ Agr] \tag{202}$$

Suppose that the language also has a rule of object-agreement inflecting the verb with an element O-A to agree with its object. If this rule applies prior to applicative, then the D-structure (201i) will be converted to (203), which will be converted in turn to (201ii), and the actual abstract form of V_4 will be (204):[99]

$$e \ \text{V}_1 \ \text{NP}_2 \ \text{NP}_3 \ (\text{by NP}_1) \tag{203}$$

$$[[[[\text{V O-A}] \ App] \ P] \ Agr] \tag{204}$$

We need not assume here that (200) is actually a movement rule; in fact, a transformational process literally corresponding to (200) is not readily formulable within the restrictive theory we have assumed. Rather, the rule adds the applicative inflection *App* thus changing the structure of assignment of Case and grammatical function, with actual order within the VP presumably a reflex of this and other factors. We might assume that *App* has the effect of causing the Verb to which it is added to assign its objective Case to the underlying benefactive, so that the underlying object now becomes a "second object" receiving Case by some other mechanism, as in "John gave Bill a book."[100]

Baker shows that the mirror principle accounts for the hierarchic structure of words in a variety of cases and observes that the principle would play a significant role in facilitating language acquisition in languages with a complex morphology. The mirror principle follows from the assumption that D-structure is "pure" in the sense of containing only elements that enter into θ-structure, thus omitting all affixes that relate only to syntactic role, and the further assumption that derivations are all of the form (201), with syntactic operations assigning affixes that "trigger" applications of Move-α.

We might implement these ideas in various ways. For example, we might continue to assume that in general the rule Move-α is applied only as a "last resort" (see p. 143), specifically, when failure to apply it will lead to a structure that violates a condition such as the Case filter. We might assume further that affixes can be added freely, incorrect choice being filtered out by other principles and by properties of the lexicon, if it leads to nonexisting words. There are further consequences concerning the precise formulation of the projection principle and other notions.

3.5.2. Modules of Grammar

Let us now consider more closely several of the modules of grammar and their interactions, and the concepts that enter into them.

3.5.2.1 *X-bar Theory*.

Let us begin with a further consideration of X-bar theory, reviewing and extending earlier remarks. Each lexical category X (X = N, V, A, P) heads a category X' (X-bar) consisting of X and its complements. Call X' a *projection* of X. We assume a further projection X'' consisting of X' and a *specifier* of X', where the specifier of N' is the determiner (DET: articles, quantifiers, possessive NP). We call X'' the *maximal projection* of X and X the head of X'' (and of X'); we will continue to use the conventional symbols NP, VP, AP, and PP for the maximal projections of N, V, A, and P, respectively. The order of elements is determined by setting parameters concerning direction of Case assignment and θ-marking and a "default" (left or right) for other cases. The order of complements is further determined by the Case adjacency principle. This much is the lexical core of the X-bar system, which may have various modifications.

Let us now extend the system to clausal structures. Assume that there is an element INFL (inflection) consisting of tense and agreement elements and modals. By phonological rules, the abstract tense and agreement elements are generally associated with an adjacent verb. INFL heads a projection INFL' consisting of the head INFL and its complement, VP. The maximal projection INFL'' consists of INFL' and its specifier, the NP subject of INFL''; this maximal projection is what we have called S. Assume further that there is another nonlexical element COMP (complementizer), which in English may be *that, for,* or null. COMP takes S as its complement and heads a projection COMP', generally called S' in the literature, which we will call C and assume to be a (defective) maximal projection with C' = C''; on the possibility of assimilating C to the general X-bar schemata, see Chomsky (forthcoming).

The general structure of a clause, then, will be as in (205), and the structure of NP will be (206), where ... stands for the complements of V and N (if any):

$$[_C \text{ COMP } [_S \text{ NP } [_{\text{INFL}'} \text{ INFL } [_{\text{VP}} \text{ V } ...]]]] \tag{205}$$

$$[_{\text{NP}} \text{ DET } [_{N'} \text{ N } ...]] \tag{206}$$

We can now define the grammatical function *object* to be the NP of X',[101] and the grammatical function *subject* to be the NP of X'', including in the latter case the NP subject of (205) and a possessive NP in the position of DET in (206). The object, then, is an internal argument s-selected and θ-marked by the head, whereas the subject is not s-selected and is θ-marked, if at all, by the X' (INFL' or N') of which it is the specifier, generally in terms of properties of the lexical head V or N alone, sometimes compositionally.

The level at which X-bar theory applies is D-structure. Movement rules may form structures that do not conform to the X-bar schemata; but at D-structure, which is a direct projection of lexical structure subject to other licensing conditions (e.g., those that guarantee the presence of subjects of predication), X-bar theory conditions are satisfied.

3.5.2.2. *C-command and Government.* We defined the *domain* of an element to be the minimal phrase in which it appears. Let us now restrict the notion to maximal projections:

The domain of α is the least maximal projection containing α. In (205), the domain of V is VP, the domain of INFL is S, and the domain of COMP is C. In (206), the domain of N is NP. We say that α *c-commands* every element of its domain that is not contained within α.

Let us say that a category α *governs* a maximal projection X'' if α and X'' c-command each other; and if α governs X'' in this sense, then α governs the specifier and the head X of X''. Thus, a head α governs its complements, the core case of government, and in a construction [$_{VP}$ V NP], where NP = (206), V governs NP, DET, and N. Furthermore, subject and predicate govern one another. Only lexical categories and their projections can be governors: N, V, A, P, NP, and VP, but not, for example, the complementizer *that* or the infinitival element of INFL. We assume that the agreement element (AGR) of INFL, which is "nominal" in the sense that it contains the features person, number, and gender, counts as a governor so that AGR governs the subject. Assume further that AGR is automatically co-indexed with the subject to express the agreement relation. We might expect the second clause of the definition of government (the noncore case) to follow on some other grounds; this may be so, but I will not pursue the matter here.

The concepts of c-command and government play a central role throughout the modules of UG, so their precise formulation entails many and complex consequences. I generally follow here an approach developed by Aoun and Sportiche (1983), with modifications suggested by Kayne (1984), Belletti and Rizzi (1981), and others.

I am restricting attention here largely to the syntactic and LF components of the language and the levels D-structure, S-structure, and LF. There is evidence that the concept of government is also relevant in the PF component. A case in point concerns the contraction rule (207) that yields such colloquial forms as (208):

want + to → wanna (207)

I don't wanna visit them (208)

As is well known, this rule is sometimes blocked. Thus, in (209), (i) is unambiguous (meaning "for which person x, you want to visit x," not "for which person x, you want x to visit"), and (ii) is impossible:

> (i) who do you wanna visit (209)
> (ii) *who do you wanna visit Tom

These facts are explained on the assumption that at the point in the PF component where the contraction rule (207) applies, the trace of wh-movement is present so that *want* and *to* are not adjacent and the rule is blocked.[102]

There are other cases beyond those of (209) in which the contraction rule (207) is blocked, for example:

> (i) I don't [need or want] to hear about it (210)
> (ii) we cannot expect [that want] to be satisfied
> (iii) they want, to be sure, a place in the sun

Aoun and Lightfoot (1984) propose that (207) is applicable only when *want* governs *to*—thus, not in such cases as (210)—and that this government requirement is general for processes of this sort. This quite natural proposal, along with trace theory, appears to cover the phenomena quite closely, providing an account for the fact that the conditions for application of the contraction rule are known without evidence, another typical case of Plato's problem. If this idea is correct, then the concept of government is relevant to the PF component.[103]

Under one suggested analysis of another class of contraction phenomena, the trace of wh-movement is also present at the point where a "destressing" rule applies as a prerequisite for subsequent application of the auxiliary reduction rule (AR) that yields "where's John" but not "I wonder where John's": Thus, destressing applies to *is* in "where is John" but not in "I wonder where John is e."[104] The level of PF itself is reduced by elimination of any category that is not required by presence of lexical material within it, and AR applies to this reduced structure—for example, to the reduced structures (211), yielding "who's here," "what do you think's happening," and so forth:

(i) who [$_\text{INFL'}$ is here]   (211)

(ii) what do you think [$_\text{INFL'}$ is happening]

Thus, within the PF component, we have *wanna*-contraction (207) and destressing applying prior to reduction of categories not required by lexical material, and AR applying after reduction. The ordering is presumably determined on more general grounds. Although trace has no phonetic content itself, it can influence phonetic form indirectly by serving as a barrier to application of other rules: the idiosyncratic contraction rule (207) and the destressing rule.

As these few remarks indicate, the question of the internal structure of the PF component is an interesting one, but we will not pursue the matter any further here.

3.5.2.3 *Binding Theory.*

The concept of empty category has played a central role throughout this discussion. We have found four kinds of empty categories: NP-trace, variable, PRO, and *pro*. NP-trace is a nonargument lacking Case, and a variable is an Ā-bound r-expression that must have Case by the visibility condition. Either PRO is bound, or it is free with (typically) an arbitrary interpretation similar to *one*, as in "one's beliefs often prove false." The element *pro* is a pure pronominal element with the sense of *he, they,* and so forth, or an expletive, an element not instantiated in English but only in the null subject languages.

Let us assume that these four types of expression are the realizations of the two basic features [a] ([anaphoric]) and [p] ([pronominal]). NP-trace is a pure anaphor [+a, −p] and *pro* a pure pronominal [−a, +p]. Variables are neither anaphoric nor pronominal, thus [−a, −p]. We then take PRO to be a pronominal anaphor [+a, +p], sharing properties of pronouns and anaphors (see Section 3.4.2). The same features cross-classify overt categories. Thus, we have the pure anaphors reflexive and reciprocal (*himself, each other*), the pure pronominals (pronouns), and the r-expressions that are neither anaphoric or pronominal (*John, the child,* etc.). The category of pronominal anaphor is lacking, not surprisingly, as we see directly.

Let us now turn to binding theory. We say that α *binds* β if α c-commands and is co-indexed with β. α *locally binds* β if α binds β and there is no γ such that α binds γ and γ binds β. The principles of binding theory determine how categories of the various types just specified may or must be bound.

We have mentioned two principles of binding theory: principle (87), repeated as (212), and the specified subject condition (SSC), illustrated by (213):

> An r-expression is A-free (in the domain of the head   (212)
> of its chain)

> (i) the men$_i$ expected [$_S$ the boys$_j$ to see them$_k$]   (213)
> (ii) the men$_i$ expected [$_S$ the boys$_j$ to see [each
>   other]$_l$]

SSC states that pronouns are free and anaphors are bound in the domain of the nearest subject; thus, *them* may not be bound by *the boys* but may be bound by *the men* in (213i), and *each other* must be bound by *the boys* in (213ii); k is distinct from j but may be identical with i, and l must be identical with j.

Clearly, pronominals and anaphors do not observe principle (212) of the binding theory. Rather, in contrast to r-expressions, anaphors must be bound and pronominals may be bound, as in:

> (i) they$_i$ like [each other]$_i$ (214)
> (ii) they$_i$ wanted Bill to like them$_{i,j}$

Replacement of the bound element by a bound r-expression yields an ungrammatical expression. Furthermore, anaphors and pronominals differ with regard to binding possibilities. Their distribution, in fact, is close to complementary: Pronominals are generally free in just those contexts where anaphors are bound. In (214), for example, *each other* and *them* cannot be interchanged to yield:

> (i) *they$_i$ like [them]$_i$ (215)
> (ii) *they$_i$ wanted Bill to like [each other]$_i$

As these examples illustrate, anaphors must be bound whereas pronominals must be free in a certain local domain.

The binding theory, then, will have the following form, where the notion "local domain" remains to be specified and (C) = (212):

(A) an anaphor is bound in a local domain (216)
(B) a pronominal is free in a local domain
(C) an r-expression is free (in the domain of the head of its chain)

One case of a local domain is given by the specified subject condition (SSC), illustrated in (213). This principle defines the domain of the closest c-commanding subject as a local domain for (216). Within this domain, an anaphor must be bound and a pronominal must be free. Note that the antecedent of an anaphor need not be a subject, although it cannot be outside of the domain of a subject:

(i) I told them$_i$ about [each other]$_i$ (217)
(ii) *I told them$_i$ that Bill liked [each other]$_i$

Similarly, a pronominal cannot be bound by a nonsubject within the domain of a subject:[105]

(i) *I told them$_i$ about them$_i$ (218)
(ii) I told them$_i$ that Bill liked them$_i$

SSC also applies in noun phrases:

(i) they$_i$ told [stories about each other$_i$] (219)
(ii) *they$_i$ heard [my stories about each other$_i$]
(iii) *they$_i$ told [stories about them$_i$]
(iv) they$_i$ heard [my stories about them$_i$]

The subject *my* blocks binding in (ii) by condition (A) and permits it in (iv) by condition (B) (cases of the SSC). SSC is inapplicable in (i) and (iii) because the NP has no subject. Thus, binding is permitted in (i) by condition (A) and blocked in (iii) by condition (B).

Suppose we interchange *tell* and *hear* in (219). This yields:

(i) they$_i$ heard [stories about each other$_i$]   (220)
(ii) *they$_i$ told [my stories about each other$_i$]
(iii) they$_i$ heard [stories about them$_i$
(iv) they$_i$ told [my stories about them$_i$]

Cases (i), (ii), and (iv) are as expected, but (iii) is not. An explanation is suggested by the fact that in (219iii), we assume that the stories are *theirs*, whereas in (220iii), we assume them to be someone else's. The representations that give the intended sense, then, are something like:

(i) *they$_i$ told [PRO$_i$ stories about them$_i$]   (221)
(ii) they$_i$ heard [PRO$_j$ stories about them$_i$]

The SSC applies properly to these representations. Perhaps, then, the DET position can include an implicit argument with the properties of PRO, as suggested in Section 3.4.2 (see the discussion of (137) and (138)). In fact, (219iii) is acceptable if we make the (implausible) assumption that someone else's stories are being told. Where this option is excluded, the form is ungrammatical:

*they$_i$ took [pictures of them$_i$]   (222)

In the sentence (220i), we also assume the stories to be someone else's, but *each other* is still allowed. Hence, presence of the implicit argument as subject is optional: If present, the interpretation is fixed depending on the indexing; if absent, the interpretation is free.

Other evidence to support this assumption, as noted by Howard Lasnik, is provided by the examples (223) discussed by Ross (1967):

(i) [the knowledge that John might fail] bothered   (223)
    him
(ii) [the possibility that John might fail] bothered
    him

In (ii), we may take *John* to be the antecedent of *him*, but in (i) we cannot (unless we are referring to some kind of unattributed general knowledge). The distinction can plausibly be attributed to the assumption that the syntactic representation of (i) includes a PRO (or related element) in the DET position, controlled by *him* as in the normal control structure (224) (see (153)):

[PRO knowing that John might fail] bothered him   (224)

In both (223i) and (224), there is a violation of condition (C) of the binding theory (216) if *him* is taken to refer to John, because now *John* is bound by PRO. The problem does not arise in (223ii), with no option for an NP in the DET position: Thus, we have "our knowledge that S" but not *"our possibility that S." The same point is illustrated in such examples as:

[the realization that John would fail] bothered him   (225)

The pronoun may take *John* as antecedent if we understand that it is someone else's realization that is under discussion (as in "the general realization that..."), but not if it is John's realization that...; in the latter case, it would be natural to assume that there is an implicit argument similar to PRO in the DET position as the subject of *realization*.

Another position from which anaphors but not bound pronominals are excluded is the subject of a tensed sentence (the nominative island condition—NIC):

(i) they expected [each other to win]   (226)
(ii) they would prefer [$_C$ for [$_S$ each other to win]]
(iii) *they expected [that each other would win]

(i) *they$_i$ expected [them$_i$ to win]   (227)
(ii) *they$_i$ would prefer [$_C$ for [$_S$ them$_i$ to win]]
(iii) they$_i$ expected [that they$_i$ would win]

In the subject position of the infinitivals (i, ii), the anaphor can appear but not the bound pronoun; the situation is reversed in the subject position of the tensed counterparts (iii). The concept of local domain will, therefore, have to be extended to this case as well.

These examples can be unified if we take the local domain for an anaphor or pronominal α in (216) to be the minimal *governing category* of α, where a governing category is a maximal projection containing both a subject and a lexical category governing α (hence, containing α). A governing category is a "complete functional complex" (CFC) in the sense that all grammatical functions compatible with its head are realized in it—the complements necessarily, by the projection principle, and the subject, which is optional unless required to license a predicate, by definition. Thus, the local domain for an anaphor or pronominal α in (216) is the least CFC containing a lexical governor of α—the minimal governing category of α (MGC(α)).

Because a governing category must have a subject, it can only be S, or NP with a subject: There is no need to stipulate the choice of governing categories for the core cases.

If α is the object or the object of a PP complement of a verb, then MGC(α) is the minimal S containing α since α is governed by the verb or preposition and S has a subject. If α is in the PP complement of a noun (including the case where α is the object of the noun after *of*-insertion) as in (219), (220), and (221), then MGC(α) is the minimal NP if the latter has a subject; otherwise, the minimal S.[106] If α is the subject of a tensed S, the latter is MGC(α) because INFL governs α (see p. 162) and S has a subject. If α is the subject of an infinitival clause β, then it may be ungoverned, in which case it is PRO, or it may be governed. In the latter case, it is governed either by the main clause verb as in (226i) and (227i), or by the complementizer *for* as in (226ii) and (227ii); these are the only possibilities. In either case, it is the CFC immediately containing β that is MGC(α), because this is the minimal category containing a subject and a governor of α.

We therefore obtain a substantial unification of the binding theory, incorporating both SSC and NIC, by defining the local domain as the minimal governing category.

The structure of the binding theory leads us to expect that in a position in which an anaphor α appears bound to its antecedent β, a pronominal γ cannot appear bound by β. Thus, there is a certain type of complementary distribution between anaphor and pronominal, as noted earlier. This expectation is generally fulfilled, but there are two well-known exceptions, both in nominal expressions:[107]

(i) the children heard [stories about each other]   (228)
(ii) the children heard [stories about them]

(i) the children like [each other's friends]   (229)
(ii) the children like [their friends]

Contrary to expectations, both the anaphor *each other* and the pronoun *they* (in *them, their*) can be bound by *the children* in (228) and (229). If the S-structure and LF representation correspond to the surface structure in (228) and (229), then we have a violation of the binding theory.

We have seen that many cases of (228) fall under the binding theory naturally when we attend to their interpretation, allowing a PRO-like element to appear, optionally, in the determiner position—hence, in (ii) but not (i). Assuming this approach to be tenable, we are left with case (229).

The contrast exhibited in (229) indicates that the relevant local domain is different in some respect for anaphors and pronominals. One would expect that this difference should fall out as an immediate consequence of the difference in their nature—namely, that anaphors must be bound whereas pronominals may be free—without any need to stipulate any further difference in the binding theory conditions for these two categories of expressions. Let us explore this possibility.[108]

As the binding theory now stands, it is satisfied by (229ii) but violated by (229i). The reason is that the embedded noun phrase counts as $MGC(\alpha)$ when α is the anaphor or the pronoun, because it contains a subject (the anaphor or the pronoun itself) and a governor of this position, namely, the head noun. What we want to say, however, is that although the noun phrase is a legitimate MGC for the pronoun, it is not the MGC for the anaphor. Rather, the MGC for the anaphor is the full clause: it is in this phrase that *each other* must be bound; we cannot, for example, have:

the children thought that [I liked [each other's   (230)
friends]]

Intuitively, it is clear why this should be the case. There is an indexing in which the pronoun satisfies the binding theory with the NP object of (229ii) taken as the relevant governing category, because the pronoun will be free in NP and pronouns are permitted to be free. But there is no possible indexing in which the anaphor satisfies the binding theory with this NP as the relevant governing category, because it cannot be bound in this NP; rather, the clause is the smallest governing category in which the anaphor can be bound. What we want to say, then, is that the relevant governing category for an expression α is the least CFC containing a governor of α in which α could satisfy the binding theory with some indexing (perhaps not the actual indexing of the expression under investigation). Thus, in (229) the clause is the relevant governing category for the anaphor, but the NP is the relevant governing category for the pronoun. Under this interpretation of binding theory, the examples (229) will be exactly as predicted.

Let us, therefore, reformulate the binding theory in these terms. Suppose we have an expression E with the indexing I, where an indexing is an association of indices with phrases of E. We say that the indexing I and the pair (α, β) are *compatible* with respect to the binding theory if α satisfies the binding theory in the local domain β under the indexing I:

> I is *BT-compatible* with (α, β) if:　　　　　　　(231)
> 　(A) α is an anaphor and is bound in β under I
> 　(B) α is a pronominal and is free in β under I
> 　(C) α is an r-expression and is free in β under I

We now add the licensing condition (232) for a category α governed by a lexical category γ in the expression E with indexing I:

> For some β such that (i) or (ii), I is BT-　(232)
> compatible with (α, β):
> 　(i) α is an r-expression and (a) if α heads its
> 　　chain or (b) otherwise
> 　　(a) $\beta = E$
> 　　(b) β is the domain of the head of the
> 　　　chain of α
> 　(ii) α is an anaphor or pronominal and β is

the least CFC containing γ for which there is an indexing J BT-compatible with (α, β)

The condition (232) now expresses the revised content of the binding theory (216).

The conditions for r-expressions are unchanged. For α an anaphor or pronominal (case (ii)), the licensing condition amounts to saying that the relevant governing category for α is the minimal one in which the binding theory could have been satisfied by some indexing. We will henceforth refer to the relevant governing category for α in this sense as the governing category for α. Notice that if α has no governor, then the licensing condition (232) is inapplicable.

The cases of anaphors and pronominals discussed earlier are unchanged under this reformulation. If α is in VP then it is governed in the VP and its governing category is the least S containing this VP, because there is always a BT-compatible indexing: if an anaphor, α can be co-indexed with the subject, and if a pronominal, α can be free. If α is the subject of a tensed clause S, then S is the governing category: if an anaphor, α can be co-indexed with the AGR element of the head INFL (the latter is not a proper antecedent, but we may take that to be irrelevant for the moment); and if a pronominal, α can be free. If α is the subject of an infinitive it either is ungoverned so that the licensing condition (232) is inapplicable, or it is governed either by *for* in COMP or by the main clause verb; in either case, the main clause S is the governing category as before.

The last case to be considered is the case of α within an NP β. If α is in the complement of N, then the NP β with N as head is the governing category if it contains a subject (possibly the "hidden pronominal" discussed earlier); and the minimal CFC containing β is the governing category if β lacks a subject, with consequences already reviewed. If α is the subject of the NP β, then it is governed by the head N and β has a subject, so it is the governing category if there is an indexing I BT-compatible with (α, β). There is such an I if α is a pronominal (namely, with α free), but there is none if α is an anaphor, so in this case the minimal CFC containing β is the governing category within which α must be bound.

One possible case is still misanalyzed, namely, where α is the complement or subject of N in an NP subject as in:

(i) the children thought that [s [NP pictures of (233) each other] were on sale

(ii) the children thought that [s [NP each other's pictures] were on sale]

(iii) the children thought that [s [NP pictures of them] were on sale]

(iv) the children thought that [s [NP their pictures] were on sale]

In all cases, α (= *each other, them, their*) can be bound by the main clause subject *the children*.[109] Case (iv) is analyzed properly, with the governing category *their pictures*. In case (iii) it may be, as before, that the determiner of the NP contains a "hidden pronominal." If so, this case is unproblematic. The assumption often seems well motivated. Compare

(i) we felt that [s [NP any criticisms of each other] (234) would be inappropriate]

(ii) we felt that [s [NP any criticisms of us] would be inappropriate]

In (i), it is *our* criticisms that we feel would be inappropriate whereas in (ii) it is someone else's criticisms, consistent with the requirements of the binding theory if we assume that the determiner of the subject of the embedded clause contains a hidden pronominal. If the NP in (233iii) lacks a hidden pronominal, then S is the governing category for *them*, and the binding theory is satisfied because the pronoun can be free in S.

Examples (233i, 233ii), however, violate the binding theory as given in (232) because S should be the governing category: S contains a governor of *each other* and a subject, and *each other* can be co-indexed with the AGR element of the INFL head of the embedded S. Evidently, this option for the indexing I must be excluded. Notice that the NP containing *each other* (*pictures of each other, each other's pictures*) is itself co-indexed with AGR in INFL, as the subject of the clause headed by INFL (see p. 162). The natural assumption, then, is that the indexing I is not BT-compatible with (α, β) if it violates the "i-within-i condition" (235), which prevents co-indexing of a phrase with a phrase that contains it under certain conditions that I will ignore here:

$$*[_i \ldots \alpha_i \ldots] \tag{235}$$

In (233i) and (233ii), then, there is no indexing BT-compatible with (*each other*, S), so that the main clause must be the governing category within which *each other* is bound.

With these modifications, the major cases are accommodated with no need to stipulate any distinction between the binding theory conditions for anaphors and pronominals, except that the former must be bound and the latter free in their respective governing categories. The different choice of governing category for anaphors and pronominals falls out as a consequence of their basic binding theory properties. Henceforth, I will assume this interpretation of the binding theory, continuing for convenience to refer to the three conditions as stated in (216). We return directly to a possible simplification of the system.

The examples of (233)—sometimes called "long-distance binding"—illustrate a difference between movement rules and anaphoric binding. The anaphor in these examples can be bound by the main clause subject, but an element cannot be raised from this position to the main clause subject position:

*[the children] seem that [[pictures (of) *e*] were on   (236)
sale]

The meaning would be: "it seems that pictures of the children were on sale." Such long-distance movement is ruled out by Case-theoretic conditions to which we will return (and also, independently, by the locality conditions on movement illustrated earlier).

Long-distance binding has other noteworthy properties. As we have seen, it is subject-oriented:[110]

they told us that [[pictures of each other] would be   (237)
on sale]

Here the binder of *each other* must be *they*, not *us*, as the sense makes clear. Subject-orientation does not hold for anaphors in simple sentences such as:

they told us about each other (themselves)   (238)

Here, either *they* or *us* may be the antecedent of *each other, themselves*.

Suppose we assume that anaphors undergo LF-movement to the INFL position leaving a trace, so that the LF representation corresponding to such sentences as (238) (similarly, (237)) is (239), where α is the anaphor:

they α_i-INFL [$_{VP}$ tell us about e_i]   (239)

It would, then, follow that α could only be bound by the subject *they* in (237), (238), and (239). Binding by the object in (238) requires adjunction to VP, giving a structure that would allow the raised anaphor to be bound by the object of V under a slight revision of the notion c-command that may well be required for other cases not discussed here. Binding theory condition (A) would now hold not of the antecedent-anaphor relation but of the anaphor-trace relation. The antecedent-anaphor relation would then be a government relation, not a binding-theoretic relation. See Lebeaux (1983) for some similar ideas.

This suggestion amounts to treating anaphora in English rather in the manner of reflexivization in the Romance languages, with a reflexive clitic binding a trace in the object position: English would have LF-movement of the anaphor corresponding to the S-structure representation in the Romance case (actually, both cases would then exist in Romance languages, with somewhat different properties). We might then attempt to reduce the differences in the properties of anaphors in these cases to differences in conditions on S-structure and on LF representation, rather in the manner of the approach to Move-*wh* discussed earlier (see pp. 152f.). At the LF level, then, there would be no overt anaphors in A-positions but only the anaphor trace. If binding theory (or at least, conditions (A) and (B)) is restricted to LF, then it will not apply to overt anaphors directly but rather to the anaphor-trace relation, which will be analogous to a clitic-trace relation. The relation will still satisfy SSC, but we might now eliminate the condition NIC for anaphors. This amounts to eliminating the option of having AGR count as an antecedent for the subject of a finite clause in the definitions (231) and (232); the governing category for such an element would then be the larger clause in which it is embedded (and (232) will be violated if the clause is not embedded). To bar an anaphor in this position, then, we would appeal not to binding theory but rather to the principle ECP (see p. 155), which excludes the trace of *wh*-movement in this position in such sentences as *"who do you think that *e* saw Bill." We therefore associate anaphors in the position of subject of finite clause not with bound pronouns but rather with variables.

This move eliminates the somewhat artificial assumption that AGR can be a binder. Now it is unnecessary to appeal to this assumption for an anaphor subject of a finite clause (see p. 173), because in this case there will be an ECP violation irrespective of binding theory. Eliminating the option of taking AGR as a binder, we may now also avoid recourse to condition (235) on BT-compatibility, thus dispensing with this condition, since the embedded clause will not be the governing category in such examples as (233i) and (233ii) in any event. We also eliminate a redundancy between ECP and NIC. Furthermore, we now have a plausible approach to the questions raised in note 107. In both of the cases mentioned there, an anaphor in the subject position of a finite clause in fact behaves in the manner of a *wh*-trace (both are permitted in the Chinese-Japanese case, and both are barred in the subjunctive case, apart from the option of successive-cyclic movement for *wh*-movement) but is dissociated in its behavior from bound pronouns, which are explained straightforwardly in the manner already discussed. In effect, then, we reduce NIC to ECP in the relevant cases.[111] Many interesting questions arise in this connection, but it is impossible to pursue them here because the required groundwork has not been laid.

We have ignored the fact that reflexives do not appear in the subject position of NP, as distinct from reciprocals. Instead, we have the phrase *X's own*:

Mary's mother likes her own friends best   (240)

Higginbotham (forthcoming) observes that *her own* has anaphoric properties here, as we see from the lack of ambiguity in
(240), the antecedent being only *Mary's mother*, not *Mary*, in
accordance with the c-command requirement.

This version of the binding theory overcomes the empirical
problems mentioned in a rather natural way, and is also conceptually simpler than earlier versions: It eliminates the *i*-
within-*i* condition (though some of the cases that fell under it
now require a different treatment) and the related concept of
"accessible subject"; it does not require extending the notion of
subject to include AGR in the definition of "governing category"
and eliminates AGR as a possible binder; and it avoids the need
for an auxiliary stipulation that the main clause is a governing
category for governed elements (see, e.g., Chomsky (1981) and
subsequent modifications). But a look at other problems in
English and at other languages quickly reveals that this discussion only touches the surface of the problems that arise, as is
well-known. See note 23.

Because NP-trace is a pure anaphor, it will satisfy condition
(A) of the binding theory (216). Therefore, it must be bound in
its governing category in the sense of (232). Various conclusions
follow for A-chains (chains headed by an element in an A-
position). In particular, if $C = (\alpha_1, \ldots, \alpha_n)$ is a chain, then in
each link (α_i, α_{i+1}), α_i c-commands α_{i+1}; that is, there are rules
advancing α to a less embedded position (raising and passive),
but no "lowering rules" moving α to a more embedded position
that it c-commands and no "sidewards rules" that move α to a
position unrelated by c-command. Our discussion of CHAINs
in Section 3.3.3.3 began with a restriction to CHAINs with this
property of advancement to a c-commanding position (see p.
133). We now see that at least for chains, the restriction is well
motivated in terms of binding theory.

In fact, there is good reason to weaken the assumption and
to allow chains to be formed freely as histories of movement,
thus allowing "lowering rules." An example would be the rule
of NP-postposing in a null-subject language such as Italian,
which derives (241ii) from (241i) by Move-α:[112]

(i) Giovanni [$_{VP}$ parla] ("Giovanni speaks")   (241)
(ii) *e* [$_{VP}$ parla Giovanni]

In this case, *e* cannot be an anaphor or it will violate binding theory condition (A). In fact, *e* behaves just like an empty expletive *pro*, and we may assume it to be this element. Then, it would follow that such postposing rules would be allowed only in a null-subject language that permits this element to appear in subject position, but not in English or French, for example (continuing to assume, as before, that an expletive such as *there* cannot be inserted in the course of a derivation; see p. 134). We can allow for this possibility by modifying slightly the convention Move-α. We have hitherto been tacitly assuming that movement to an A-position leaves a trace with the features [+a, −p] (an anaphor), whereas movement to an A-position leaves a trace with the features [−a, −p] (an r-expression, a variable). Suppose we allow movement to an $\bar{A}$-position, such as the adjoined position in (241), to leave as its trace the element [−a, +p] (the pure pronominal *pro*). This option can be allowed freely; it will be meaningful only if this element is left as a trace of movement in a position in which it is licensed—specifically, as subject of a tensed sentence in a null-subject language.[113]

If this option is adopted, then in (241ii) we have the chain (*Giovanni*, *e*), formed by movement, but also the CHAIN (*e*, *Giovanni*), an expletive-argument pair. Neither of these satisfies the general chain property (171) that we developed, and largely derived, under the more restrictive assumption of the earlier discussion. This property, then, holds as before for CHAINs involving only A-positions, but need not hold for CHAINs containing $\bar{A}$-positions, as in (241ii).

Although movement is free, the only possible cases will be movement of α to a c-commanding position, leaving a trace *e* and forming the chain (α, *e*), or movement of α to a c-commanded position, leaving *pro* and forming the expletive-argument pair (pro, α). The requirement that such pairs share the properties of links of a chain restricts the possibilities of movement to a narrow class of cases. In particular, if α is moved from position X to position Y, then either (X, Y) or (Y, X) meets the binding theory condition (A) on links of a chain.

The requirement that expletive-argument pairs share the properties of chain links, so far stipulated, should follow from binding theory. This result would follow if expletives are not permitted to appear in LF representations. That is, at LF all CHAINs are chains; only arguments or their traces appear in A-positions—a rather natural requirement given the role of LF as representing the contribution of the language to semantic interpretation. We may assume that the expletive α can be eliminated, in accordance with the condition on recoverability of deletion, only if α is replaced by a co-indexed element β, hence by movement of β to the position occupied by α, forming a chain (α, e). This chain will violate binding theory unless the expletive-argument pair (α, β) had the properties of a chain link to begin with, so that this property of S-structure CHAINs is now derived from binding theory, which applies at LF. We cannot, for example, have such sentences as (242) with *there* linked to *several books* so that we have plural agreement in the main clause:

there were decided that several books would be on   (242)
reserve

This structure would now be eliminated at LF, because a violation of binding theory (or perhaps ECP; see p. 176) would result from movement of *several books* to the main clause subject position occupied by *there*. There would also be a violation of the chain condition (171) in this case of movement to an A-position. Notice also that at least at LF, we can now eliminate the condition (188), which voids a binding theory violation in the case of an argument bound by a nonargument. There are a number of complications in pursuing this idea, but it might be worth exploring. Note that if we adopt it, we can dispense with the concept **CHAIN**, except as a descriptive artifact at S-structure. We will have only chains, at S-structure and LF.

The requirement that each link of a chain satisfy condition (A) restricts the class of permissible derivations. Consider for example:

(i) *[a book] is unusual [for John to read e]   (243)
(ii) e is unusual [for John to read [a book]]

> (iii) *[a book] is unusual [for there to be read *e*]
> (iv) *e* is unusual [for there to be read [a book]]

We cannot derive (i) from the D-structure (ii) because of the SSC, but this derivation is also blocked by the "last resort" condition (170) that bars Case-marked trace. To avoid this redundancy, we might consider the example (iii) derived from (iv). In this case, (170) is inapplicable because the passive verb does not assign Case. But recall that in this structure, *there* must be co-indexed with *a book* in (iv), hence with *e* in (iii), so, in fact, (243iii) does not violate SSC because the trace is bound (by *there*) in its governing category, the embedded S. In fact, (243iii) is not a violation of binding theory at all, as we have constructed the latter, or of any other condition so far discussed. One might argue that (243iii) violates a uniqueness requirement on maximal CHAINS; here the trace *e* in (iii) appears in two maximal CHAINs, the chain ([*a book*], *e*) and the expletive-argument pair (*there*, *e*), and it would be natural to require that two distinct maximal CHAINs cannot terminate in the same position.[114] Another possibility is to pursue the idea of the preceding paragraph, which would require LF-movement of *e* in (243iii) to the position of *there*, yielding (244) as the LF representation corresponding to (243iii):

> (i) *[a book] is unusual [for *e* to be read *e'*]   (244)

This structure, however, is ruled out by the principle that prohibits raising to derive (245ii) from (245i), presumably the condition ECP, which we have not discussed here (see p. 155):

> (i) *e* is illegal [for John to drive]   (245)
> (ii) John is illegal [for *e* to drive]

Under either alternative, (243iii) is not a binding theory violation. The corresponding examples without *for* would be barred by (171), because the chain (*e*, *e'*) in (244) would now lack Case.

In fact, it is not clear that there are any cases in which condition (A) alone blocks NP-movement, except for the requirement that trace must be bound so that movement is to a c-commanding position; although perhaps, if the idea just proposed proves feasible, condition (A) may also explain the properties of expletive-argument pairs. There is, then, a certain degree of redundancy in the system. Often it has proven useful to adopt the working assumption that UG does not tolerate such redundancy and to redesign its principles so as to avoid them; perhaps, the same is true in this case as well. This working assumption is not at all an obvious one in the case of a biological system, where one might expect considerable redundancy on functional grounds. Nevertheless, when explored it has generally proven to be justified—a rather curious fact.

These questions aside, certain properties of chains, such as the binding condition for links, follow from general principles concerning anaphors and, therefore, need not be stipulated. In fact, abstracting from Case, the distribution of NP-trace is virtually that of anaphors, as illustrated in the comparison of *each other, e*:

(i)(a) they saw each other   (246)
    (b) they were seen *e*
(ii)(a) they expect [each other to like Bill]
     (b) they seem [*e* to like Bill]
(iii)(a) their [destruction of each other]
      (b) their [destruction *e*]

Apart from Case, apparent differences in the distribution of overt anaphors and NP-trace reduce to other independent factors, such as the bounding theory conditions on movement mentioned earlier and ECP, which we have not discussed. These similarities provide further evidence of a somewhat abstract sort for the existence of NP-trace.

As noted, in each link (α, β) of a chain of A-positions, α binds β. But there also appears to be a stronger condition:

if (α, β) is a link of a chain, then α locally binds β (247)

There can be no γ such that α binds γ and γ binds β. This condition, in fact, also extends to CHAINs more generally. In Chomsky (1981), where the concept of chain is introduced, property (247) is simply stipulated, but it seems that several cases of the principle, and perhaps all, may be derivable from independent assumptions.[115]

We have just examined one ungrammatical construction violating (247), namely (243iii). Here, perhaps, the result follows from the uniqueness condition proposed for maximal CHAINs or from the requirement that expletives be eliminated at LF. We have also discussed another instance of (247) in the case of $\bar{A}$-chains, namely, the case of strong crossover, illustrated in the fact that (248i) has the interpretation of (249) but (248ii) does not.

> (i) who e thinks he is intelligent   (248)
> (ii) who does he think e is intelligent

> for which person x, x thinks x is intelligent   (249)

In both (i) and (ii), *who* binds e. But it is impossible for *who* to bind *he*, which, in turn, binds e. This case of (247) follows from the binding theory principle (C) of (216), which requires that r-expressions must be A-free in certain domains.

The property (247) also holds of A-binding in such constructions as:[116]

> *John$_i$ is believed that [$_\alpha$ he$_i$ likes e_i]   (250)

Here *John* derives from the D-structure position of e_i. This is not a binding theory violation, because e_i is bound by he$_i$ within its governing category α. However, it is a violation of (171), which bars Case-marked NP-trace. We will consider below several other cases that violate (247) for various independent reasons, although it is not entirely clear that the condition can be reduced to others in its entirety. As Rizzi notes, it is rather curious that various special cases of (247) should be derivable in separate ways, as if there were a "conspiracy" to ensure local binding.

There is some reason to suspect that the local binding conditions (247) may be too strong, and that, in fact, only the cases derived on other grounds are valid. Consider:

(i) they seem to each other [*e* to like Bill]   (251)
(ii) it seems to him [that John is a failure]
(iii) it seems to his friends [that John is a failure]

In (ii), *him* cannot take *John* as antecedent, although it can in (iii). Therefore, *him* c-commands *John* in (ii), invoking condition (C) of the binding theory. The *to*-phrase does not act as a maximal projection barring c-command in this case; rather, it is as if the phrase is an NP Case-marked by *to*.

Assuming now that the structure of (i) is the same in relevant respects,[117] it follows that *each other* c-commands and, thus, binds *e*, the trace of *they*. Nevertheless, *they* binds both *each other* and *e*, violating the local binding condition (247). This case, however, does not violate other principles.

Consider now the status of PRO, which we have taken to be a pronominal anaphor. If PRO is governed, then it is subject to the licensing condition (232). But this condition can never be satisfied, because whatever the indexing I, there can be no β such that I is BT-compatible with (PRO, β); as an anaphor, PRO would have to be bound in β under I, and as a pronominal it would have to be free in β under I. Therefore, PRO cannot be governed.[118]

We thus derive the basic property determining the distribution of PRO, as discussed earlier:

PRO is ungoverned   (252)

PRO is therefore restricted to the subject position of infinitives and gerunds, the basic ungoverned positions. PRO cannot be a complement, the subject of a finite clause, or the subject of a nongerund NP as in *PRO story* (meaning "someone or other's story"), because these are governed positions.

Notice that if there were an overt pronominal anaphor, it too would have to be ungoverned, hence, excluded from all the standard Case-marking positions. But being overt, it must be Case-marked by the Case filter. Therefore it could exist only if it were restricted to ungoverned Case-marked positions, which are marginal at best.

We have been regarding a variable as an r-expression, with the features [−a, −p], which is the trace of movement to an

Ā-position. It follows that a variable is locally Ā-bound by an operator. Nothing requires an empty category locally Ā-bound by an operator to be a variable, however. In particular, PRO can have this property, as illustrated in (253) and (254):[119]

> (i) [PRO getting his teeth filled] generally upsets   (253)
> John
> (ii) *[PRO shaving himself] convinced Mary to trust John

> (i) who does [PRO getting his teeth filled] gener-   (254)
> ally upset e
> (ii) *who did [PRO shaving himself] convince Mary to trust e

The examples (253) illustrate certain control properties of PRO; it can be controlled by *John* in (i) but not (ii); see pp. 128f. These properties are duplicated in (254), where the variable e controls PRO. The parallelism extends more generally and shows that we have PRO, not a variable, in the subject position of the gerund; in fact, variables cannot appear in this position as we can see by replacing e by *John* in (254i), forcing the subject of the gerund to be a variable:

> *who does [e getting his teeth filled] generally upset   (255)
> John

Although locally bound by *who* in (254i), PRO is not a variable bound by the operator *who*.

There are further complexities that I will not consider here; see the references cited earlier for discussion. We have, however, the rudiments of a simple and straightforward version of binding theory that includes a fair range of cases.

3.5.2.4   Theta Theory.   Consider theta theory next. Its fundamental principle is the theta criterion, which expresses the intuitive idea that each argument is assigned its θ-role in exactly one θ-position (namely, at D-structure), and that each assignable θ-role must be assigned to an argument. We have formulated this principle as (168), which sets up a one-to-one relation between argument chains (actually CHAINs, though at LF we will have only chains if the proposal concerning expletive replacement at LF is tenable) and θ-positions: Each such chain contains exactly one θ-position, and each such position appears in one and only one argument chain (which, furthermore, must meet the visibility condition). As discussed in Section 3.4.3, it follows that movement is always to a non-θ-position.

This formulation—essentially that of Chomsky (1981)—may be slightly too strong. A possible counterexample in Italian is discussed by Burzio (forthcoming), following an earlier analysis by Luigi Rizzi. The case concerns the impersonal clitic *si*, with essentially the meaning of arbitrary PRO and impersonal *one*. I will not review the analysis, which involves a number of complexities and open questions. The potential problem is illustrated by such sentences as (256i) with the structure (256ii):

    (i) alcuni articoli si leggeranno ("one reads some   (256) articles")
    (ii) NP_1 si_2 $-V$ e_3

Take the subscripts here to be positions. The phrase *alcuni articoli* has been moved, by a rule of object preposing, from its D-structure position 3 as object of *leggere* to the subject position 1. Burzio argues, however, that *si* has moved from the subject position 1, leaving a trace, to the clitic position 2; the trace is then filled by object preposing. If so, we have two overlapping chains, and object preposing has moved an element into the θ-position 1. If this analysis is correct,[120] then the theta criterion as formulated must be slightly revised. Instead of requiring a one-to-one relation between θ-positions and chains containing them, we require only a one-to-one relation between θ-positions and chains that they θ-mark, assuming now that a chain is θ-marked by the element in its final position.

Returning to (256) under the proposed analysis, we have the two chains:

    (i) (2, 1)   (257)
    (ii) (1, 3)

The first is the chain of *si*, the second the chain of *alcuni articoli*. Although we have movement into the θ-position by object preposing, nevertheless, the required one-to-one relation between θ-marking and chains is preserved: *si* is θ-marked by position 1 in chain (257i), and *alcuni articoli* is θ-marked by position 3 in chain (257ii).

Whether or not this analysis is correct, the example does illustrate that the precise formulation of the intuition that θ-marking of arguments is unique is a rather delicate matter; slightly different formulations yield possible empirical differences that must be investigated. This situation is typical, as we have seen, and is to be expected in a computational system of the sort we have presupposed throughout.

3.5.2.5. *Case Theory.* Let us turn next to Case theory. The basic ideas originated from the study of infinitival clauses with subjects. We find the typical configuration of data (258), illustrating that the clause can appear after a preposition or a verb (as in (i), (ii), and (iii)) but not after a noun or an adjective ((iv) and (v); compare (vi) and (vii)), or, in fact, in any other position (e.g., (viii) and (ix); compare (x), etc.):

    (i) for [John to be the winner] is unlikely   (258)
    (ii) I'd prefer for [John to be the winner]
    (iii) I believe [John to be the winner]
    (iv) *the belief [John to be the winner]
    (v) *proud [John to be the winner]
    (vi) the belief [that John is the winner]
    (vii) proud [that John is the winner]
  (viii) *[John to be the winner] is unlikely
    (ix) *I wonder to whom [John to give the book]
    (x) I wonder [to whom John is to give the book]

To generate just the right forms in cases of this sort would require a rather complex rule system. A more plausible approach is to seek some "output condition," some condition on S-structure that "filters out" unwanted cases, and then to allow simple rules to apply without contextual constraints. The first attempt along these lines postulated a filter serving as a kind of template to rule out unwanted S-structures. The data of (258) follow from a filter that bars S-structures on the form NP-*to*-VP, where NP is not PRO, unless the construction follows V or P. Thus, in (258) (iv), (v), (viii), and (ix) are barred, whereas (i), (ii), (iii) are admitted by the *unless*-clause. An approach of this sort was developed in Chomsky and Lasnik (1977) as part of a more general effort to deal with complex phenomena in terms of a modular approach that dispenses with rich and elaborate systems of phrase structure and transformational rules.

Although the filter is descriptively adequate over a wide range and does contribute to factoring out simple components that interact to yield complex effects, nevertheless, it seems rather *ad hoc*. Vergnaud observed that its effects could largely be accommodated[121] by the Case filter (34). Then in (258) (iv), (v), (viii), and (ix) are barred by lack of Case on the subject *John* of the infinitive, but (i), (ii), (iii) are admitted because V and P assign Case to *John*. We can proceed further, reducing the case filter to theta theory by recourse to the visibility condition as discussed earlier, with further consequences as indicated.[122] The apparent diversity of languages is now further reduced. All are subject to a core system of Case assignment, though only in some languages is there a morphological realization. In English, largely lacking morphological Case, the core properties of Case assignment are nevertheless manifested in such paradigms as (258), and also in the Case adjacency condition on phrase structure, the Case requirement on variables, and so forth.

Case theory now deals with the question of how Case is assigned. This question depends crucially on decisions concerning other subsystems of UG. The modular system of UG is a tightly knit and intricate structure so that any specific proposal has wide-ranging consequences, and many questions remain unresolved as to how the basic notions should be formulated. I will outline one possible approach, a modified version of Chomsky (1981), continuing with the assumptions sketched so far.

If the category α has a Case to assign, then it may assign it to an element that it governs. In the structure (259), for example, if V is transitive it assigns objective Case to NP and to DET and N:

$$[_{VP} \text{ V } [_{NP} \text{ DET } [_{N'} \text{ N } \dots]]] \tag{259}$$

Prepositions assign (oblique) Case in the same way. The agreement element of INFL is associated (we have assumed, co-indexed) with the subject, which it governs since they share all maximal projections, and assigns it nominative Case. The possessive element POSS is affixed to the subject of an NP, serving as the realization of Case for the NP to which it is affixed. Thus, Case is assigned to the subject *John* in *John's book* and *John's reading the book*.[123] Note that Case is uniformly assigned under government.

Possessive noun phrases have certain well-known distributional peculiarities:

    (i) a book of John's (is on the table)   (260)
    (ii) that book of John's
   (iii) *the book of John's
   (iv) the book of John's that you read
    (v) *John's book that you read
   (vi) John's book

In general, the phrase *of John's*, which has something of the character of a restrictive relative clause, can appear with any determiner except the definite article (unless a restrictive modifier such as "that you read" or "with a blue cover" appears), and the gap in the distribution of phrases of the type [DET-N-of NP's] is filled by the phrase [NP's N], which, furthermore, has exactly the meaning of the missing option (thus, (vi) means "the book of John's," not "a book of John's"). The data suggest that (vi) may be a secondary form, derived from (iii) by an instance of Move-α, in which case there are no gaps in the distribution of [DET-N-of NP's] constructions, although X-bar considerations would still indicate that such structures as "their destruction of the city," and "their refusal to leave" are directly generated at D-structure in the form [SPEC N'], with SPEC = NP, receiving genitive Case in the normal way.[124]

Let us return now to the constructions of (258), repeated here:

    (i) for [John to be the winner] is unlikely   (261)
    (ii) I'd prefer for [John to be the winner]
   (iii) I believe [John to be the winner]

   (iv) *the belief [John to be the winner]
    (v) *proud [John to be the winner]
   (vi) the belief [that John is the winner]
  (vii) proud [that John is the winner]
 (viii) *[John to be the winner] is unlikely
   (ix) *I wonder to whom [John to give the book]
    (x) I wonder [to whom John is to give the book]

We are concerned with the Case of *John*. In the ungrammatical examples, no Case is assigned and *John* violates the Case filter. In (vi), (vii), and (x) *John* receives nominative Case as subject of a finite clause with tense and agreement. In (i) and (ii), the complementizer *for* governs S and therefore governs its specifier, the subject *John*, assigning it Case. This leaves only (iii) to be explained.

    Notice that *believe* in (261iii) contrasts with *try*, as illustrated below:

   (i) I believe [$_\alpha$ John to be the winner]   (262)
  (ii) *I believe [$_\alpha$ PRO to be the winner]
 (iii) *I tried [$_\alpha$ John to be the winner]
 (iv) I tried [$_\alpha$ PRO to be the winner]

These results follow if we assume that *try* selects C and *believe* selects S,[125] so that $\alpha = S$ in (i) and (ii) and $\alpha = C$ in (iii) and (iv). In (iii) and (iv), then, the complement of *try* is:

$$[_C [_{COMP} e] [_S \text{NP to be the winner}]] \qquad (263)$$

The verbs *believe* and *try* govern their complements, S and C, respectively. Furthermore, *believe* governs the subject of S, *John* (the specifier of S), but *try* governs only C and its head, COMP. Thus, *believe* is able to Case-mark *John* in (262i), but *try* is unable to Case-mark *John* in (262iii), which therefore violates the Case filter. Structures such as (262iii) would be possible only if COMP were *for*, itself a Case assigner; and, indeed, constructions of this form are grammatical in dialects of English that allow *try* to take a *for*-infinitive complement.[126]

    This explains (262i) and (262iii). What about (262ii) and (262iv)? Their status follows from the basic property (252) that determines the distribution of PRO. This property follows from the principles of binding theory under plausible assumptions, as we have seen. From (252) it follows that PRO can appear only as the subject of an infinitive or gerund, and in the former case, it cannot appear as the infinitival subject of the complement of a verb such as *believe*, because this position is governed. But it can appear as the infinitival subject of the complement of *try*, which is ungoverned.

In general, a verb selects a full clause C, not S; C, not S, is the normal canonical structural realization (CSR) of proposition (see p. 87). Thus, *try*, not *believe*, illustrates the general case; such examples as (262i) (=(261iii)) are often called "exceptional Case-marking" constructions. In languages very much like English (French and German, for example) these constructions do not exist, and the counterpart of *believe* behaves like *try* in English in this respect. We assume, then, that the exceptional Case-marking property of *believe*-type verbs (generally, epistemic verbs) in English must be specifically learned, from sentences such as (261iii).

Consider the nominal constructions analogous to (262), namely:

(i) *the belief [$_\alpha$ John to be the winner] (264)
(ii) *the belief [$_\alpha$ PRO to be the winner]
(iii) *the attempt [$_\alpha$ John to be the winner]
(iv) the attempt [$_\alpha$ PRO to be the winner]

The examples (iii) and (iv) are explained as before: *attempt*, like *try*, selects C, so that PRO may appear in the ungoverned subject position in (iv), and *John* is barred by the Case filter in (iii), exactly as in the corresponding verb phrases. Case (ii) is analogous to (262ii). The nominal form of *believe* retains the lexical property of selecting S, not C, so that PRO is in a governed position as before, violating (252). Turning to (i), the noun *belief* does not assign objective Case, so this form too is excluded, even though *John* is in a governed position.

The distribution of infinitival clauses with overt subject is now largely explained. They can appear only in positions where Case is assigned, i.e., after a verb or preposition. Endowed with Case theory along with the other subtheories of UG, the language learner knows without specific instruction that grammatical and ungrammatical structures are as indicated in the preceding examples. Again, the need to stipulate elaborate rule systems or to explain how they can possibly be learned is overcome.

One major problem remains, however. We noticed earlier that English allows an "escape" from Case filter violations by the rule of *of*-insertion, which applies to give such examples as (58iii) and 65iii), repeated here:

> (i) I persuaded John [of the importance of going   (265)
>   to college]
> (ii) John is uncertain [of the time]

We might ask, then, why this rule does not apply in (264i), giving (266) and thus voiding the Case filter violation:

> the belief [of John to be the winner]   (266)

The same question arises elsewhere; thus, *of*-insertion does not apply in:

> (i) there was [$_{VP}$ killed (of) John]   (267)
> (ii) it seems [$_S$ (of) John to be happy]
> (iii) it is certain [$_S$ (of) John to be happy]

If *of*-insertion were to apply in these cases, it would be unnecessary to apply the rule Move-α, moving *John* to the position occupied by expletive *there* or *it* and giving (268), to escape the Case filter violation:[127]

> (i) John was [$_{VP}$ killed *e*]   (268)
> (ii) John seems [$_S$ *e* to be happy]
> (iii) John is certain [$_S$ *e* to be happy]

It is necessary, then, to specify the domain of the rule of *of*-insertion more carefully and to account for its specific properties, as far as possible.

The problem is an interesting one for the reasons discussed in Section 3.5.1. The rule is rather marginal—and in this case, arguably part of the periphery rather than core grammar—and it seems likely that evidence concerning its application is limited. The question, as throughout, is why the language learner does not generalize to unwanted cases on the basis of the examples presented. To the extent that relevant (i.e., positive) evidence is, indeed, meager, the properties of the rule will follow from UG and may, therefore, give us some insight into the detailed structure of the general system of principles.

As discussed earlier, the "functional role" of the rule of *of*-insertion and comparable rules in other languages is to regularize certain paradigms. Thus, the projection principle predicts the presence of NP in certain positions, but the Case filter bars its presence. Two examples discussed earlier were (265i, 265ii). More broadly, X-bar theory leads us to expect that nouns and adjectives should have essentially the same complement structures as verbs. Thus, for example, alongside of *discover America* or *destroy the city*, we should find such representations as (269):

(i) $[_{N'}$ discovery $[_{NP}$ America$]]$ (269)
(ii) $[_{N'}$ destruction $[_{NP}$ the city$]]$

But Case theory bars these structures, because *America* and *the city* lack Case. The rule of *of*-insertion has the functional role of permitting the representations licensed by X-bar theory, where *of* is a semantically empty Case-marker. Given the D-structure form (270i) licensed by X-bar theory, we must use some device to assign Case to the object, either an application of Move-α and the genitive assignment rule to yield (270ii), or *of*-insertion to yield (270iii); adjective phrases such as (271i) permit *of*-insertion to yield (271ii) and require it, since noun phrases with genitive Case do not appear in the specifier position of adjectives (there is no adjectival counterpart to "John's book":

(i) the [destruction [the city]]   (270)
(ii) [the city]'s destruction *e*
(iii) the [destruction [of the city]]

(i) proud [John]   (271)
(ii) proud [of John]

The expression (270ii) is, in effect, the "passive" of (270i), just as (268i) is the passive counterpart of (267i).[128]

Suppose we revise the version of Case theory outlined earlier, regarding nouns and adjectives as Case-assigners along with verbs and prepositions.[129] We distinguish the "structural Cases" objective and nominative, assigned in terms of S-structure position, from the "inherent Cases" assigned at D-structure. The latter include the oblique Case assigned by prepositions and now also genitive Case, which we assume to be assigned by nouns and adjectives just as verbs normally assign objective Case. Inherent Case is associated with θ-marking while structural Case is not, as we should expect for processes that apply at D- and S-structure, respectively. Thus, we assume that inherent Case is assigned by α to NP if and only if α θ-marks NP, while structural Case is assigned independently of θ-marking.[130]

Now all lexical categories assign Case: P, N, and A assign inherent Case at D-structure, whereas V (along with INFL containing AGR; usually as in English, finite INFL) assigns structural Case at S-structure. The NP complement of any lexical category may be Case-marked, and V may assign structural Case to an NP that it governs but does not θ-mark, as in the exceptional Case-marking constructions.

It is plausible to assume that the direction of Case-marking for lexical categories is uniform and, in the unmarked case, corresponds to the head parameter of X-bar theory. In English, then, Case-marking by a lexical category should be uniformly to the right.[131] If we assume this condition to be generally valid, then genitive Case will be assigned to the complement of a noun or adjective. But as illustrated in (270), genitive Case can be realized in either the complement or subject position in the case of a noun phrase. Therefore, we must distinguish Case-assignment, at D-structure, from Case-realization, at S-structure. Both Case-assignment and Case-realization fall under government: At D-structure, N governs and θ-marks its complement and assigns Case to it; at S-structure, N governs both the complement and the subject, so that Case can be realized in either position. Let us proceed to investigate these assumptions.

Assume further that the association of inherent Case and θ-marking extends to Case-realization as well as Case-assignment. Thus we have the following uniformity condition:

If α is an inherent Case-marker, then α Case-marks   (272)
NP if and only if θ-marks the chain headed by NP

Here "Case-marking" includes Case-assignment and Case-realization. Because Case-assignment is at D-structure, the chain headed by NP will be the trivial single-membered chain (NP) in this case. This extension amounts to the requirement that inherent Case must be realized on NP under government by the category that θ-marks NP at D-structure.

Returning to (270), repeated here, genitive Case is assigned to the complement in (i) and is realized in the same position in (iii) but is realized in the subject position in (ii):

  (i) the [destruction [the city]]   (270)
  (ii) [the city]'s destruction *e*
  (iii) the [destruction [of the city]]

Case-assignment and both instances of Case-realization satisfy the uniformity condition.

Genitive Case is realized morphologically by affixation of some element to the NP: *of* in complement position, the possessive element POSS in subject position. These specific mechanisms arguably belong to the periphery rather than core grammar in the sense described earlier. Each has certain properties that must be made explicit. Let us consider them in turn.

The rule of *of*-insertion is a "default case," applying only when there is no preposition available that inherently assigns the appropriate θ-rule, as there is in such constructions as:

  (i) our promise to John   (273)
  (ii) the order to John to leave

Similarly, the rule cannot adjoin *of* to an indirect object to yield (274i) corresponding to (274ii), because *to* assigns the θ-role of goal as in (274iii), (274iv), where *of* is properly inserted as a default (see note 130):

  (i) *the gift of John a book   (274)
  (ii) give John a book

(iii) the gift to John of a book
(iv) the gift of a book to John

Turning to POSS-insertion, recall that alongside of nominalizations such as (270ii), genitive Case can be realized on the
subject of a noun phrase:

(i) [John's story] disturbed me   (275)
(ii) [John's reading the book] disturbed me

In (ii), *reading the book* θ-marks *John*, and the uniformity
condition is met if we think of it as also Case-marking *John*. In
the case of (i), however, no lexical head θ-marks *John*, unless
we assume, following Gruber (1976) and M. Anderson (1983),
that a "possessional θ-role" is assigned in this structural position, perhaps under government by the concrete noun *story*, in
which case the uniformity condition would again be met.
Abstract nouns, in contrast, would assign some specific θ-role
to their subjects. The distinction, which is fairly general, is
illustrated by such examples as (276), noted by Mona Anderson:

(i) John's reconstruction(s) of an eighteenth-   (276)
   century village
(ii) John's reconstruction of the crime

In (276i), the head noun is concrete and the semantic role of
John ranges over the possibilities that fall under the category
"possessional"; in (276ii), *John* is the agent.[132] There are various
controversial questions about these structures; let us assume
that they are settled in such a way as to satisfy the uniformity
condition.

The context in which POSS is inserted is:

$[_{NP} NP—]$ (277)

In (275i), $\alpha = N'$; in (275ii), $\alpha = VP$, and there is presumably
further clausal structure. In a language lacking the equivalent
of (277), movement from the complement of α to the specifier
position is impossible. Because (277) is restricted to NP, move-

ment from the complement of α to the specifier position is restricted to $\alpha = N$ or gerunds such as "John's having been appointed." The restriction to NP presumably follows from X-bar theoretic considerations.

If the uniformity conditions (272) for POSS-insertion is stated in terms of chains, not CHAINs, then it will be impossible to assign POSS to expletives as in (278i–278iii). If the condition is generally valid, such forms as (278iv) will also be barred, because *seem* does not θ-mark the chain headed by *John*.

   (i) *there's destruction of the city   (278)
   (ii) *there's having been too much rain last year
  (iii) *it's seeming that John is intelligent
  (iv) *John's seeming to be intelligent

In large measure, the conclusion seems correct. Various consequences ensue for structures of the form "it is obvious (believed, certain,...) that S," which do permit POSS-insertion,[133] some of them related to the question of expletive-argument pairs violating (171), discussed on p. 137. Note that this approach gives an independent way to block (278i), which was excluded in earlier discussion on the basis of condition (171) (see (172)). Restriction of the uniformity condition to chains, not CHAINs, follows directly from the theory of expletive replacement, which eliminates the concept CHAIN (see p. 179). The fact that the uniformity condition applies at S-structure is also natural, given that Case has manifestations both at PF and at LF.

These assumptions, which seem minimal, exclude the possibility of a PRO complement to an inherent Case-marker. Suppose we have such a construction, as in (279), where $\alpha = N$, A, or P:

$$[_{\alpha''} \text{SPEC} [_{\alpha'} \alpha \text{ PRO}]] \tag{279}$$

The position of PRO is necessarily θ-marked at D-structure, as discussed earlier, because this is a complement position (PRO is an internal argument, the object of α). By (252), PRO must move from this position to an ungoverned position, forming a chain (PRO, e). PRO cannot move to the position of SPEC because this position is governed by α. Therefore, it must move to some more remote position, one that is ungoverned, as in (280ii), derived from the D-structure (280i):

> (i) it is difficult [e to be believed that he was (280)
>   [proud PRO]]
> (ii) it is difficult [PRO to be believed that he was
>   [proud e]]

The meaning would be "it is difficult for it to be believed that he was proud of someone or other," a fine meaning, but not expressed by (ii). The reason is that (ii) violates the uniformity condition: *proud* is an inherent Case-marker which θ-marks the chain (PRO, e), but it does not Case-mark PRO. Thus, the structure is ill-formed. One might assume that (ii) is a violation of condition (A) of the binding theory (216), but that would not be true if *he* is co-indexed with PRO.[134] Notice that in this case (280) is a violation of (247), which requires local binding for links of a chain. Hence, this case of (247) too is derivable from other considerations.

Another possible violation of (247) is provided by the D-structures (281), where *John* is the complement of the noun *pictures* and is, therefore, θ-marked and assigned genitive Case by *pictures* at D-structure:[135]

> (i) it seems that [(his$_j$) pictures John$_i$] are on sale (281)
> (ii) the story about [(his$_j$) pictures John $_i$] (is silly)
> (iii) reading the book about [(his$_j$) pictures John $_i$]
>   (is silly)

With *his* missing or $j \neq i$, genitive Case may be realized by *of*-insertion in all three cases. If *his* is present with $j = i$, we have a straightforward violation of condition (C) of the binding theory (216).

Suppose instead we were to apply Move-α, yielding:

> (i) John$_i$ seems that [(his$_j$) pictures e_i] are on sale (282)
> (ii) John$_i$ story about [(his$_j$) pictures e_i] (is silly)
> (iii) John$_i$ reading the book about [(his$_j$ pictures e_i]
>   (is silly)

With $j \neq i$, we have a violation of condition (A) of the binding theory (216). Suppose that *his* either is missing or is present with $i = j$; the latter case violates (247), because the chain (*John, e*) is now not a case of local binding.[136]

In (282), *John* is Case-marked by main clause INFL, *story* and *reading the book*, respectively. Assuming that "Case-marking" in the definition (167) does not include Case-assignment,[137] there is no violation of the requirement that a chain can only have one Case-marked position. However, there is Case conflict in (i) because *John* is assigned nominative Case at S-structure and genitive Case at D-structure, a violation of the uniformity condition in all three cases, and a violation of the theta criterion if *John* is in a θ-marked position in (ii), (iii). Therefore, such constructions as (282) are impossible and (247) once again is not violated.

Consider now (270), or more generally, the D-structures (283) that surface as (284):

(i) the [$_{N'}$ destruction [$_{NP}$ the city]]   (283)
(ii) they [$_{N'}$ destruction [$_{NP}$ the city]]

(i) (a) the destruction of the city   (284)
    (b) the city's destruction
(ii) their destruction of the city

The D-structure representations (283) cannot surface in this form because of the Case filter. In (i), *destruction* θ-marks its complement *the city* and, therefore, assigns it genitive Case. We now have two options: *destruction* may realize Case in this position by *of*-insertion, yielding (284ia); or Move-α may apply, yielding (285), with the chain (*the city, e*):

[$_{NP}$ the city] [$_{N'}$ destruction e]   (285)

The rule (277) of POSS-insertion applies to this structure, yielding the surface form (284ib). This satisfies the uniformity condition, because *destruction* realizes Case on the head of the chain that it θ-marks. In (283ii), the Move-α option is voided because the target position is already occupied. Therefore, *of*-insertion must apply to yield *of the city*. But *destruction* also governs the subject *they* and θ-marks it, assigning it the θ-role of agent exactly as in the corresponding clause. Therefore, by the uniformity condition, *destruction* assigns genitive Case to *they*. Now POSS-insertion applies forming *they* + POSS = *their*, finally yielding (284ii).

A question arises about the effect of movement applied to an element α assigned Case at D-structure: Does the Case move with the element, or does it remain in place on the trace? In different terms, is Case assigned to the NP or to the position it occupies? The crucial structure is (285). Recall that the condition (170) bars Case-marked NP-trace, thus making movement a "last resort." To satisfy the principle, then, we must assume that in (285), the trace is not Case-marked. We therefore conclude that case moves with the element moved; Case is assigned to the NP, not the position it occupies. Alternatively, we might assume that (170) refers to realized Case, not assigned Case.

Suppose we were to adopt the principle (190), repeated here, considered but not adopted in Section 3.4.3 (p. 144):

A binding relation between an argument and a   (190)
Case-marked nonargument is not subject to binding
theory

The advantage of this principle was that it incorporated both the requirement that NP-trace cannot be Case-marked (thus yielding the general chain condition (171) in full generality) and also the requirement that an argument is not bound by a nonargument. But there are problems concerning the structure (285).

First, because (190) bars Case-marked NP-trace, we must again assume that in (285) the trace is not Case-marked. Second, (190) voids a binding theory violation in the case of an argument c-commanded by a Case-marked nonargument. In (285), the subject *the city* is c-commanded by its trace, which will yield a binding theory violation unless the trace is Case-marked so that the violation is voided by (190). We therefore have a contradiction: The trace must be Case-marked to void the binding theory violation under (190) but must be non–Case-marked to satisfy the requirement that trace not be Case-marked under (190). The contradiction arises however we construe "Case-marking" in

(190): as including Case-assignment, Case-realization, or both. This is one reason why we did not adopt (190).

Not adopting (190), we have to assume that Case-marked trace is barred, one case of the principle that Case can only appear on the head of a chain (see (170)). We also have to assume the principle (188) requiring that an argument not be bound by a nonargument, thus voiding the binding theory violation in (285). (Recall that the major cases of (188), though not the one in question here, are accounted for by the requirement that expletives be eliminated at LF; see p. 179). Both assumptions would follow from (190) if the contradiction just noted can be overcome by some reformulation, for example, by defining "c-command" for binding theory along the lines of Reinhart (1976). We saw that condition (170) applied to CHAINs more generally. The choices among the options is not entirely clear. We have assumed (170) rather than (190), although with reservations. Thus, one case of the general condition (171) on chains, namely, case (170), remains a stipulation, although the remainder is derived on independent gerunds.

Let us now review the problematic examples (265), (266), (267), and (270), repeated here, which initiated these considerations:

> (i) I persuaded John [of the importance of going   (286) to college]
> (ii) John is uncertain [of the time]
> (iii) *the belief [of John to be the winner]
> (iv) *there was [$_{VP}$ killed (of) John]
> (v) *it seems [$_S$ (of) John to be happy]
> (vi) *it is certain [$_S$ (of) John to be happy]
> (vii) *the [destruction [the city]]
> (viii) [the city]'s destruction e
> (ix) the [destruction [of the city]]
> (x) *proud [John]
> (xi) proud [of John]

In (i) and (ii), genitive Case is assigned to the NP at D-structure and is realized in the same position by *of*-insertion at S-structure, these being the only options since Move-α is impossible, lacking any possible target (or in (ii), because of the restriction to NP in (277); see also note 130). In (iii), genitive Case is not assigned to *John* because it is not θ-marked by *belief*, so the structure is barred by the Case filter. In (iv) and (v), *John* is not assigned genitive Case since the governor is not a noun or adjective; independently, in (iv) the passive morphology removes the capacity to assign Case, and in (v) the governor *seem* does not θ-mark *John*. The same reason bars Case-assignment to *John* in (vi), although it is governed by the adjective *certain* (compare (ii), where *the time* is both governed and θ-marked by *uncertain* as its complement). The S-structures corresponding to (iv)–(vi) must, therefore, be (268). In the D-structures (vii) and (x), genitive Case is assigned to *the city* and to *John*, respectively. In the latter case, it must be realized by *of*-insertion, yielding (xi); in the former, it may be realized by *of*-insertion, yielding (ix), or, after application of Move-α, it may be realized by POSS-insertion, yielding (viii).

The uniformity condition (272) may have some consequences for the phenomenon of "preposition stranding," as in (287i) and (287ii) derived from (288i) and (288ii), respectively:[138]

    (i) *John was given a book to *e*   (287)
    (ii) who did you give the book to *e*

    (i) *e* was given a book to John   (288)
    (ii) you gave the book to who

Consider first the passive case, case (i). The preposition *to* is an inherent Case-marker, which θ-marks and assigns oblique Case to its object *John* at the D-structure (288i). At the S-structure (287i), *to* θ-marks the chain headed by *John* and therefore, by the uniformity condition, *to* must Case-mark *John*, which is impossible. Thus, cases such as (i) are ruled out as ill-formed. But the argument is not compelling if we continue to accept the "last resort" principle (170) that bars Case-marked trace, because this condition will suffice to bar (287i), unless we assume again that the inherent Case is "moved" with the NP to which it is assigned; see p. 179. Examples such as "the bed was slept in" presumably derive by a reanalysis process that treats *sleep in* as a single verb that loses its Case-assigning property under passive morphology.

Turning to (ii), if we understand "chain" in (272) to include Ā-chains, then the S-structure (ii) is barred because *to*, which θ-marks the trace, does not Case-mark *who*, the head of the A-chain. If we restrict (272) to A-chains, then (287ii) satisfies the condition: *to* θ-marks and Case-marks the A-chain consisting just of the trace.

We might conclude, then, that NP-movement stranding a preposition is ruled out uniformly whereas the status of stranding under movement to an Ā-position (e.g., *wh*-movement) is subject to variation, depending on the interpretation of (272), which could be parametrized.

Alternatively, we might extend (272) to Ā chains, thus concluding that (287ii) is a marked structure, to be accounted for by special properties of English, perhaps related to the "weak" Case realization of English. Perhaps, the oblique Case assigned by prepositions is not distinguished from objective Case in English, as suggested by Richard Kayne, who draws a number of interesting conclusions from the assumption.

Further questions arise in connection with the complementizer *for* as in (261i) and (261ii), repeated here:

    (i) for [John to be the winner] is unlikely   (289)
    (ii) I'd prefer for [John to be the winner]

We have assumed that *for* Case-marks *John*, but this is inconsistent with the uniformity condition if *for* is an inherent Case-marker because *for* does not θ-mark *John*. We might again resort to Kayne's suggestion that in English, prepositions assign objective rather than oblique Case, so that the only inherent Case-markers would be N and A, assigning genitive Case. English, then, would have the degenerate Case system (nominative, objective, genitive), lacking oblique. Case-marking is now permissible in (289), and we regard these to be marked constructions, possible in a language with a degenerate Case system.[139]

Summarizing this discussion of Case theory, we continue to assume the Case filter as determined by the visibility condition on θ-marking. Case theory determines the properties of Case-marking. We distinguish between the structural Cases, nominative and objective, assigned in terms of S-structure position, and the inherent Cases, oblique and genitive, assigned at D-structure and associated with θ-marking by the uniformity condition. Genitive Case is realized either by POSS-insertion or *of*-insertion. Because the realization of genitive Case depends on S-structure position, we distinguish Case-assignment at D-structure from Case-realization at S-structure for genitive Case, both subject to the uniformity condition. The rule of *of*-insertion, which has the functional role of removing Case filter restrictions on the projection principle, is a default rule, applied only when no preposition is available to assign the required θ-role.

Apart from these properties of Case theory, we have assumed principles of X-bar theory and binding theory, the theta criterion, Move-α and its properties (specifically, those of bounding theory, which we have illustrated but not discussed), and the condition (171) on CHAINs,[140] along with a few auxiliary assumptions. In addition, we have several general principles such as the projection principle and FI (full interpretation). Some of the possibilities of parametric variation have been illustrated, along with certain marked options such as exceptional Case-marking.

From these assumptions, a variety of consequences follow as described, some general, some dependent on specific properties of English, which themselves are subject to general principles.

Recall that this analysis represents one selection among a maze of options. The assumptions are natural and straightforward but obviously far from uniquely determined by the relevant data. A number of no less natural and straightforward assumptions have been put forth within the same general framework, and other quite plausible approaches have also been advanced, some with substantial empirical support. One would naturally expect that further inquiry into English and other languages will show that the assumptions proposed here are wrong, at least in detail, quite possibly in general conception. We look forward, then, to improvement or replacement in other terms. Nevertheless, the conclusions reached in this discussion seem to me likely to be qualitatively correct in a certain sense. That is, phenomena of the kind reviewed are explained in terms of simple principles of UG of some generality, specified and extended with some language-specific options and, further, determined through the interaction of various modules of language—probably by computations of some intricacy, that is, with a certain depth of deductive structure. Conclusions of this sort are implicit in the empirical conditions of Plato's problem, and in several domains, there has been encouraging progress in giving them a substantive form.

The general idea that the language faculty involves a pre-cisely articulated computational system—fairly simple in its basic principles when modules are properly distinguished, but quite intricate in the consequences that are produced—seems reasonably well established. As we have remarked earlier, this is not at all an obvious property of a biological system. Indeed, it is in many respects a very surprising property. Nevertheless, the evidence supporting it is quite substantial, and this conclusion is likely to withstand the inevitable revisions in the systems of UG that have been tentatively proposed in the past years.

NOTES

1. For various interpretations of this procedure, essentially that of Chomsky (1975a; 1955–56) and (1965), see Chomsky (1975b). There is important recent work on formalization of possible procedures of language acquisition; see Wexler and Culicover (1980) and Berwick (1982). For critical discussion of various misinterpretations of this general approach, see Lightfoot (1981) and Bracken (1984).

2. For example, Hyams (1983) argues that early stages of language acquisition proceed on the assumption that the language is like Italian or Spanish in not requiring an explicit subject, a decision later reversed in the acquisition of English.

3. On uniformities of maturation, see Gleitman (1981). See Borer and Wexler (1984) for ideas as to how to explain some of the phenomena of child language on the assumption that certain princi-ples of UG are not available at early stages of language growth. On the general issue, see Chomsky (1975b, 1980b) and Berwick (1982).

4. Cf. Tomas (1957). Peirce's invocation of natural selection as a *deus ex machina* to account for successful theory construction in science will not do, however; see Chomsky (1968, 1975b).

5. See Chomsky (1965), pp. 61–62), (1980b, pp. 120–122), Ber-wick and Weinberg (1984). On the generative capacity of UG, suppose a set of levels $L_1, \ldots L_n$ to be given in the sense of p. 46,

where L_1 is the system of universal phonetics that specifies the class of possible sentences s_1, s_2,.... The rule system R assigns to each s_i a structure $S_i^R = (m_1^i, \ldots, m_n^i)$, where m_j^i is the marker assigned to s_i at the level L_j, $m_1^i = s_i$ (m_j^i may be null, indicating that R assigns no marker to s_i at L_j). Then R generates the set of structures $\{S_i^R\}$. UG permits the maximal variety of rule systems, in one sense of this notion, if it provides a rule system for each recursively enumerable set of structures. If the notion E-language is somehow defined in terms of the set of generated structures, then we may regard UG as maximal if it provides a rule system for each recursively enumerable E-language.

6. Note that the conclusion is unaffected by the existence of other types of idiomatic constructions that are not of NP-V-NP form, for example, "the roof fell in on X." For discussion of these matters, from similar although not identical points of view, see Chomsky (1981) and Marantz (1984). For different approaches, see, among others, Bresnan (1982), Perlmutter (1983a), and Rothstein (1983).

7. See Whitman (1982) and Saito (1985); on further complications, see Huang (1982).

8. Called "deep structures" in earlier work. I have stopped using the term because it led to too much misinterpretation; see Chomsky (1980b).

9. See Chomsky (1966).

10. This is evident from the earliest publications in generative grammar, which are primarily concerned with the problem of designing the theory of linguistic structure (UG) so that the rule systems selected will be adequate to explain semantic properties of expressions. It has often been assumed that semantic considerations were excluded in this early work, but on the basis of a serious misinterpretation of a very different position: namely, that syntactic properties apparently cannot be defined in semantic terms, at least in the ways that were commonly proposed. This is a wholly different matter. For further discussion, see Chomsky (1977), Chapter 1; Hornstein (1984).

11. The status and properties of LF are empirical matters, not to be settled in terms of considerations of valid inference and the like. See Chomsky (1980b).

12. Note that this is not a uniform category; for example, the violation in (27viii) is much "weaker" than the others, a fact that also must be explained.

13. This actually appeared in two earlier published versions; I will collapse the three here, although they made somewhat different proposals as to the relevant principles. It is often supposed that the attempt to reduce the richness and variety of transformational rules was motivated by concern over generative capacity; see, for example,

Johnson-Laird (1983), who asserts that this "reappraisal of transformational grammar" began in the late 1970s as a consequence of the
observation by Stanley Peters and Robert Ritchie that an unconstrained
grammar of this sort could generate every recursively enumerable set
(more interestingly, they showed that a simple formal property sufficed
to reduce generative capacity to a much narrower class containing
only recursive sets). This assertion is doubly wrong: The work began
in the early 1960s for other reasons and was unaffected by this observation; moreover, it had been pointed out years before that this conclusion, if valid, would have no empirical import (see note 5). Johnson-
Laird also believes that the Peters-Ritchie result had other "embarrassing consequences," specifically in undermining "Chomsky's
'universal base' hypothesis." Such a hypothesis had indeed been proposed,
but I had never accepted it; furthermore, the hypothesis would be
unaffected by this observation, essentially for the reasons already
noted.

14.   We might take *wh-* to be a determiner in the category of
some, any, every, with phonological rules spelling out *wh-one* as
who, and so forth. There are interesting questions here, which I will
ignore, concerning "relational" nouns such as *friend* as distinct from
nonrelational ones such as *book*. Many of these questions remain
open.

15.   See Chomsky (1965, 1977) and Chomsky and Lasnik (1977).

16.   See Rouveret and Vergnaud (1980), Vergnaud (1982), and
Chomsky (1980a, 1981).

17.   Here and henceforth I will capitalize the word "Case" in
its technical usage to avoid confusion.

18.   See Borer (1983, 1984a) for discussion of how the properties
of the passive morpheme apply differently for principled reasons in
the lexical and syntactic components; for a somewhat different
approach, see Fabb (1984).

19.   On these matters, see Chomsky (1981), following proposals
of Rizzi (1982a), Burzio (forthcoming) and others; more recent work,
some cited below, suggests other possibilities along somewhat different
lines, which I will ignore here. The topics I am reviewing are under
active investigation, and many alternative ideas are being pursued
more or less within the general framework outlined here.

20.   In some cases, it might be wholly determined as a reflex of
properties of the phrase structure. On other possible parameters
associated with the general rule Move-α, see Baltin (1982).

21.   On how the parameter might be formulated, and other
variants beyond those mentioned here, see Lasnik and Saito (1984).

22.   On some of the relevant parameters for (40), see Rizzi
(1982a).

23.   This assumption is known to be too simple as it stands. See Lasnik (1980), who argues that it is necessary to return to the more complex indexing system of Chomsky (1980a). See Higginbotham (1983a) and Finer (1984) for modifications to deal with these and other problems; Higginbotham argues that the asymmetry of the antecedent-anaphor relation should be built into the notation; Finer proposes a system of dual indexing to express set inclusion and intersection. I will ignore these questions here. The question of exactly what the operative principles of binding theory are has been subject to considerable study over the past several years. One influential early paper was Lasnik (1976). See Chomsky (1981) for further discussion and references; also Reinhart (1983), Higginbotham (1983a), (forthcoming), Manzini (1983a), Bouchard (1984), Pica (1984), and Freidin (forthcoming), among others. See also the cross-linguistic study by Yang (1983), presenting and analyzing parametric variation in binding theory.

24.   We specify that X is a *distinct* element to allow, for example, "he$_i$ said that he$_i$ would be there," where the second occurrence of *he* takes the first as its antecedent. As formulated, the principle now excludes the grammatical expression "John hit himself"; we return to this question directly.

25.   The term is Thomas Wasow's; see Wasow (1979), based on a 1972 MIT Ph.D. dissertation. The study of cross-over was initiated by Paul Postal (1971).

26.   Strong cross-over in this case is excluded by other principles as well, in particular, by the fact that pronouns cannot be locally bound by operators in languages such as English that lack resumptive pronouns (pronouns locally bound by operators), and quite generally even in languages with resumptive pronouns in such structures as (42i); see Chomsky (1982) for discussion of this and some other analyses on somewhat different assumptions; see also Higginbotham (1983a). I will continue to rely here on the binding theory principle, which generalizes in various ways as we shall see.

27.   Howard Lasnik observes that in Thai, for example, whereas pronouns cannot bind their antecedents, the principle does not seem to extend to pairs of r-expressions.

28.   We limit ourselves here to noun phrases, although the observation should be generalized.

29.   Joseph Aoun has proposed an interesting extension of binding theory to Ā-binding as well; see Aoun (1982), (1985). I will put aside these ideas, since they bear primarily on aspects of grammar that will not be discussed here.

30.   Note that forms of the latter type are possible, particularly when the NP is complex, but as derived structures formed by an

additional rule moving the NP to the right. There is some evidence that this rule of "Heavy NP-shift" is in the syntactic component and that, like others, it leaves a trace; see Chomsky (1982), based on observations by Elisabet Engdahl. On Case adjacency, see Stowell (1981).

31. On these matters see Chomsky (1981), Stowell (1981), Koopman (1984), and Travis (1984), among other work.

32. For various ideas on just how the projection principle should be understood, see Chomsky (1981), Borer (1983, 1984a), Pesetsky (1983); for more general discussion of the topic and a somewhat different interpretation, see Marantz (1984).

33. This assumes the head of the relative clause to be the phrase *the man*, in an A-position—an assumption that might be questioned. Other examples with clearer import will appear below.

34. See Huang (1982), who suggests that r-expressions might be regarded at LF as variables quite generally.

35. The following remarks are based on Pesetsky (1983), modifying ideas of Grimshaw (1981).

36. See p. 82. Actually the result follows only for (58i, 58ii). To extend it to case (58iii) further specification is required, presumably relating to interactions between Case and theta theory.

37. The conception is, in this regard, not unlike the dependency-grammar approach to syntactic structure that derives from Lesniewski and Ajdukiewicz, later Y. Bar-Hillel, and others, although the operative principles here are considerably different.

38. Burzio (forthcoming) argues that in Italian, emphatic pronouns that correspond roughly to *himself* as in (iii) are restricted to non–Case-marked positions—in particular, the position of NP-trace.

39. We are ignoring here many important and controversial issues concerning this conclusion; see Chomsky (1981), Stowell (1981), Safir (forthcoming), and much subsequent work. Notice that in (80), the requirement that the trace have Case cannot be derived from extension of the Case filter to *who* on the assumption that phonetically realized elements require Case, since the same is true in relatives and other constructions with an empty operator, for example, (53) and others to which we will return.

40. To be precise, a chain consists of positions—that is, particular occurrences of elements. A chain may then be regarded as a linearized history of movement—a sequence of positions with no repetitions—to disallow movement back to a vacated position. It may be that no other conditions need be imposed on chains, all others following from principles of UG. We leave these questions aside here

and will present chains in the informal notation that has become conventional. On an alternative conception of chains, see below, pp. 156f.

41.   There have been several formulations of this idea since the basic intuition was expressed by Freidin (1978); see Bresnan (1982), Chomsky (1981), and Marantz (1984), among others, and Section 3.5.2.4 below.

42.   Following Williams (1980), who develops predication theory to cover a much more extensive range in this and subsequent work. See also Rothstein (1983). The formal definition of the theta criterion in Chomsky (1981, p. 335) corresponds to (83). The informal earlier discussion assumes a unique assignment of θ-roles to arguments, a fact that has led to some confusion.

43.   To be precise, we now have to specify that the chain in question is not the chain headed by the r-expression itself, because the expression is trivially A-free in this chain.

44.   For reasons to which we return, failure to θ-mark the subject is associated with failure to Case-mark the object and, thus, follows from the assumption that the sole syntactic property of the passive form is to "absorb" the Case-assigning property of the verb; see p. 74.

45.   It may also be that PRO has an inherent number; thus, arbitrary PRO is plural in Italian but singular in Spanish, as we can see from adjective agreement. For a different interpretation of these facts, see Bouchard (1984).

46.   See Giorgi (1983).

47.   As noted, the "analogic" interpretation of (I-4) and (I-5) is also dubious; see p. 8.

48.   See Chomsky (1981, 1982) for further discussion of this and other cases presented here.

49.   We might say that we have substantial evidence for the "psychological reality" of these constructs, to use a misleading term that has been subject to much abuse; see Chomsky (1980b).

50.   See pp. 156f., below; see Chomsky (1981) for some alternatives.

51.   See, for example, the proposal outlined by Johnson-Laird (1983), following Stanley Peters, to enrich phrase structure grammars to permit *wh-* structures to be derived without trace but with a different indication of the required associations. Phenomena of the kind just reviewed would remain unexplained in this enriched theory. Like many others, Johnson-Laird regards it as an advantage of the theory he outlines that it does not employ the rule Move-α. Even in isolation from the neglected empirical facts, the argument lacks merit. The UG properties of Move-α (e.g., the locality properties of bounding

theory) have to be stated somehow. Even apart from this, it is difficult to see why complication of phrase structure rules in the manner he or others propose is "simpler" or provides fewer accessible grammars than the rule-free system incorporating Move-α as a principle; if anything, the opposite seems true. As noted earlier, questions of generative capacity are beside the point, contrary to what is commonly assumed.

52.   We cannot explain the presence of *it* in (i), for example, on the basis of the conclusion to which we return that verbs must assign a θ-role, because that conclusion, in turn, rests on the assumption in question here. Note, however, that that discussion, on one interpretation, requires that some kind of θ-role be assigned to the subject position of *rain*. On this matter, see Chomsky (1981).

53.   In the case of *there*, we might assume that the general reason for its appearance lies in Case and theta theory, because *rain* must be in a Case-marked chain to be visible for θ-marking. See the discussion of (69), above. This argument would not carry over to *it*, however.

54.   Among others, see Rizzi (1982a), Burzio (forthcoming), and the review of some results of theirs and others in Chomsky (1981). For a different approach, see Borer (1984b).

55.   See Rothstein (1983) for elaboration and extension to other cases, such as PPs. See also Zagona (1982). Fabb (1984) suggests a reduction of the principle to Case theory in terms of a more general approach with other consequences. Many interesting questions arise concerning causative and other constructions where the principle appears to be violated. There is a substantial literature during the past few years dealing with this topic, including a number of the references cited here.

56.   Or, independently of that discussion, if we adopt a stronger form of the projection principle as in Chomsky (1981).

57.   The appearance of *one* in examples (iii) and (iv) is consistent with the assumption that the bracketed string of (121) is indeed a phrase, clausal in character with a subject, as implied by the projection principle. See the discussion of (72).

58.   On these matters, see Manzini (1983a), Keyser and Roeper (1984), and Roeper (1984); see also Koster and May (1982).

59.   Related observations hold in a null subject language such as Italian, in which the analogue of "*e* [vp sank the boat]," with "the boat" remaining in the object position, is a permissible variant to "the boat sank." The empty category here is expletive, not PRO, analogous to English *there* in "there arrived three men." See Burzio (forthcoming) for extensive discussion.

60. Case (iib) is perhaps problematic, because some poorly understood element of modality may be involved; cf. "the articles can be filed without reading them."

61. Roeper (1984) notes such examples as "the game was played barefoot (nude)," which seem to violate the paradigm illustrated. Luigi Rizzi suggests that "nude" may actually be adverbial, not adjectival, despite the morphology, as in some other languages. See Roeper (1984) for further discussion.

62. The relevant properties are more general; we keep to special cases here. See Montalbetti (1984) for a full discussion. In particular, Montalbetti shows that this property of pronouns provides still further evidence for the quantifier-variable structure of sentences such as (104), discussed earlier.

63. Examples such as (140i) are somewhat marginal. Verbs of the *decide* class vary rather idiosyncratically as to whether they permit the construction at all: cf. "it is often preferred (*wanted, *tried) to spend a sabbatical in Europe." Even the verbs that marginally permit such impersonal passives never permit passives with NP-movement: *"John was preferred (decided, wanted, etc.) to win." The reason cannot be that these verbs do not have passive morphology, as indicated by the impersonal passives or such forms as "the meat is preferred raw." What blocks NP-movement may be the empty category principle (ECP), which we are not considering here; see Chomsky (1981) and Lasnik and Saito (1984) for discussion of such cases in these terms, variously understood. For different approaches, see Aoun (1982) and Zubizarreta (1982).

64. On the possibility of reducing control theory to binding theory, and a discussion of other relevant work, see Manzini (1983a); see Giorgi (1983) for an extension of Manzini's approach to other cases. There are a number of other approaches within the general framework of this discussion, among them Bouchard (1984), Koster (1984), Sportiche (1983), and earlier work cited there.

65. See Hornstein (1984) for some recent discussion.

66. See the discussion of (137) and (138) above and Section 3.5.2.3.

67. We reconsider examples (i) and (ii) in Section 3.5.2.3. Certain anaphorlike properties of bound but not locally bound PRO are illustrated by constructions involving subjunctive, although only very marginally in English; see Giorgi (1983), Picallo (1984), and references cited there.

68. See also Epstein (1984) and Roeper (1984).

69. A *for*-phrase is possible in (158) and (159i–iii), but, it appears, as subject of the embedded clause, as distinct from (157).

Note that (158) is in fact ambiguous. The implausible reading, with *the crowd* as controller, is forced under *wh*-movement of *the meeting*: "which meeting is the crowd too angry to hold." Other considerations entail that *wh*-movement is possible only when the phrase "to hold the meeting" is within the adjective phrase headed by "too angry," thus with control by the subject "the crowd."

70.   One failure of correspondence is that expletive-argument pairs do not cross an S-boundary; for example, we do not have *"there seems [a unicorn to be in the garden]" corresponding to the raising structure "a unicorn seems [*e* to be in the garden]." For discussion of the relation between chain links and (expletive, NP) pairs see Burzio (forthcoming); also Chomsky (1981). For other approaches to these questions, see Safir (forthcoming), Pollock (1983), Belletti (1984), Borer (1984b), and Reuland (1984). For more on different types of expletives, see Travis (1984), among others. We will overlook a number of problems concerning expletives that would have to be addressed in a fuller treatment.

71.   The condition fails for idiom chunks, as in "tabs were kept *t* on John," where the chain (*tabs, t*) lacks a θ-role. I will ignore this case here. The natural way to account for it is to extend the visibility condition from a condition on θ-marking to a broader condition on LF interpretation, including both θ-marking and idiom interpretation.

72.   In part, the impossibility of such CHAIN-links follows for chains from the principles of binding theory, in part from other considerations not developed here; for expletive-argument pairs the result then follows from the assumption, to which we return, that these share the properties of chain-links.

73.   We assume here that each position P is in one and only one maximal CHAIN, returning to the question in Section 3.5.2.3.

74.   On the assumption (166) that at D-structure the nonargument α was already linked to an argument, which was necessarily in a θ-position, movement of α to a θ-position creates a CHAIN containing two θ-positions. See Chomsky (1981) for discussion of the property that movement is always to a non-θ-position on slightly different assumptions.

75.   In Section 3.4.2, we tentatively concluded that *offer* in (176ii) does not assign a subject θ-role to an unrealized lexical argument, as a passive form does; see the discussion of (137) and (138).

76.   Certain verbs take objects but do not Case-mark them. These satisfy the generalization: They do not θ-mark their subjects. See Perlmutter (1983b) and Burzio (forthcoming). We will leave this issue aside because the really persuasive evidence derives from null subject languages with properties not developed here.

77. But see the discussion of (75)–(77) and references of note 70.

78. For argument along quite different lines that verbs such as *believe* and *say* Case-mark their clausal complements, see Stowell (1981). See Picallo (1984) for supporting evidence for Stowell's assumptions based on properties of Romance subjunctives. If the earlier discussion is correct, the actual D-structure source of (ii) is something like "John said something" or "John said *wh*-thing." See p. 71.

79. On this assumption, see note 71 and the references of note 70.

80. Or need not be assigned; see Section 3.5.2.3.

81. Any relation, some have argued; see Williams (1982b), Higginbotham (1983a). See M. Anderson (1983) for an argument to the contrary and general discussion. We return to the question briefly below.

82. See Borer (1983, 1984a) for a different perspective on this matter.

83. See, for example, Sportiche (1983) for extensive discussion within a somewhat different framework.

84. A case that remains open is raising of an expletive from a Case-marked position not blocked by (190). It seems that such cases cannot arise for other reasons. This case would also be covered by a suggestion concerning expletive-argument pairs to which we return in Section 3.5.2.3.

85. See Kayne (1975); also Kayne (1984) for a selection of papers that have had a major impact on the development of the field. There is also now extensive and very illuminating work from standpoints similar to the one outlined here on many other languages, including many non-Indo-European languages.

86. See Wexler and Culicover (1980) and Wexler (1982) for development of a theory of acquisition based on the assumption that the evidence available involves only a very limited degree of embedding, in a sense made precise. See also Berwick (1982) and Berwick and Weinberg (1984).

87. See Hyams (1983) for discussion of this matter in connection with the null subject parameter.

88. The phenomenon was first studied by Tarald Taraldsen. See Chomsky (1982) for discussion and review of work by Taraldsen and Elisabet Engdahl, which has since been extended in interesting ways.

89. See Osherson, Stob, and Weinstein (1983). One must be cautious in relating their results to our concerns here. They are

considering E-language, not I-language, and are restricting attention to weak rather than strong generative capacity of grammars (i.e., to the class of sentences enumerated by a grammar). They take a learning function f to "identify" (i.e., to "learn") a language L if it converges on a grammar of L for any text (a text is an infinite sequence of sentences drawn from L and exhausting L), with no requirement that f converge on the same grammar for all texts. The results are, however, very suggestive and rather surprising. On these matters, see the references of note 86; see also Baker and McCarthy (1981) and Wanner and Gleitman (1982).

90.   On this topic, see Berwick (1982) and Barton (1984). See also Fodor, Bever, and Garrett (1974), for a somewhat similar conception. On some misinterpretations of theorems concerning parsing of context-free languages and related discussion, see Berwick and Weinberg (1984).

91.   See, for example, Kayne (1984), and Rizzi (1982a). For more general discussion, see Lightfoot (1979).

92.   On the ECP, see Chomsky (1981), Huang (1982), Kayne (1984), Lasnik and Saito (1984), and much other work. This is a very lively area of current research, and several alternative approaches are being actively pursued. See, among many others, Aoun (1982, 1985), Longobardi (1983), and Pesetsky (1983).

93.   On this matter, see Koster (1978), Chomsky (1981, 1982), Rizzi (1982b), and Sportiche (1983), among others.

94.   Thus, certain languages seem to have bounded LF-movement of wh-phrases, for example, Kikuyu (see Bergvall, 1982). If so, and if there is furthermore no parametric variation in the LF component, then it is necessary either to recast the discussion of LF-movement presented earlier, or to find some relevant features that are subject to parametric variation and that determine this difference, given the structure of UG. These problems are by no means trivial.

95.   See, among others, Chomsky (1977), May (1977, forthcoming), Huang (1982), Higginbotham (1983a), and Hornstein (1984).

96.   Recall that this is not required if the complement requires no Case—e.g., if it is a clause rather than an NP—or if the language permits some other mode of assigning Case, as in the null subject languages; see p. 74.

97.   See Baker (1985); see also Marantz (1984), which contains a wealth of information and enlightening analysis on these and related topics. See also Borer (1983, 1984a).

98.   These are intended as abstract representations of the hierarchical structure of morphology, independent of whether the affixes are suffixes or prefixes, or sometimes infixes or elements that induce internal phonological changes of one or another sort.

99.   Baker gives such an example with O-A realized by internal phonological change (suppletion) of the underlying stem. In the same language (Huichol), the surface object may also agree with the verb so that by the mirror principle, suppletion marks the D-structure object, and the external inflection marks the S-structure object.

100.   On double-object verbs and their grammatical functions, see Marantz (1984). Note that the applicative process must precede passivization if Case assignment is obligatory, or it would assign Case to the NP-trace left by passive, contradicting the general chain principle (171).

101.   As noted earlier, the concept object may have a more complex definition for the case of more than one NP of X'; see note 100.

102.   Note that PRO in the structure underlying (208) and (209i) does not block contraction, as distinct from *wh*-trace. The crucial distinction, presumably, is that *wh*-trace is Case-marked and PRO is not. It might be that only Case-marked trace is "visible" for the contraction rule, or it might be, following Pesetsky (1983), that PRO does not intervene between *want* and *to* (so that the structure underlying (208) is actually "who do you want [[to visit] PRO]"), an option permitted for PRO in these rule-free systems but not for *wh*-trace, which must be adjacent to its Case-marker by the Case adjacency principle.

103.   Aoun and Lightfoot take INFL to be the head of the full clause C. If COMP is the head of C, as we have assumed, their general analysis would apply if C has been deleted by the time the contraction rule (207) has applied, perhaps as a reflex of deletion of its head *for*, under one set of assumptions; there are several possibilities open in this case. For further evidence that government plays a role in the PF component, see Saito (1985) with regard to ECP, a principle that involves government. Examples (210i, ii) are from Postal and Pullum (1982). The idea of introducing government has been suggested independently by Bouchard (1984), among others.

104.   See Schachter (1984) and references cited. Schachter argues that the analysis suggested here is impossible because the reduced structures (211) are barred by the projection principle, but the latter does not apply in the PF component for principled reasons. The more complex syntactic rule system that Schachter assumes therefore seems unnecessary.

105.   Apart from the simplest cases, such as (215i), condition (B) of the binding theory is often weak. See Bouchard (1984) for discussion of this point and an analysis of the relation between conditions (A) and (B) in different terms. As observed first by Paul Postal, condition (B) extends, although somewhat weakly, from dis-

tinct to disjoint reference, as illustrated in such sets as "I expected him to like us" and "I expected us to like him," where the second is less acceptable than the first. Condition (A) is also sometimes overridden in colloquial speech; I have, for example, occasionally heard such sentences as "they didn't know what each other should do," a violation of the binding theory as presented here; see Lebeaux (1983). I will overlook such matters here, although they raise interesting questions.

106.   Assuming that the NP is not the subject of this S; we will return to this case. If the minimal NP containing α lacks a subject but is contained within NP' with a subject, then NP' = MGC(α) (assuming that NP' does not contain S containing α).

107.   There are several other major classes of exceptions. One type is illustrated in subjunctives in the Romance languages and others where α in a sentence analogous to "John wants that α leave" cannot be an anaphor or a pronoun bound by *John*. Thus, in this position neither an anaphor nor a pronoun bound by the main clause subject can appear. A complementary case is illustrated by Chinese-Japanese, where the subject of a tensed clause can be either a bound anaphor or a bound pronoun. See Picallo (1984) for discussion of cases of the first type, Huang (1982) and Aoun (1985) for discussion of cases of the second type. We will return to a somewhat different perspective on these cases.

108.   The following is in the spirit of Huang (1983). See Chomsky (1981) for discussion of earlier proposals and Manzini (1983a) for a different approach designed to extend also to control theory.

109.   Some speakers find (i) and (ii) somewhat marginal, but they are certainly better than a comparable binding theory violation such as *"the children thought that [I had bought [pictures of each other] ([each other's pictures])]."

110.   Recall that long-distance control does not have this property; see (146) and (147). As noted earlier, the relevant facts are less clear than the exposition assumes.

111.   For an argument on somewhat similar grounds that ECP should be, in part, reduced to NIC, see Aoun (1985). For some related considerations, see Kayne (1984).

112.   Investigation of this topic largely derives from ideas of Luigi Rizzi; see Rizzi (1982a). For various treatments, see Borer (1984b), Burzio (forthcoming), Chomsky (1981), Hyams (1983), Jaeggli (1982), Safir (forthcoming), Travis (1984), and Zagona (1982), among others.

113.   In fact, we should presumably allow any kind of empty category to be left as a trace of any movement rule, with other conditions determining the legitimacy of the choice.

114. This requirement could well be too strong. It would, for example, be violated if the trace of a clitic can be a variable bound by an operator in COMP. See Aoun (1982).

115. On some of the cases to be addressed, see Rizzi (1982b), who presents crucial evidence drawn from cliticization in Romance languages. It may be that these phenomena can be explained, in part at least, in terms of a crossing constraint on binding.

116. On such constructions and the problems they raise, see Lasnik (1984).

117. That it may not be has been suggested by Aoun (1982).

118. For a similar conclusion under the earlier version of the binding theory (216), along with the additional assumption that the full clause is a governing category for any governed element, see Chomsky (1981).

119. See Brody (1984) and Safir (1984).

120. An alternative would be to assume that *si* is a clitic in D-structure and that the relation of subject position to *si* is that of an expletive-argument CHAIN, so that we have no overlapping chains, but overlapping CHAINs. If *si* can itself serve as subject (perhaps in the position of INFL), then the position to which *questi articoli* moves is not a θ-position. There is a considerable literature on this topic, and a number of alternative analyses have been explored. See Belletti (1982); and see Manzini (1983b) for a unified theory of the various functions of the clitic *si* and its variants in the Romance languages.

121. Although not completely. See Levin (1983) for one attempt to deal with the residue.

122. See the references cited earlier. Note that we cannot reduce the Case filter to the requirement that nouns must have Case, because it holds as well for nominal expressions that have no nominal heads—for example, gerunds and infinitivals, which cannot appear in non–Case-marked subject position, as in the following structures analogous to (258iv): *"the belief [[John's winning] to be unlikely]," *"the belief [[for John to win] to be unlikely]." In fact, even prepositional phrases that appear in the subject position—which we may assume to be an NP position—must satisfy the Case filter; compare "[on the table] is the best place for that typewriter," *"the decision [[on the table] to be the best place for that typewriter] was a mistake."

123. On the latter constructions, see Reuland (1983a) and Fabb (1984), among others.

124. Note that there is a related nominal form *destruction* with a slightly different sense, as in "we were amazed at the destruction," referring not to the act but to its results. There are other

possibilities that I will not explore for analysis of the constructions of (260), which raise many questions: For example, why do we have both *of* and possessive *'s*; why do we not have "the concert of yesterday's" corresponding to "yesterday's concert"; why do we have "a friend of mine" rather than "a friend of me" (a frequent error of non-native speakers)? See M. Anderson (1983) for discussion and a possible analysis.

125. Alternatively, we may suppose that both verbs select C and that an exceptional process of C-deletion takes place after *believe*—the usual assumption in the literature, although other ideas have also been proposed. See Kayne (1984), and Chomsky (1981) for some discussion.

126. As we have defined "government," if *believe* governs NP in "John believes [NP to VP]," it also governs the specifier and head of NP. Consider then a structure such as "John believes [[$_\alpha$ PRO reading books] to be fun]." Here *believe* governs α, but we do not want it to govern PRO, the specifier of α; see (252). Thus, we must assume some barrier to government here. One possibility is that $\alpha =$ NP dominating S, which would, in fact, bar government of PRO by *believe*.

127. Note that constructions similar to (267i), although without *of*-insertion, are marginally possible when the object is indefinite, as in "there were seen several men from England." The same "definiteness effect" is observed in the regular structures "there is a man (*the man) in the room," and so forth. On these matters, see Safir (forthcoming) and references cited, and Reuland (1984), among other studies. The assumption that the embedded clause in (ii) and (iii) is S rather than C relates to questions concerning ECP (see p. 155), not considered here.

128. The application of Move-α as in (270ii) is constrained rather narrowly by certain semantic conditions. See Anderson (1979). A consequence is that there can be no NP-movement if there is no semantic relation at all to the head of the NP, as in the nominalizations of exceptional Case-marking constructions. Thus, there are no such forms as "John's belief to be intelligent" from the D -structure "the belief [John to be intelligent]." Furthermore, quite apart from locality conditions on movement (which are often weak), we cannot have such forms as "John seems that his belief [t to be intelligent] was unfounded," with *John* moving from the position of the trace—a violation of the local binding requirement (247) on chains discussed earlier but not a binding theory violation if *his* binds the trace, as Lasnik (1980) observes. It may be that these constraints can be reduced to ECP, but I will not pursue this issue here because the principle has not been developed. See Lasnik and Saito (1984).

129. See van Riemsdijk (1981); and see Manzini (1983b) for general background for the discussion here. The inherent Case assigned at D-structure is not to be confused with the Case we assumed to be "inherent" in PRO; cf. p. 104.

130. In addition to the normal case of *of*-insertion before a complement, it can be adjoined to the postposed subject of a nominal as in "the victory of John's friends," "the departure of John's friends"; often these are nominalizations of "unaccusatives" or "ergatives" in the sense of Perlmutter (1983b) and Burzio (forthcoming). See also (260). The exact conditions are not well understood. We ignore here a number of other questions, among them assignment of inherent Case by verbs; for example, *helfen* ("help") in German assigns dative rather than accusative. In terms of the present analysis, we must also assume that *persuade* assigns genitive to its "second object" as an inherent Case in (265i).

131. See Koopman (1984) and Travis (1984).

132. See M. Anderson (1983) for discussion, in slightly different terms. See also the discussion of (260) above and note 124.

133. See the discussion of (73)–(77). Mark Baker observes that the distinction between (278ii) and the structural Case analogue "there having been too much rain," etc. (the ACC-*ing* construction) follows, as do comparable facts concerning idioms: e.g., *"the paying of heed," *"heed's being paid," "heed being paid."

134. See Lasnik (1984).

135. Recall that θ-marking is obligatory, by the definition of D-structure, and genitive Case-assignment follows by the uniformity condition (272).

136. Note that these examples are also violations of bounding theory, analogous to *"the man who [[pictures of *e*] are on sale]," but the violation is far more severe in (282), suggesting that more than a bounding theory violation is involved in this case. Quite commonly, bounding theory violations are "weaker" than many others.

137. The assumption may be necessary to allow (270ii); see p. 199.

138. On these matters, see van Riemsdijk (1978), Hornstein and Weinberg (1981), Kayne (1984), Aoun (1982), Huang (1982), and Borer (1983, 1984a), among others.

139. Further questions need to be resolved. Thus, it follows from the above that in the D-structure "I saw [pictures [$_\alpha$ John]]," α is assigned genitive Case realized by *of*-insertion, but *John* receives objective Case from *of* at the S-structure [$_\alpha$ *of* [*John*]] so as to allow "who did you see pictures of." It is also necessary to determine exactly how θ-role and Case are assigned in such examples

as (288), where both the verb and the preposition play a role; see Marantz (1984). A number of other questions have also been left unsettled, even for the restricted case of English.

140.   Recall that (171) was derived apart from (170), and that it holds only for CHAINs consisting of A-positions; see p. 178.

4   Questions about Rules

4.1.   SOME SKEPTICAL DOUBTS

We have, so far, considered the first two of the questions (1) of Chapter 1 that express the essential research program in generative grammar: (1i) what constitutes knowledge of language, and (1ii) how does it arise? As for (1i), to know the language L (an I-language) is to be in a certain state S_L of the language faculty, one of the components of the mind/brain. L, the language known (or had, or internalized) in the state S_L, is a system with two components: core and periphery. There is a fixed initial state S_0 of the language faculty consisting of a system of principles associated with certain parameters of variation and a markedness system with several components of its own. The proposed answer to (1ii) is that the state S_L is attained by setting parameters of S_0 in one of the permissible ways, yielding the core, and adding a periphery of marked exceptions on the basis of specific experience, in accordance with the markedness principles of S_0. The core, then, consists of the set of values selected for parameters of the core system of S_0; this is the essential part of what is "learned," if that is the correct term for this process of fixing knowledge of a particular language. The grammar of the language L is the linguist's theory of L, consisting of a core grammar and an account of the periphery.

These proposed answers to the questions (1i) and (1ii) are presented at a certain level of abstraction from (largely unknown) mechanisms. This level of abstraction is appropriate in that by moving to it, we are able to discover and formulate explanatory principles of some significance, principles that should, furthermore, help guide the search for mechanisms.

The result of this process of parameter determination and periphery formation is a full and richly articulated system of knowledge. Much of what is known lacks relevant grounding in experience, justification, or good reasons and is not derived by any general reliable procedures. The same may well be true of large areas of what might be called "commonsense knowledge and understanding," and if the model of Peircean abduction is correct, it may also be true, to a significant extent, of scientific knowledge as well, although in this case argument and evidence are required to justify knowledge claims.[1] Along these lines, we can develop a possible answer to our variant of "Plato's problem."

I have so far said little about question (1iii), how knowledge of language is put to use, apart from a few remarks about the perceptual aspect of this problem. With regard to the far more obscure production aspect, the commonsense answer is that use of language is rule-guided behavior: We have (generally tacit) knowledge of the rules of language and we use them in constructing "free expressions" in Jespersen's sense. Some questions have been raised as to whether the concept of rule in the conventional sense is an appropriate one for the elements of language. Let us put these aside for the moment and assume that it is indeed legitimate to regard the language as a rule system or to project a rule system in some manner from the language that a person knows. Let us assume, then, that the commonsense picture is more or less correct, with the modifications already discussed: in particular, the abstraction from the sociopolitical and normative-teleological elements of the commonsense notions of language and rule (see Chapter 2).

An attempt to provide some substance to this commonsense account runs into numerous problems, some of them classic ones. In the first place, there are what we might call the "Cartesian problems." In the Cartesian view, the "beast-machine" is "compelled" to act in a certain way when its parts are arranged in a particular manner, but a creature with a mind is only "incited or inclined" to do so because "the Soul, despite the disposition of the body, can prevent these movements when it has the ability to reflect on its actions and when the body is able to obey" (La Forge). Human action, including the use of rules of language, is free and indeterminate. Descartes believed that these matters may surpass human understanding: We may not "have intelligence enough" to gain any real understanding of them, although "we are so conscious of the liberty and indifference which exists in us that there is nothing that we comprehend more clearly and perfectly" and "it would be absurd to doubt that of which we inwardly experience and perceive as existing within ourselves just because we do not comprehend a matter which from its nature we know to be incomprehensible." One can question various aspects of this formulation: for example, that we literally "know" the matter to be incomprehensible, and that the limits are not merely those of human intelligence but rather of undifferentiated mind, not part of the biological world at all. But even so, it is difficult to avoid the conclusion that serious problems are touched on here, perhaps impenetrable mysteries for the human mind, which is, after all, a specific biological system and not a "universal instrument which can serve for all contingencies," as Descartes held in another context. There is no more reason to suppose humans to be capable of solving every problem they can formulate than to expect rats to be able to solve any maze.[2]

A second class of problems concerning rule following are what we might call the "Wittgensteinian problems."[3] This topic has been greatly clarified by Saul Kripke's recent exegesis and analysis (Kripke, 1982). I will not enter into the textual question of whether Kripke's version of Wittgenstein is the correct one, but will merely assume that it is and will refer to Kripke's Wittgenstein henceforth as "Wittgenstein"; the quotes below are from Kripke, unless otherwise indicated. Kripke does not specifically endorse the picture he presents, but it is undoubtedly an influential and important one, and one that appears to be highly relevant to the concerns of generative grammar, as Kripke stresses several times. Of the various general critiques that have been presented over the years concerning the program and conceptual framework of generative grammar, this seems to me the most interesting.

Kripke suggests that "our understanding of the notion of 'competence' [equivalently, "knowledge of language," as used above] is dependent on our understanding of the idea of 'following a rule,'" so that Wittgenstein's skeptical paradox concerning rule following crucially bears on the central questions addressed in generative grammar. Furthermore, if we accept Wittgenstein's solution to his skeptical paradox, then

> the notion of 'competence' will be seen in a light radically different from the way it implicitly is seen in much of the literature of linguistics. For *if* statements attributing rule following are neither to be regarded as stating facts, nor to be thought of as *explaining* our behavior...[as Wittgenstein concludes], it would seem that the *use* of the ideas of rules and of competence in linguistics needs serious reconsideration, even if these notions are not rendered 'meaningless.'

One aspect of the account given earlier, and of the work reviewed, is that it is presented in the framework of individual psychology: Knowledge of language (competence) is taken to be a state of the individual mind/brain. Wittgenstein's solution to the skeptical paradox concerning rule following is crucially framed in terms of a community of language users. Furthermore, the preceding account assumed that the statements of grammar and UG are not different in principle from the statements of natural science theories; they are factual, in whatever sense statements about valence or chemical structure or visual processing mechanisms are factual and involve truth claims. We can look forward to the day when these statements will be incorporated into a broader theory concerning mechanisms which will explain why they are true (or why they are not) at the level of abstraction at which they are formulated. But all of this appears to be undermined by Wittgenstein's solution to his skeptical paradox. As Kripke puts it, generative grammar "seems to give an explanation of the type Wittgenstein would not permit." Thus, "Depending on one's standpoint, one might view the tension revealed here between modern linguistics and Wittgenstein's sceptical critique as casting doubt on the linguistics, or on Wittgenstein's sceptical critique—or both." He further observes that the issue has nothing to do with whether rules are explicitly stated—with whether people have access to the rules that constitute their knowledge, in our terms. Note also that the questions arise even under the abstraction from the sociopolitical and normative-teleological aspects of the commonsense notion of language, that is, under the idealizations we have assumed.[4]

Wittgenstein's skeptical paradox, in brief, is this. Given a rule R, there is no fact about my past experience (including my conscious mental states) that justifies my belief that the next application of R does or does not conform to my intentions. There is, Wittgenstein argues, no fact about me that tells me whether I am following R or R', which coincides with R in past cases but not future ones. Specifically, there is no way for me to know whether I am following the rule of addition or another rule (involving "quus," not "plus") which gives the answer 5 for all pairs beyond the numbers for which I have previously given sums; "there was no *fact* about me that constituted my having meant plus rather than quus," and more generally, "there can be no such thing as meaning anything by any word." Each application of a rule is "a leap in the dark." My application of a rule "is an unjustified stab in the dark. I apply the rule *blindly*." The argument is not limited to use of concepts but extends to any kind of rule application.

In short, if I follow R, I do so without reasons. I am just so constituted. So far, these conclusions offer no serious challenge to the account discussed earlier. I follow R because S_0 maps the data presented into S_L, which incorporates R; then "I apply the rule R blindly." There is no answer to Wittgenstein's skeptic and there need be none. My knowledge, in this instance, is ungrounded. I know that $27 + 5 = 32$, that this thing is a desk, that in a certain sentence a pronoun cannot be referentially dependent on a certain noun phrase, and so forth, as a consequence of knowing rules, which I follow (or I may not for some reason, perhaps by choice, thus giving wrong answers). But I have no grounds for my knowledge in any useful general sense of the term and no reasons for following the rules: I just do it. If I had been differently constituted, with a different structure of mind/brain (S_0' instead of S_0), I would have come to know and follow different rules (or none) on the basis of the same experience, or I might have constructed different experience from the same physical events in my environment.

The apparent problem for our account arises when we consider a different question: How can I tell whether you are following R or R'? Under what circumstances does it make sense for me to attribute rule following to you? When is this attribution correct or justified? Here we may distinguish two cases: my doing so as a person in ordinary life, and my doing so as a scientist seeking to discover the truth about the language faculty. The first case raises a question of description: When do I, in fact, attribute to you a particular instance of rule following? Both cases raise questions of justification: When am I entitled, as a person in ordinary life or as a scientist, to say that you are following a rule?

Consider the first case: ascription of rule following in ordinary life. Wittgenstein holds that I am entitled to say that you are following R if you give the responses I am inclined to give and you interact properly with my community, and if the practice of attributing the rule R to you has a role and utility in our communal life. Then I "take you into the community" to which I belong. The community attributes a concept (rule) to an individual as long as he or she conforms to the behavior of the community, its "form of life." Deviant behavior is rare as a matter of "brute fact"; hence, this practice of attributing concepts and rules is a useful one. Because attribution of rule following requires reference to the practices of a community, there can be no "private language." There is no substance or sense to the idea of a person following a rule privately. It seems that the "individual psychology" framework of generative grammar is undermined.

Wittgenstein holds, then, that "If we confine ourselves to looking at one person alone, his psychological states and his external behavior, this is as far as we can go. We can say that he acts confidently at each application of a rule...there can be no facts about him in virtue of which he accords with his intentions or not." "If one person is considered in isolation, the notion of a rule as guiding the person who adopts it can have *no* substantive content," so that the statements of a generative grammar, which appear to consider a person in isolation, can have no substantive content. But "The situation is very different if we widen our gaze from consideration of the rule follower alone and allow ourselves to consider him as interacting with a wider community. Others will then have justification conditions for attributing correct or incorrect rule following to the subject...," namely, if his responses coincide with theirs. There are no truth conditions for "Jones is following rule R," because there is no fact of the matter; and more generally, we should not seek truth conditions for the expressions of ordinary language but rather assertability conditions.

As for the assertability conditions, Jones is entitled to say "I mean addition by 'plus,'" subject to various provisos, "whenever he has the feeling of confidence . . . that he can give 'correct' responses in new cases." His inclination to go on in a certain way is to be regarded as "primitive." Smith is entitled to say that Jones means addition by "plus" if he judges that Jones is inclined to give the answers to addition problems that he, Smith, is inclined to give; and since as a matter of brute fact the community is roughly uniform in its practices, this "game" of attributing rule following has a role and utility in our lives. Smith's behavior too is "a primitive part of the language game."

Recall that Wittgenstein's solution is not intended to reform language use, but to describe it, to show why it is fine as it is. It must therefore be descriptively adequate. But this account is very far from descriptively adequate; it simply does not work for standard cases of attribution of rule following. Possibly, the discussion is obscured by concentrating on cases that are felt to be deep in their character and implications, and that certainly are deeply embedded in the philosophical tradition, specifically, attribution of concepts. These are, furthermore, cases where there is understood to be some normative standard of correctness. Let us consider, however, typical cases of attribution of rule following that are less "loaded" in this sense.

At a certain stage of language growth, children characteristically overgeneralize: They say *sleeped* instead of *slept*, *brang* (on the analogy of *sang*) instead of *brought*, and so forth. We have no difficulty in attributing to them rules for formation of past tense, rules that we recognize to be different from our own. In this case, we will say that their rules are "incorrect," meaning different from those of the adult community or a selected portion of it. Here we invoke the normative-teleological aspect of the commonsense notion of language. If all adults were to die from some sudden disease, the "language would change" and these irregularities would be erased. The child's rule would now be "correct" for the new language. In accordance with the move suggested earlier, we may, then, say that the child is following a rule of his or her language at the time, one of the possible human languages, but not exactly ours.

To avoid the issue of the normative-teleological aspect of the commonsense notion, consider a different case. Suppose that we have visitors from a dialect area different from ours where lax and tense /i/ are merged before /g/, so that the words *regal* and *wriggle* are pronounced the same way, with an intermediate vowel; or where people say "I want for to do it myself" or "he went to symphony" instead of "I want to do it myself" and "he went to the symphony." Again, we would say that they are following rules, even though their responses are not those we are inclined to give, and we do not take them into our linguistic community in these respects. They do not share our "form of life" or interact with our community in the relevant sense. In such cases there is no question of "correctness" any more than in the choice between English and French. Furthermore, our conclusion that they are following rules different from our own has no obvious role or utility in our lives, although the conclusion is more likely to be drawn in this case than in the case of conformity to our practice; under the latter circumstances, such questions are commonly ignored. It might be that the usual case of attribution of rule following is when the responses do *not* accord with ours, when they are unexpected and unfamiliar. Few people other than linguists would be inclined to say that Jones is following condition (B) of the binding theory when he understands *them* to be free in reference, not dependent on *the men*, in "the men expected to like them." This case, although unusual in practice, does follow the Wittgensteinian paradigm; normal cases do not.

The same applies to attribution of concepts. Like many people, I learned the word *livid* from the phrase *livid with rage*. In my language at the time, it meant something like "flushed" or "red." Later, my linguistic knowledge and practice changed, and in my current language it means something like "pale." I have no difficulty in attributing a different rule (my earlier one) to someone who I see follows it. Similarly, it is standard to attribute concepts different from ours to children and foreigners, or speakers of other languages. In the *plus-quus* case, we would, as players of the normal language game, attribute one or the other concept to people by inspecting their behavior, although in one case their responses would not accord with our own. There may be a question as to *how* we do it, but there seems little doubt that we do do it. Furthermore, none of this seems to have much if any utility in our lives.

In standard cases of attribution of rule following, such as those mentioned, the rules in question may or may not be followed in behavior. The child who overgeneralizes, for example, may choose not to apply his or her rule for forming the past tense of *sleep* in some particular case, or might not follow the rule for some other reason (and might, perversely, even say *slept,* violating the rule). Our visitors might pronounce *regal* and *wriggle* with a tense-lax vowel distinction (as we do), possibly by choice, thus violating what is their rule at the time (but keeping this rule, though violating it), and so forth. Thus, even when we drop any of the various normative considerations, the rules are not descriptions of behavior or of regularities in behavior (in principle, our visitors might choose to violate their rule most or all of the time, for one reason or another). The problem of determining when the rule is being followed, and when not, may be a difficult empirical one, but there seems little doubt that it does arise in the manner just indicated.

One of the centerpieces of Kripke's discussion is paragraph 202 of the *Philosophical Investigations:*[5]

> ... to *think* one is obeying a rule is not to obey a rule. Hence it is not possible to obey a rule 'privately'; otherwise thinking one was obeying a rule would be the same thing as obeying it.

This passage misconstrues our attribution of rule following in ordinary language or science, and the argument it presents is not valid. The premise is correct: Jones may or may not be following a rule whatever he is thinking, either because he doesn't think about rules at all or because his self-analysis is wrong for one reason or another (in general, the account that people give for their behavior is highly unreliable, even when they feel that they can offer one). It is correct, then, that thinking one is obeying the rule is not the same thing as obeying it. But the conclusion does not follow. If we say that Jones is obeying a rule "privately," and hence that he is obeying a rule, nothing follows at all about whether he thinks that he is obeying the rule. In fact, we do say that Jones obeys a rule "privately"—that is just the way we play the game and no reason has been advanced as to why we should do otherwise—even if he thinks he is obeying a different rule or has no idea about rule following (and is responding differently than we would). Correspondingly, we must avoid the temptation to assume some notion of "accessibility to consciousness" with regard to mental states and their contents. This seems inconsistent with the way we use the relevant concepts in normal discourse, however deeply rooted the assumption may be in various philosophical theories, and it is an assumption that can only stand in the way of a descriptively adequate or genuinely explanatory theory of mind.

At the very end of his discussion (p. 110), Kripke brings up a case that might be construed as being of the kind discussed above, where attribution of rule following violates the Wittgensteinian paradigm: the case of Robinson Crusoe, not part of any community. Kripke asks whether the Wittgensteinian argument against the possibility of a "private language" entails "that Robinson Crusoe, isolated on an island, cannot be said to follow any rules, no matter what he does," referring to a passage where Wittgenstein discusses the "somewhat similar question" of a person playing a familiar game translated by some rule into a different modality. If Robinson Crusoe's responses are those we would be inclined to give, then this case raises no new questions; it is essentially the same as the case of our meeting people whose responses agree with our own, so that we attribute rule following to them in accordance with the Wittgensteinian paradigm, which as Kripke outlines it does not ask whether they are part of a community but rather whether we can take them into our community. The case becomes interesting, however, if Robinson Crusoe gives responses different from ours, that is, speaks a language of his own, shared by no community, in particular not our community. If the case is understood this way, then it does serve as a—rather exotic—example of the type discussed earlier. Let us interpret Kripke's discussion to include this case—noting, however, that this may not be what was intended—and ask how his account, so construed, applies to the cases discussed earlier (quite normal cases, so it seems).

Kripke argues that we can still attribute rule following to Robinson Crusoe in accordance with the Wittgensteinian solution. Namely, we regard him as a *person* who acquires rules under certain experiences, although not our rules, because we had different experiences. Then we can take him into the broader community of persons, who share our "form of life" in a broader sense. "Our community can assert of any individual that he follows a rule if he passes the tests for rule following applied to any member of the community," that is, if he acts in the manner of rule follower although he doesn't give our responses. This would include the cases discussed earlier but at the cost of abandoning any consequences of the "private language argument" that bear on the attribution of rules within the framework of individual psychology.

Consider more closely the statement that "Our community can assert of any individual that he follows a rule if he passes the tests for rule following applied to any member of the community." Assuming that Robinson Crusoe passes the tests for rule following in the community of persons, we can say that "he follows a rule." But which rule does he follow? Here, the Wittgensteinian paradigm is no help. The extension of the Wittgensteinian paradigm to the Robinson Crusoe case is inadequate to the task at hand, even if we accept it as legitimate.

Recall Wittgenstein's solution to his skeptical paradox: "The situation is very different if we widen our gaze from consideration of the rule follower alone and allow ourselves to consider him as interacting with a wider community. Others will then have justification conditions for attributing correct or incorrect rule following to the subject...," namely, if his responses coincide with theirs. But Robinson Crusoe does not interact with the wider community of persons to which we assign him on the basis of his behavior. Therefore, the Wittgensteinian solution does not apply to the Robinson Crusoe case: As formulated, it does not permit us to consider Robinson Crusoe to be a rule follower, because he does not interact with the community of persons, and it clearly does not permit us to determine which rule he is following. The first defect might be overcome by modifying the Wittgensteinian paradigm along the lines of the interpretation of Kripke's remarks sketched above, but the second is a defect of principle. Recall that this is a perfectly normal case in which we attribute not only the general property of rule following but also the following of particular rules. The defects in the analysis are therefore rather serious.

Furthermore, there seems to be a crucial equivocation in the concept "form of life," which plays a central role in the argument just sketched. The term is defined (by Kripke) to refer to "the set of responses in which we agree, and the way they interweave with our activities" (p. 96). In this sense, I take you into the community sharing my "form of life" if your responses are like mine, in accordance with the Wittgensteinian paradigm for attribution of rule following. But in this sense, Robinson Crusoe, in the case we are considering, does not share our "form of life," and the solution collapses if intended to capture normal usage. We cannot attribute rule following to Robinson Crusoe, or in standard cases of the sort mentioned earlier. But Kripke also suggests a metaphorical usage of the phrase "form of life." In this extended sense, the "form of life" (he gives the term in quotes, indicating that it is a metaphorical extension) refers to the "highly species-specific constraints" that "lead a child to project, on the basis of exposure to a limited corpus of sentences, a variety of new sentences for new situations" (p. 97n). Here, the "form of life" refers to characteristic species behavior. It is this sense that is relevant to attribution of rule following or possession of concepts when the behavior does not match our own. Robinson Crusoe shares our "form of life" in this extended sense, although we need some further method to determine which rules he follows, which concepts he uses.

In the terms of the earlier discussion, the distinction is one of level of description: The technical usage of "form of life" is at the level of particular grammar (the attained language); in the extended sense it is at the level of UG (S_0). We might modify the Wittgensteinian solution to incorporate this distinction explicitly, so that it begins to approach normal usage. If we do, however, we derive a very different analysis of the "practice" of attributing concepts and rule-governed behavior, one that undermines the private language argument and the consequences drawn from it. A member of the species might well have unique experience that yields a unique rule system, a private language, although we could "take him into our community" in the broader sense of "form of life."

Indeed, this is not only the normal case but arguably the only case, if we investigate a person's language in sufficient detail. That is, we can expect Jones's language to be different from ours in at least some respects, and a correct analysis of rule following should be holistic, accounting for Jones's following of a particular rule not in isolation but against the background of (tacit or explicit assumptions about) his whole language and no doubt much more. This conclusion, in fact, is implicit in the Wittgensteinian approach. In these broader respects we can hardly expect Jones to be like us.

Returning to the statement that "If one person is considered in isolation, the notion of a rule as guiding the person who adopts it can have *no* substantive content" (p. 89)—the conclusion that seemed to undermine the individual psychology framework of generative grammar—we see that this must be understood as referring not to an individual whose behavior is unique but to someone "considered in isolation" in the sense that he is not considered as a person, like us. But now the argument against private language is defanged. We consider Robinson Crusoe to be a person, like us. He has a private language with its own rules, which we discover and attribute to him by some means other than those allowed in Wittgenstein's solution to the skeptical paradox.

Note that we might also say that if a sample of water is "considered in isolation," not regarded as water, then we can say nothing about its chemical constitution and so forth; and we can say nothing about a fruit fly in a genetics experiment if we do not consider it as a member of the class of fruit flies. An entity becomes an object of inquiry (scientific or commonsense) only under a particular description, only insofar as it is assigned to a particular natural kind. We investigate a particular thing (already tacitly assuming some framework of description and understanding in accord with which it is a thing), tentatively decide that it is a sample of water, and then learn about its properties by investigating it and other samples. Similarly, we decide that Robinson Crusoe is a person on the basis of certain of his characteristics, and then determine the rules of his language by investigating his behavior and reactions and those of others, with different rules, who belong to the same natural kind. But there are no interesting conclusions to be drawn from this, beyond those that hold of descriptive commentary (scientific or otherwise) quite generally and hence are not relevant here.

We may ask how, in ordinary life, we assign Robinson Crusoe to the category of persons and what the sense of this attribution is; and whether, as scientists, we are entitled to say that this attribution amounts to a factual claim that Robinson Crusoe shares with other persons some actual property—specifically, the initial state S_0 of the language faculty—so that given his experience he follows the rules of the attained state $S_{L'}$, not our rules. The answer to the first question seems to be an intuitive and vague version of the scientist's answer: To be a person is to be an entity of a certain kind, with certain properties; we decide that Robinson Crusoe is an entity of this type, with these properties of personhood, by investigating what he does under various conditions. The status of these judgments becomes clearer when we consider the second question, to which we turn directly.

Keeping to the first question, we are led back, I think, to something like the Cartesian conception of "other minds." According to this view, I attribute to you a mind like mine if you pass tests that indicate that your behavior exhibits intelligence,[6] where to "exhibit intelligence" is to exceed the limits of mechanism in the sense of Cartesian contact mechanics. If a variety of such experiments succeed in showing this, then "I would not be reasonable if I did not conclude that [the subjects] are like me," possessing a mind (Cordemoy). The major tests outlined by the Cartesians, including Descartes himself, involve what I have called elsewhere "the creative aspect of language use," the use of language that is unbounded, stimulus-free, appropriate to situations, coherent, and evoking appropriate thoughts in me. Or if your behavior reflects understanding and the exercise of will and choice as distinct from mechanical response, then I attribute to you possession of mind, a power that exceeds the bounds of Cartesian contact mechanics (as does, in fact, the motion of the heavenly bodies, as Newton subsequently showed, thus undermining the mind-body problem as Descartes formulated it since there is no longer any clear content to the notion of body). By various tests, I try to determine whether your "cognoscitive power" is "properly called mind," that is, whether it is not "purely passive" but rather "forms new ideas in the fancy or attends to those already formed," not completely under the control of sense or imagination or memory (*Rules for the Direction of the Mind*). If so, I "take you into my community" in the broader sense; I take you to be a person, sharing my "form of life" in the metaphorical sense (at the level of UG), and I assume that you follow rules as I would under similar past/present conditions, although the rules I attribute to you are not mine—our responses differ, and we do not share a "form of life" in the technical sense. There is no issue of "utility" in all of this. I just make these determinations, without reasons, just as I follow rules, without reasons, as a reflection of my nature.

The Kripke-Wittgenstein dismissal of the Cartesian position is based on Humean arguments (namely, that we have no impression of self) that do not seem to me to bear on the relevant aspects of Cartesian thought, because they fail to take into account the respects in which attribution of mind is a theoretical move, part of a pattern of explanation based on assumptions with regard to the limitations of mechanics. We surely need not accept Cartesian mechanics or metaphysics or the beast-machine conclusions, nor need we accept the model of conscious testing and theory construction for normal usage. But the kernel of thinking seems plausible enough, and it is not unlike the extension of the Wittgensteinian paradigm, considered above, to the cases that clearly violate the formulation in terms of "interaction with a wider community" and the technical notion of "form of life." On the Cartesian assumptions, I attribute to you rules (though perhaps not mine), rules that I would have followed had I had your experience. I do this because you seem to be a person, exhibiting characteristic features of will and choice, the creative aspect of language use, and other indications of intelligence (and for Cordemoy, looking like me). Further analysis, however, is required to explain how I assign particular rules to you.

Summarizing, Kripke's Wittgenstein holds that

(I)   "To judge whether an individual is indeed following a given rule in particular applications" is to determine "whether his responses agree with their own."

(II) We therefore reject the "'private model' of rule following," according to which "the notion of a person following a given rule is to be analyzed simply in terms of facts about the rule follower and the rule follower alone, without reference to his membership in a wider community."

(III)   "Our community can assert of any individual that he
follows a rule if he passes the tests for rule following
applied to any member of the community."

As for (I), it is not true in standard cases. We regularly
judge that people are following rules when their responses
differ from our own. As for (III), it is tenable if we understand it
to mean that whether or not an individual's "responses agree
with [our] own," we may assert that he or she follows rules if he
or she passes the tests for rule following, not with respect to
particular rules or with reference to any particular community
of rule users, but more generally: He or she acts as a person,
passing the tests for "other minds" in roughly the Cartesian
sense (with the provisos noted). By virtue of such facts about the
individual (which are not facts about the individual's experience
and mental life), we "take him into the community" of persons
and assume him to be following rules like ours, though perhaps
not our rules. It remains to determine what these rules are by
observation, applying our own intuitive methods and criteria,
whatever they may be—evidently not those of the Wittgensteinian paradigm. All of this is done without reasons, just as we
follow rules ourselves without having reasons (*"blindly"*).
Contrary to (II), there seems nothing objectionable about the
"private model" of rule following, nor is any serious alternative
proposed to it, at least in any sense relevant to the explanations
and concepts involving "competence" or "knowledge of language" in generative grammar; reference to a community of
users of a language seems beside the point.
    All of this has to do with the way, as persons, we attribute
rule following without much if any reflection to others we take
to be persons (and also, probably, to nonpersons in some cases).
But it does not yet deal with the objection that there is no fact of
the matter. This issue arises when we consider the second
question raised earlier: What about our conclusion, as scientists,
that Jones is following the rule R? Here we need reasons and
justification. Can they be given?
    The approach sketched earlier holds that we should proceed
as follows. We amass evidence about Jones, his behavior, his
judgments, his history, his physiology, or whatever else may
bear on the matter. We also consider comparable evidence

about others, which is relevant on the plausible empirical assumption that their genetic endowment is in relevant respects the same as his, just as we regard a particular sample of water as water, and a particular fruit fly as a fruit fly. We then try (in principle) to construct a complete theory, the best one we can, of relevant aspects of how Jones is constructed—of the kind of "machine" he is, if one likes.

One heavy empirical condition is that this theory must incorporate a theory of the initial state that suffices to yield both the account of Jones's language (given relevant experience) and the account of the state attained by others (given their different experience). This theory is about Jones's capacities and how they are realized, these being facts about Jones. At the same time it is a theory about persons, the category to which we take Jones to belong as an empirical assumption.

Suppose that our best theory takes the initial state to incorporate as one component the initial state S_0 of the language faculty (a distinct component of the mind/brain), certain processing mechanisms, a certain organization and size of memory, a theory of random errors and malfunctions (parts wearing out or whatever), and so forth, all of this as a species characteristic. This theory provides an account of the current state of the person as incorporating a particular language L, which is a particular realization of the principles of S_0 with values of parameters fixed (its core) and a periphery added. Then we conclude that the person follows the rules of L or those projected from it,[7] which determine what expressions mean for him, their correct forms for him, and so forth. This approach is not immune to general skeptical arguments—inductive uncertainty, Hilary Putnam's antirealist arguments, and others. But these are not relevant here, because they bear on science more generally. It is not clear that there are any further skeptical arguments that apply. A particular theory of this sort may certainly be wrong and may be shown to be wrong, for example, if the theory UG of S_0 proposed to account for Jones's language (and, thus, to explain facts about Jones's judgments and behavior, in the explanatory model discussed earlier) fails with respect to someone else, say a speaker of Japanese. In fact, this has repeatedly been the case and is surely the case with regard to current theories. It seems clear, then, that these theories are empirical ones, which could also be right.

Kripke argues against a "dispositional" account of rule following and concludes that the account must be "normative," not "descriptive" (p. 37). As he notes, the preceding account is not dispositional (it says little about what a person is disposed to say under particular circumstances), and it is also not "causal (neurophysiological)." Furthermore, the account is not "functionalist"; it does not "regard psychology as given by a set of causal connections, analogous to the *causal* operations of a machine,"[8] although it has causal aspects: namely, with regard to the apparently deterministic passage from S_0 to the attained state S_L, and (at least in part) with regard to the operations of a parsing mechanism that uses the language. But the account of "competence" is descriptive: It deals with the configuration and structure of the mind/brain and takes one element of it, the component L, to be an instantiation of a certain general system that is one part of the human biological endowment. We could regard this instantiation as a particular program (machine), although guarding against implications that it determines behavior. Thus, an account can be descriptive although it is neither dispositional nor causal (neurophysiological or functional), in Kripke's sense.

Kripke argues, however, that what program a machine is following is not an objective fact about the machine, and that we can distinguish between a machine's malfunctioning and its following its program only in terms of the intention of the designer: "Whether a machine ever malfunctions and, if so, when, is not a property of the machine itself as a physical object but is well defined only in terms of its program, as stipulated by its designer." If a machine fell from the sky, there would be no answer to the question: "What program is it following?"

In our case there is no designer, but, nevertheless, we do assert that the machine incorporates a particular program. This assertion is part of a more general account of the properties of the mind/brain, an account that defines "malfunction" and "intrusion of extraneous factors," and is answerable to a wide range of empirical evidence, including evidence concerning the person's history and concerning speakers of other languages, and in principle much else: physiology, psychological experiment, brain damage, biochemistry, and so forth. Our assumption is that the person before us has a language with particular rules and principles along with other systems that interact with it as a matter of mental/physiological fact, and which we might think of as a particular machine program with a particular data structure, and so forth. There may be empirical problems in sorting out the effects of these interacting systems, but these seem to be problems of natural science. In this world, with its regularities, the problems do not seem hopelessly difficult. Indeed, they have been addressed with some success.

It should furthermore be noted that there is no necessary restriction to human behavior here. It might be appropriate to describe the way a sheep dog collects the flock, or the way a spider spins a web, or the way a cockroach walks in terms of rule following, with reference to an underlying "competence" consisting of a system of rules of some sort—a faculty that might be intact although unusable, or might be misused for some reason in particular cases, and that underlies abilities that might be impaired, lost, recovered, or whatever.

Although the matter is not strictly relevant here, it seems to me that Kripke's conclusions about machines of the usual sort are too strong. Suppose that a machine fell from the sky, say an IBM PC with a particular operating system and a particular program stored in machine memory. Could we distinguish hardware, operating system, particular program? It seems that we could learn something about the matter by investigating input-output properties. For example, we might ask what aspects of the machine's functioning can be affected just through use of the keyboard and what can be changed by inserting a new board, or by going inside the microprocessor and manipulating the circuitry, and so forth. We could distinguish properties of this specific device from those that hold of any device made up of such components (properties of random behavior or distribution of output). We could develop a theory of the machine, distinguishing hardware, memory, operating system, program, and perhaps more. It is hard to see how this would would be crucially different in the respects relevant here from a theory of other physical systems, say the interior of the sun, an internal combustion engine, or the organization of neurobehavioral units (reflexes, oscillators, and servomechanisms) that explain how a cockroach walks.[9]

Wittgenstein's skeptic goes beyond his argument when he concludes that there are no facts of the matter. What he has shown is that the facts concerning Jones's past behavior and conscious mental states are not sufficient to establish that Jones is following the rule R, but it does not follow that "there can be no facts about him in virtue of which he accords with his intentions or not," that is, in virtue of which he can be said to follow the rule R. Kripke notes that there might be a neurophysiological theory that would explain a person's behavior, but this would not be to the point because it does not have the required prescriptive force: It does not provide justification and, thus, does not answer the skeptic; and furthermore, such theories would not be relevant to ascription of rule following by others who know nothing of these matters but do ascribe rule following. But it does not follow that we must accept the skeptical conclusion that there is no fact as to whether Jones means plus or quus, or whether he follows the rules of binding theory, or the rule that merges tense and lax /i/ before /g/. The approach just outlined leads to confirmable theories as to whether indeed Jones follows these rules.

The entire discussion is, in fact, a familiar one. The approach we have outlined is a variant of what Richard Popkin (1979) calls the "constructive scepticism" developed by Mersenne and Gassendi in response to the skeptical crisis of the seventeenth century, their "new outlook,...doubting our abilities to find grounds for our knowledge" and recognizing that "the secrets of nature, of things-in-themselves, are forever hidden from us," while "accepting and increasing the knowledge itself"—a position based on "the recognition that absolutely certain grounds could not be given for our knowledge, and yet that we possess standards for evaluating the reliability and applicability of what we have found out about the world"; essentially, the standard outlook of modern science.

Wittgenstein holds that there is a crucial difference between the case of Robinson Crusoe (or any rule follower) and the case of a molecule of water or benzene. In the latter case, we regard a particular entity as a sample of water or benzene and then determine its properties, which are real properties of that sample. In the case of Robinson Crusoe, we regard him as a person and thus consider him a rule follower who behaves as we would had we had his experiences; and somehow, though not by the Wittgensteinian paradigm, we identify particular rules that he follows—commonly, not ours. In our terms, we assume that he has a language faculty that shares with ours the state S_0 and attains a state S_L different from ours, on the basis of which we can develop an account for his current perceptions and actions. But, Wittgenstein holds, we are not entitled to go on to assert that the initial state S_0 or the attained state of knowledge S_L are real properties of this individual, that statements about them are true or false. There is no fact of the matter about Robinson Crusoe, or about persons in general, apart from the facts about communities. However, his arguments fall far short of establishing this conclusion except insofar as they reduce to standard skeptical doubts concerning scientific procedure and hence are not relevant here. And his account leaves as a complete mystery our practice of assigning rules to Robinson Crusoe, an exotic instance of what is in fact a standard case, as noted.

We should stress again that there are differences among these examples. The structure of a molecule of water or benzene determines how either substance will behave in a chemical experiment, but the structure of Jones's language does not determine what he will say, although it does determine (fairly closely) how he understands what he hears; and the structure of his initial state S_0 determines (again, fairly closely, perhaps very closely) what his language will be, given experience. Our theory of Jones—a grammar G of his language, a theory UG of the initial state of his language faculty—is a descriptive theory of his attained or initial competence, his knowledge system and its origins. Our theory is not a causal or dispositional theory concerning his behavior.

The rules of Jones's language are sometimes said to have "prescriptive force," but the term should be used with caution. These rules are not like the normative rules of ethics, for example. They entail nothing about what Jones ought to do (perhaps he should not observe the rules for one reason or another; they would still be his rules). And the question of the norm in some community is irrelevant for reasons already discussed. But whatever we conclude about the status of the rules, our theories about them are descriptive. We have every right to assert (tentatively, these being empirical matters) that it is a fact about Jones that his language has the rules R, R',...: rules of pronunciation, rules of binding theory determining the antecedent for a pronoun, rules determining the meaning of "John is too stubborn to talk to" by a computational process, and so forth. It is a fact about Jones that with certain experiences, he understands *livid* to mean "flushed," and that with other experiences he would understand it to mean "pale." These are facts about Jones and his properties; in the case of S_0, they are facts about the category of persons to which we assign Jones as we proceed to determine his specific properties. These properties of Jones enter into his behavior and understanding but do not determine his behavior, not even his inclinations or dispositions. But throughout, this is discourse about facts, facts about Jones. We can learn a good deal about such facts and already have done so.

Here, I think, an observation of Paul Horwich's is to the point. We may take Wittgenstein's skeptic to have undermined the "naive" claim

> that there *must* exist inner states of understanding which explain our behavior. But that is not to question that there could be good a posteriori grounds for accepting such a picture. Nor is it to deny that, in either case, facts about meaning are as fully-fledged as facts ever manage to be (Horwich, 1984).

The same observation holds for rule following over a broader domain.

This seems to me correct, although I should add again that reference to a community seems to add nothing substantive to the discussion except under something like the Cartesian interpretation, moving to the level at which "form of life" corresponds to UG, that is, to attribution of "personhood"—a move that does not impugn the private model of rule following (and that is probably too narrow in its restriction to personhood as a matter of descriptive fact concerning normal usage and possibly potential science).

As persons, we attribute rule following to Jones on the basis of what we observe about him, perhaps without having reasons that justify this move. One might, but need not, adopt the intellectualized Cartesian account in this case. As scientists, we do attempt to develop a rather complex account in terms of postulated mental/physical states with elements that are not generally accessible to conscious introspection. The classical problems about rule following remain unanswered; we have nothing like a "causal" account of behavior or any reason to believe that one exists. It also may be that the best theory will depart from the model of rule following altogether in any standard sense of the notion of rule, both for the receptive and the productive side of linguistic behavior, perhaps on the grounds already discussed, perhaps others.[10]

4.2. ON ATTRIBUTION OF RULE SYSTEMS AND RULE FOLLOWING

The discussion of the preceding section assumed the propriety of commonsense talk about rule following. This discussion accepted the view of rule systems of the sort rejected under the second conceptual shift discussed earlier, although in fact it could have been recast in terms of a principles-and-parameters model. Under this reformulation, we would not say, as scientists, that a person follows the rule of phrase structure (1) and the rules of passive and question-formation to yield (2):

$$VP \rightarrow V\ NP\ C \tag{1}$$

who was persuaded to like them (2)

Rather, the person uses the lexical properties of *persuade* under the projection principle, and the principles of Case adjacency, Move-α, binding theory, and so on, with values of the parameters fixed in a particular way. In earlier chapters, we regarded the question of choice among these and other theories as a matter of fact, and the skeptical considerations just reviewed do not seem to impugn this practice in any way.

Let us now put aside commonsense usage and the question of how, in ordinary life, we conclude that Jones is a rule follower who observes such-and-such rules. We are concerned now with the sense and legitimacy of the technical usage of our earlier discussion. Suppose that we find that the best theory we can construct attributes to Jones a certain mental structure S_L incorporating the I-language that includes the rule R and explains his behavior in terms of this attribution. Are we then entitled to say that Jones follows R, or that his behavior is governed by R, as we have done so far?[11] Specifically, are we entitled to conclude from studies such as those outlined earlier that a person is following rules—say, those arrived at in the earlier discussion—when he assigns an interpretation to (2) or (3):

John is too stubborn to talk to   (3)

It is of little interest to ask whether such principles as the projection principle or the binding theory conditions should be called "rules"; the latter term is too vague to allow an answer, and the answer would be of no significance in any event. We will refer to these principles, in UG and in their parametrized versions in particular grammars, as "rules," but merely as a convenience; nothing turns on the matter. The more interesting question is whether we are entitled to hold that the person is in fact observing or somehow using the principles we are led to postulate in our study of the initial and attained state. Is behavior governed or guided by these "rules," as we shall call them? Do the rules we postulate play what some call "a causal role" in behavior?[12] Do the principles formulated in UG concerning the initial state S_0 have "causal efficacy" in bringing about the attained state S_L?

My assumption so far (as in earlier work) has been that we are entitled to propose that the rule R is a constituent element of Jones's language (I-language) if the best theory we can construct dealing with all relevant evidence assigns R as a constituent element of the language abstracted from Jones's attained state of knowledge. Furthermore, we are entitled to propose that Jones follows R in doing such-and-such (say, interpreting (2) and (3) in the manner he does) if, in this best theory, our account of his doing such-and-such invokes R as a constituent of his language. And if R is a constituent element of the initial state as determined by our best theory, and invoking R is part of our best account of why the attained state has such-and-such properties that then enter into behavior, we are entitled to propose that R has "causal efficacy" in producing these consequences. These assumptions have been regarded as highly controversial along with the underlying assumption that psychological explanation, insofar as it involves rule following, is in principle part of the natural sciences.

Some analyses of rule following that appear to deny the legitimacy of this usage impose requirements so strong as to exclude the standard cases of commonsense usage as well; for example, Dennett's proposal (1983) that we can speak of rule following only if there is a "very strong resemblance" to the case where we actually refer to an explicit representation of the rule in a formula (say, on a page, or as a "physically structured object, a *formula* or *string* or *tokening*...," somewhere in the brain). As he seems to interpret "resemblance," this proposal would rule out virtually all standard cases of rule following, linguistic or other, because they are not accompanied by recourse to such objects on a page or written in the brain. Or if something weaker is intended, it is entirely unclear wht it might be or what bearing it might have on the cases that Dennett is discussing or that concern us (as he holds that his account does). Dennett's further observation that rule systems might be only "tacitly represented" in the sense in which addition is represented in a hand calculator is correct but uninformative. Such possibilities cannot be excluded *a priori*. The question is one of best theory. It is also of no interest to observe, as Dennett and others do, that for every account that explains "input-output" relations in terms of rules, there is another with the same input-output properties that does not involve rules. We assume that this is so (for example, an account in terms of brain cells), but the question is whether in these terms we can formulate the applicable explanatory principles, provide explanations for a variety of facts within and across languages, or even state facts about words, phrases, repetitions, and so on—surely facts, if anything is. I will put aside objections of this nature, which are beside the point.

Many have taken exception to the idea, expressed by Jespersen and others since, that the speaker is "guided" by a perhaps unconscious "notion of structure" in forming free expressions or interpreting them. Quine, for example, has held that this is an "enigmatic doctrine," perhaps pure "folly," and that we may legitimately speak of "guiding" only when rules are consciously applied to "cause" behavior—surely not what happens in the ordinary use of language. Otherwise we may speak only of behavior as "fitting" one or another system of rules: "Bodies obey, in this sense, the law of falling bodies, and English speakers obey, in this sense, any and all of the extensionally equivalent systems of grammar that demarcate the right totality of well-formed English sentences," the E-language (Quine, 1972); and we must refrain from inputing "psychological reality" to one or another system to which behavior conforms.

It is folly, then, to claim that one of a set of "extensionally equivalent systems of grammar" is correctly attributed to the speaker-hearer as a property that is physically encoded in some manner, whereas some other one merely happens to fit the speaker's behavior but does not correctly represent his knowledge. And it would be further folly to seek evidence that would distinguish two proposed grammars that generate the same sentences while attributing very different structural properties to them: say, a grammar that analyzed "John hit Bill" as a three-word sentence and another that analyzed it as a two-word sentence, the words being *Johnhi* and *tBill*; or a grammar that assigned to the sentence (4) the phrase structure indicated by brackets, as contrasted with a grammar that assigned it the phrase structure (5):

[his father] [convinced Bill [that he should go to [a   (4)
good college]]]

[his] [father convinced] [Bill that he] [should go to a   (5)
good] [college]

Our explanations of the facts concerning the use and understanding of such examples as (2) and (3), however successful they might be, do not bear on any facts about the language faculty or even on its existence. There is no truth of the matter in such cases as those we have been discussing throughout, if we take Quine's position literally, just as there is no sense to the question of which of two grammars that generate the well-formed sentences of arithmetic in some notation is the "true" grammar.

Similar attitudes are revealed in certain approaches to the theory of meaning inspired by the work of Donald Davidson.

Michael Dummett describes Davidson's approach as holding that "the proper method" for the study of meaning

> is to ask, for any given language, what body of knowledge would be required for someone to be able, in virtue of his explicit possession of that knowledge, to speak and understand the language. Here it is not maintained that any actual speaker really has such a body of knowledge, however tacitly or implicitly.

What the speaker does fits the theory in Quine's sense, but we must not go on to say that the speaker actually "has" the body of knowledge expressed in the theory. Dummett concedes that this way of "giving an illuminating account of what is involved in speaking and understanding the language" is "somewhat roundabout unless ability to speak a language actually does involve having such knowledge." He appears to be saying that it is somehow illegitimate to attribute possession of such knowledge to the speaker, even though knowledge of language may be "a genuine instance of knowledge." Something is lacking, some kind of relevant evidence, to prevent the account from being illegitimate, either unconfirmed or perhaps vacuous in principle.[13]

Many others have argued in a similar vein. John Searle, for example, holds that even if the rules proposed as elements of the attained state S_L explain the facts concerning such examples as (2) and (3), and the theory UG of S_0 explains why the attained state is of this form, thus providing a still deeper explanation for these facts, still this is not enough:

> Additional evidence is required to show that they are rules that the agent is actually following, and not mere hypotheses or generalizations that correctly describe his behavior. It is not enough to get rules that have the right predictive powers; there must be some independent reason for supposing that the rules are functioning causally.

Searle holds that I have provided no evidence that the rules are more than "mere hypotheses" describing behavior.

Note that the rules proposed are not hypotheses describing behavior, for reasons already discussed, although they are of course "mere hypotheses"—that is, theories of grammar and UG are empirical theories, not part of mathematics. Furthermore, it is not in doubt that evidence has been provided, however one may assess its strength, that the initial and attained states have the structure postulated in these attempts at explanation. So the objection must be that evidence that certain rules are constituent elements of the state attained does not bear on the question of whether the agent is following these rules, whether they are "functioning causally"; something more is needed. And evidence that certain assumptions about the constituent elements of the initial state offer a deeper explanation for facts about the agent's behavior does not in any way support the conclusion that these elements have "causal efficacy" in bringing about the state containing rules that the agent is in fact following.[14] The objection must be, then, that even if there is evidence that S_0 includes the principle P and Jones's attained state S_L includes the rule R, and even if these conclusions are specifically and crucially invoked in the best account of Jones's behavior, still none of this would provide any reason to believe that R is a rule that Jones is following or that P has "causal efficacy."

I think that the qualms expressed by these and many other commentators are misplaced. To see why, let us compare three kinds of fact:

(i) When Jones is dropped, he falls   (6)

(ii) Jones understands (2) and (3) in the manner indicated

(iii) Jones has acquired the knowledge that the facts are as they are on the basis of a certain exposure to data

How do we proceed to explain these facts?

In each case, we proceed by attributing to the person certain properties: in case (6i), mass; in case (6ii), an attained state S_L incorporating a language (an I-language); in case (6iii), an initial state S_0. Returning to Quine's example, Jones obeys the law of falling bodies because of some property that he has: mass. This property does not suffice to explain why he obeys the "laws of grammar," so we therefore have to attribute to him other properties, those of S_0 and S_L, just as we attribute properties beyond mass to a molecule of water or benzene or to a cell of the body to explain their behavior.

Quine's comparison, which is common in the literature, is completely beside the point. A more accurate rendition of his statement quoted above would be the following: English speakers obey any and all of the extensionally equivalent systems of grammar that demarcate the right totality of well-formed English sentences in the sense in which bodies obey any and all of the extensionally equivalent theories that demarcate some set of phenomena projected in some undetermined manner from some arbitrarily selected proper subpart of the evidence relevant to physics. This terminological proposal, for that is all that it is, is of no interest to physics or to linguistics.

What is the nature of the states we attribute to Jones? As already discussed, we want to develop the best theory of Jones's behavior, and we find that this best theory attributes to Jones a language faculty with these states, which we can then attempt to characterize at various levels: in terms of neural elements or in terms of general properties of these elements at a certain level of abstraction. At the second level, we propose certain principles, parameters, representations, modes of computation, and so forth, and we seek to explain the facts in these terms, taking this account tentatively to express the truth about the language faculty. Although there are distinctions (see p. 241), we do the same when we attribute a certain structure to a molecule of water or benzene, to a cell of the body, to the sun to account for light emissions, or to a machine of some sort. If our best theory accounts for Jones's behavior by invoking these rules and other elements, we conclude that they enter into Jones's behavior and guide it, that they play a "causal role" in the sense of this discussion. Let us consider more closely whether these moves are legitimate.

The argument at issue has two steps: The first step involves the tentative conclusion that the statements of the best theory of the language faculty are true; the second, that the elements (rules, etc.) invoked to explain Jones's behavior in the best theory we can construct in fact guide his behavior. Let us consider these steps in turn.

The first step seems unproblematic: We try to construct the best theory of all the evidence and tentatively accept its statements as true. Two theories of the state attained S_L (two grammars of the I-language abstracted from this state) might yield the same judgments of grammaticality or form-meaning correspondence (or any other subset of relevant facts), but yet differ in that one is a better theory and/or accords better with other evidence, so that one will be chosen over the other as factually correct. There are innumerable ways in which this might happen, and we cannot offer strict "criteria" to determine such a choice any more than we can anywhere in rational inquiry. Theory G of S_L might conform to some theory UG of the initial state that is verified for other languages too, while theory G' might not—a familiar case. Or theory G' might contain superfluous rules to specify facts determined by a proper subpart of G' that is essentially equivalent to G, as, for example, in the case of a theory G' that provides explicit phrase structure rules to bar *"who did John see Bill?" although in fact the conclusion follows from other parts of anyone's theory (see p. 99). Or we might find relevant evidence from the brain sciences to select between G and G'. In short, we are trying to discover the truth about the language faculty, opportunistically using any kind of evidence that we can find, and relying on the vague principles used throughout rational inquiry to find more elegant, deeper, and more empirically adequate theories.

Evidently, we will try to choose among "extensionally equivalent" theories of the state attained, meaning theories that coincide on some subpart of the evidence (e.g., grammaticality judgments, form-meaning correspondences, or whatever) or that coincide on "all the evidence" but differ in depth, insightfulness, redundancy, and other characteristics. This is just standard scientific practice. There is no general reason to doubt that these efforts deal with questions of fact; and apart from empirical uncertainties, there is no reason to hesitate to regard their conclusions as (tentatively) true of the language faculty. As Tyler Burge (1984) observes:

> ...questions of ontology, reduction, and causation generally, are epistemically posterior to questions about the success of explanatory and descriptive practices. One cannot reasonably criticize a purported explanatory or descriptive practice primarily by appeal to some prior conception of what a "good entity" is, or of what individuation or reference should be like, or of what the overall structure of science (or

knowledge) should turn out to look like. Questions of what exists, how things are individuated, and what reduces to what, are questions that arise by reference to going explanatory and descriptive practices. By themselves, proposed answers to these questions cannot be used to judge an otherwise successful mode of explanation and description.

The assumption that there is a distinct language faculty of the sort discussed is a relatively "successful mode of explanation and description," indeed the only one known in general terms.

Questions of a similar sort were raised in nineteenth-century science. In an interesting review of the period, John Heilbron (1964) observes that

> the practicing physicist who was also a philosopher of science was (and perhaps still is?) something of a split personality. In the former capacity, the scientist might reason, write and speak as if his concepts were more real than [those of] his colleagues; in the latter role, somewhat self-conscious, perhaps, in the presence of those colleagues, he professes that his concepts have nothing more to recommend them than the convenience they offer in the arrangement of his ideas. In a study as rarified as the mathematical physics of the end of the last century it was probably impossible for most people to make progress without committing themselves so completely to their ideas that the philosophical line between the convenient concept and the ultimate reality vanished in practice. Yet at the end of the nineteenth century, one could not avoid the influence of Kant, with his insistence that the world of the noumena is forever closed to us; nor that of Comte and Mill, with their assurances that the aim of "true" science, positive science, is simply accurate description of the phenomenological world.

Thus on the one hand, Boltzmann described his molecular theory of gases as nothing but a convenient analogy, and Poincaré held that we have no reason for holding to a belief in the existence of matter apart from its convenience for explaining phenomena, and no reason to choose between ethereal-mechanical or electromagnetic theories of light; we accept the molecular theory of gases, he held, only because we are familiar with the game of billiards. Yet on the other hand, Heilbron continues, "One has the impression from the way the concepts atom, ion, molecule and ether were used by scientists in everyday problems that many practicing physicists and chemists considered these particles as real as vacuum pumps and spectroscopes." Skepticism with regard to the realist stance diminished in practice as evidence converged (e.g., different ways of calculating the number of molecules in a volume of gas, results which, according to Lorentz, made it "no longer possible to doubt reasonably the real existence of molecules and atoms, i.e., of very small particles of matter separated one from another") and as more successful theories were advanced (e.g., Bohr's theory of the atom).

With all the many distinctions that should be drawn, the study of mind—language in particular—is in a somewhat similar state today. We proceed in practice by taking a realist stance toward theoretical discourse. Although many feel that this stance is somehow illegitimate, that it goes beyond the evidence, the issues are not crucially different from those that arise in any intellectual work of significance. The significant questions have to do with the pesuasiveness and explanatory power of the theories and the quality and scale of the evidence bearing on them. No issue of principle arises in connection with the first step of the argument.

Let us turn now to the second step of the argument. Suppose that our most successful mode of explanation and description attributes to Jones an initial and attained state including certain rules (principles with parameters fixed or rules of other sorts) and explains Jones's behavior in these terms; that is, the rules form a central part of the best account of his use and understanding of language and are directly and crucially invoked in explaining it in the best theory we can devise. Are we now entitled to say that the rules of the attained state guide Jones's understanding and enter into his behavior, and that the rules of the initial state have "causal efficacy" in bringing about the attained state? Are these *further* claims, beyond the claim that our best theory of Jones attributes to him encoded rules that operate in this way? Since the first step of the argument exhausted the methods of science, if something else is involved in this second step, then it goes beyond the natural sciences; and indeed it is sometimes argued that psychological explanation is unlike explanation in the natural sciences and cannot be assimilated to the natural science model because of its crucial reference to the "causal efficacy" of the rules that guide behavior.

I cannot see that anything is involved in attributing causal efficacy to rules beyond the claim that these rules are constituent elements of the states postulated in an explanatory theory of behavior and enter into our best account of this behavior.[15] We will say that our theories of S_0 and S_L involve encoded rules that guide Jones's behavior when our best theories attribute these rules to Jones and resort to them in accounting for his behavior: an unsurprising answer, but one that cannot be improved upon. Clearly, we cannot obtain more evidence than all the evidence, or find better theories than the best theory. Nor is there any hope of identifying a kind of magical evidence that plays some unique role in determining that the rules attributed to Jones and invoked to explain his behavior in the best theory of all the evidence in fact guide Jones's behavior.

Returning to Searle's critique, his position is that to show that a person is following the rule R, one must show that the content of the rule plays a causal role in the production of the rule-governed behavior. What kind of evidence could confirm this conclusion, beyond best theory considerations of the sort just indicated? One possibility is that nothing more is required, in which case recourse to this condition is mere incantation. A second possibility is that more evidence is required than all the evidence and a better theory is required than the best theory; this we may dismiss. The only other possibility is that some special kind of evidence is required to show that the computational principles that constitute part of Jones's knowledge and are involved in his use of language (and hence have "psychological reality," if that hopelessly misleading and pointless term is invoked) are indeed rules that Jones is following. What kind of evidence would this be? Some have held that access to consciousness would count as such evidence, but this is plainly wrong, as already noted; this is generally evidence of the least useful and relevant sort, far weaker than evidence of the kinds adduced earlier. Other kinds of evidence that one can imagine (neurophysiological, etc.) might well be valuable, but they have no magical status beyond that of the evidence regularly adduced to establish theories of knowledge and behavior. In fact, the quest seems entirely misguided, whether at the level of grammar or UG.

Consider a specific example (borrowed from Searle). Let us say that Jones follows the rule R: Drive on the right-hand side of the road. Consider now the rule R': Stay on the side which is such that the steering wheel of the car is nearest to the center line of the road. Suppose we want to determine whether Jones is following R or R', both of which correctly describe ordinary behavior. How then would we proceed?

We might ask Jones what rule he is following, but this possibility arises only because of the triviality of the example and is not available in the general case, for example, the case of following a rule of pronunciation or syntax. Furthermore, such evidence is at best very weak because people's judgments as to why they do what they do are rarely informative or trustworthy.[16] So other approaches are necessary.

We would try to construct other cases that would distinguish the two rules. For simplicity, assume that Jones consistently follows his rule, either R or R'. An obvious test would be to try Jones in a British-made car with the steering wheel on the right. Suppose we discover that Jones follows R and violates R', which must then be revised to R'': Stay on the side which is such that the steering wheel of the car is nearest to (farthest from) the center line of the road if the steering wheel is on the left (respectively, right). In the context of normal science, we would presumably terminate the inquiry right here, but let us proceed.

Suppose we test Jones on a multilane highway, and we find that he veers right (i.e., away from the center line) to avoid a head-on collision with a car coming toward him on the right-hand side. Then we have evidence that he follows R, not R'', and we must somehow modify R' to R'''. Or we may try the same experiment on some area with no demarcated center line (say, a beach) and find the same results, again supporting R over R''. In principle, we could seek neurological evidence. Suppose that some drug X affects the brain in such a way as to eliminate the notion "right" while leaving whatever concepts appear in R', whereas some drug Y has the opposite effects. Suppose we find that after taking X Jones loses the capacity in question while Y does not affect the capacity. Then we have evidence for R over R'. One can imagine many kinds of evidence; it is simply a matter of ingenuity and feasibility. This is exactly how we would proceed, in the general case, to determine whether it is R or R' that Jones is following, and to determine which rule is "causally efficacious" in his behavior.

In short, we try to find the best theory of all the evidence, and if that theory invokes R to explain Jones's behavior, we say that Jones is following R.

Suppose that our efforts to distinguish R and R' are in vain. To turn to a language case, suppose that R and R' are two rules proposed to account for the facts concerning (2) or (3), and the two yield equally good theories of all the evidence. We now face a true indeterminacy, not of the uninteresting sort that we know always exists in an empirical discipline, but of a real and significant sort. How do we proceed at this point?

We ask: What is it about these theories that makes them work? Is there some deeper level at which the theories are really identical, the latter being the right level for our theory of language? We ask whether the two theories are overly concrete realizations of the same system of principles that should be formulated at this more abstract level—more or less in the way that rotations of a plane figure and elementary operations of arithmetic are two realizations of the principles of group theory. We try to find a more abstract principle P incorporating just the relevant features shared by R and R' without the extra structure that differentiates these rules. If we succeed, we then conclude that this deeper principle P is the actual rule that John is following. This is the right way to deal with significant indeterminacies, which are not some lethal defect or source of paradox, as assumed in much current philosophical discussion, but rather constitute important evidence that can guide our thinking in theory formation.

Incidentally, we should expect something of the sort just described in actual practice; we should expect that the actual theories we work with for concreteness are "too concrete," that is, involve elements that are really playing no explanatory role and that we should try to eliminate as we seek to discover what is really doing the work of explanation. It is a difficult but important task to compare successful theories in this manner and to use this analysis to progress toward the correct theory of the language faculty.[17]

So far, this is standard scientific practice. We say that Jones is following R if R is attributed to Jones's language (or its initial state) at the relevant level of abstraction in the best theory of all the evidence and the best account of Jones's behavior invokes the rule R, just as attribution of mass to Jones is invoked in the best theory explaining how he falls. But the argument we are considering holds that this does not satisfy the requirements for establishing that Jones is following R. We have to show, further, that the form or semantic content of R plays a "causal role" in Jones's behavior. But this makes no sense at all.

As already observed, it makes little sense to try to identify specific kinds of evidence or specific criteria that play just the role of identifying R as a rule that Jones follows.[18] To return to the analogy discussed before (with provisos indicated), suppose that we are nineteenth-century chemists postulating valences, benzene rings, properties expressed in the periodic table, and so forth. Suppose someone were to ask what justification we have for doing so and we were to say: This is the best theory we can devise to deal with all the evidence we have. Would it be reasonable to demand more? For example, to demand specific criteria to determine whether there are elements with a valence of 2? Would it have been reasonable to ask nineteenth-century chemists to state explicitly the conditions that would justify their saying that the entities they postulate are "represented" in physical mechanisms?

All of this seems senseless. In no domain is there any hope of satisfying demands of this kind. The chemists could do no more than observe that the entities they postulate form part of the best theory of all the evidence, and that they would like to learn what physical mechanisms of some different order account for these facts. To say that Jones follows rule R is to say no more than that the best account of Jones's behavior invokes the rule R of Jones's attained state (and uses the mode of computation postulated, etc.). We cannot go beyond the best theory of all the evidence we have. There is no reason to depart from the usual procedure of the sciences, taking a realist stance with regard to theoretical terms. There is no reason to suppose that some crucial evidence is missing when we conclude that Jones is following R on the grounds that the best theory accounting for Jones's behavior includes R as an operative rule, entering into explanations of this behavior. As Demopoulos and Matthews (1983) observe, "the apparent theoretical indispensability of appeals to grammatically characterized internal states in the explanation of linguistic behavior is surely the best sort of reason for attributing to these states [and, we may add, to their relevant constituent elements] a causal role in the production of behavior."

We do, of course, assume that the rules are somehow represented in physical mechanisms, and, like the nineteenth-century chemist, we look forward to the day when something will be learned about exactly how this takes place. But there is no point in a demand that we give answers to questions that no one yet understands and concerning which no one yet has any idea what would be relevant evidence.

Turning back to some of the objections mentioned at the beginning of this section, recall that Dummett asks us to seek a formulation of the body of knowledge that would be required to speak and understand "any given language." But what does it mean to refer to "a given language"? An infinite class of expressions, or expressions paired with meaning or use conditions, or actions, or whatever, is never "given." What is "given" is some finite object, a finite set of observed phenomena. On the basis of observed phenomena, the child's mind constructs a language (an I-language); the child comes to know a language. The linguist attempts to discover the nature of this process of coming to know a language, and to determine what body of knowledge has been acquired, thus affording the ability to speak and understand. The linguist's grammars and theory of UG are theoretical proposals as to what is known and how it comes to be known. They offer the only possible kind of answer (although in practice, no doubt, the wrong answers in part at least) to Dummett's demand.

What about Dummett's apparent belief that some kind of relevant evidence is lacking that would legitimate the assumption that a particular theory concerning the knowledge attained is the correct one, the correct characterization of what the speaker-hearer knows? This seems to me seriously in error.

True, we always want more evidence, and evidence of more varied types, but there is no defect of principle in the kinds of evidence we have, no defect of principle that other kinds of evidence would remedy. In fact, the kinds of evidence we have carry us rather far toward determining the properties of the system that constitutes "knowledge of a given language." We naturally will seek evidence that carries us even further, but the study of language and meaning is hardly unique in this regard. In fact, the qualms that Dummett attributes to the Davidsonian view and that he appears to share are no more relevant here than in any other empirical inquiry.

Dummett's argument that we are not entitled to impute unconscious knowledge of the rules of language appears to be based on the belief that this is somehow circular or vacuous, like the pseudoexplanation that a band stretches when pulled *because* it is elastic (recall that he does regard knowledge of language as a "genuine instance of knowledge," although by "language" here he presumably means some version of E-language). He alleges further that I "never expressly [adduce] evidence that our linguistic competence is based on unconscious knowledge at all, rather than being a skill," an ability to speak and understand based on reflexes or feedback mechanisms or whatever. Understanding may be "simply a practical ability—say, to respond appropriately," and we therefore achieve nothing by attributing unconscious knowledge of the rules of language. "The difficulty is, however, that we have no idea what structure and character knowledge, conceived as an internal state, may have, apart from the structure of what is known." We identify knowledge "solely by its manifestations." "We therefore need much more than Chomsky offers us about how, in general, unconscious knowledge is manifested if we are to understand or evaluate his theory." We need some kind of independent check, beyond the structure of what is known, to make the explanation nonvacuous. Let us consider these objections in turn.

It cannot be that our account, say, of what is involved in understanding (2) or (3) is circular and vacuous, since it clearly could be wrong and we can easily produce hypothetical evidence that would disconfirm it; as discussed earlier, it is based on principles that have a broad range of empirical consequences.

Hence the account is in no way similar to the pseudoexplanation of the stretching of a band. It is simply false that no evidence has been adduced that our linguistic abilities are based on rules and principles that are somehow represented in the mind (as to whether this should be called "knowledge," see the next section); certainly evidence has been presented, however one estimates its force, and many other kinds of evidence that would be relevant if obtainable have been sketched. Someone who believes that this kind of understanding is "simply a practical ability," a "skill" of some sort, owes it to us to provide some account of the nature of this ability or skill; otherwise, the proposal is empty (see also pp. 9–13). Consider the statement that we have no idea what the structure and character of an internal state of knowledge may be apart from the structure of what is known. Dummett is unclear about what he thinks "is known," but he seems to mean that what is known is that sentences mean such-and such, the elements of E-language in some version. But what, then, is *the structure* of what is known"? This is hopelessly obscure. On the other hand, we have quite a good idea of the structure and character of (possession of) knowledge as an internal state, and we have nontrivial theories concerning the matter; these theories are based on evidence as to what "is known" in Dummett's sense, and in principle much else, and are certainly not vacuous or circular. To say that we identify knowledge (or the structure of knowledge, or the internal state of knowledge, or the system of rules constituting knowledge, etc.) "solely by its manifestations" is true only in the sense that the nineteenth-century chemist identified the structure of benzene "solely by its manifestations." In fact, we identify the system of knowledge of language that accounts for facts concerning (2), (3), and so forth by such manifestations of this knowledge as the judgments concerning referential dependence, by judgments concerning other expressions, by behavior of speakers of other languages, and in principle in many other ways as discussed earlier. We have quite extensive accounts of how not only in general, but also in many specific cases, "unconscious knowledge is manifested," and if these do not serve to indicate how we are to understand or to evaluate the theory that incorporates these cases, Dummett owes us a reason as to why they do not and as to how the situation is different, in principle, from familiar cases in the empirical sciences. Dummett's objections amount to saying that we confirm a theory by determining how it accounts for available evidence, and therefore we have no basis for affirming the principles of the theory.

Perhaps the fear is that the evidence is all "of the same sort," primarily informant judgments, and that other types of evidence are necessary. As an objection of principle, this is plainly without merit; these phenomena certainly constitute evidence, and in fact the evidence they provide does suffice to confirm or to refute proposed theories and even leads to empirical theories of some scope and depth. As an objection of a narrower sort, one can take it seriously as an argument that the evidential base is too narrow to carry conviction; one who believes this might ask what other kinds of evidence would strengthen or undermine the theories we are led to construct on the basis of the (not inconsiderable) evidence that we can now readily obtain. In practice, what has been proposed along these lines has not been very informative, but certainly any improvement in this regard will be welcome.[19]

As for Quine's conclusion, he assumes that the possibilities are exhausted when we speak of behavior as "guided" by conscious rules that "cause" it or as simply fitting rules we state. But there is no reason to accept this conclusion. Behavior is guided by the rules and principles of a system of knowledge, and these are, in fact, generally not accessible to conscious awareness. The conclusion is perfectly intelligible and in fact is the only one yet formulated that appears to be at all warranted by the known facts. On these assumptions, we can explain a good deal about the ways in which linguistic expressions are used and understood, although we cannot predict what people will say. Our behavior is not "caused" by our knowledge, or by the rules and principles that constitute it. In fact, we do not know how our behavior is caused, or whether it is proper to think of it as caused at all, but that is another matter entirely. As for Quine's tacit assumption that the notion of E-language or of grammars extensionally equivalent over E-language is relatively unproblematic as compared with I-languages and their grammars, that is incorrect for reasons already discussed (see pp. 26–31).

In general, there seems to be no force to a wide range of objections of this nature in the philosophical literature, many of which I have discussed elsewhere.[20]

There are, to be sure, further distinctions to be made with regard to how the rules of language (the principles of S_0, etc.) are used. We mentioned earlier the classical view that the use of these rules in speech is free and indeterminate. To rephrase the point in the terms of contemporary discussion: the cognitive system involved in use of language is "cognitively penetrable" in the sense of Pylyshyn (1984) and other current work; that is, our goals, beliefs, expectations, and so forth clearly enter into our decision to use the rules in one way or another, and principles of rational inference and the like may also play a role in these decisions. This is true not only of what we decide to say but of how we decide to say it, and similar factors enter at some level into determining how we understand what we hear.

Consider, for example, the pronunciation rule P, discussed earlier, that merges lax and tense /i/ before /g/ in dialects in which *regal* and *wriggle* are pronounced alike. A speaker of this dialect may choose to ignore the rule, and to apply instead the rule of the standard dialect, for one reason or another; this may be done, in fact, without any awareness of what the rule is or even that it exists. Or consider again the "garden path" sentence (7) (see Chapter 2, note 12):

the horse raced past the barn fell (7)

In normal circumstances, a speaker of English presented with (7) will judge that it is not a sentence; this decision is presumably reached by applying the rules R_1 that interpret "the horse raced past the barn" as a clause, so that *fell* has no role and the principle FI (full interpretation) is violated. But with prior instruction or experience, the same speaker might well use the different rules R_2, interpreting "the horse raced past the barn" as a reduced relative clause construction, the subject of "fell," so that (7) is given the meaning "the horse that was raced past the barn fell." It is entirely possible that quite different rules are used in the two cases, so that the process of sentence perception is cognitively penetrable, influenced by factors that might involve expectations, reasoning, and so on.

But while the system of language use is cognitively penetrable in this sense, the system of principles of S_0 presumably is not; it merely functions as a kind of automatism. In normal cases, the same is true of the system of speech perception and much of speech production; it may well be true, for example, that the rules R_3 used in parsing such sentences as (3), repeated here, form a cognitively impenetrable set:

John is too stubborn to talk to   (8)

There is a distinction to be made between cognitively impenetrable systems that constitute what Pylyshyn (1984) calls "functional architecture" and systems that involve reference to goals, beliefs, and so forth, and perhaps inference of one sort or another. In Pylyshyn's terms, the distinction is between the "symbolic (or syntactic) level" and the "semantic (or intentional) level," each to be distinguished from a third level, the "biological (or physical) level" at which description and explanation are in terms of laws of physics, biochemistry, and so forth.

In these terms, most of our discussion so far has been at the "symbolic level," not the "semantic-intentional level." It is at the symbolic level that we have proposed a system of rules, representations, and computations to account for the facts. Notice that it would be rather odd to argue that rules and representations enter into the cognitively penetrable system of language use—e.g., the rule of pronunciation P or the rules R_1, R_2, and FI that enter into the interpretation of (7)—but that these very same entities are not rules and representations when they constitute elements of the symbolic level; or that the rules R_1, R_2, and FI exist at the symbolic level only if the system using them in parsing is cognitively penetrable as suggested, but not, say, if parsing actually provides both interpretations of (7) (namely, by using R_1, R_2, and FI, if that is what the best theory asserts) and some other system selects between them; or that we are not entitled to speak of rules and representations at the symbolic level when we provide an explanation for the interpretation of (8) and similar cases in terms of R_3 and the representations involved; or that we cannot speak of the principles of S_0 in these terms, even though these principles (or their parametrized variants) are elements of the cognitively penetrable system of language use, at the semantic-intentional level. Rather, it seems that at each level we are entitled to postulate rules and representations, and to hold that these are involved in language use, when "best theory" considerations of the sort discussed lead to this conclusion.[21]

4.3. ON KNOWLEDGE OF RULES

Much of the interest of the study of language, in my opinion, lies in the fact that it offers an approach to the classical problem that I called "Plato's problem": the problem of explaining how we can know what we do know. Plato's answer was that much of what we know is inborn, "remembered" from an earlier existence. Leibniz argued that the idea is basically correct, but must be "purged of the error of preexistence." Much of our knowledge is innate, he held, virtually present in the mind even if not clearly articulated. This is true of the propositions of arithmetic and geometry, and also of "the in-built principles of the sciences," and of practical knowledge. Within a different philosophical tradition, David Hume spoke of those parts of our knowledge that are derived "from the original hand of nature," echoing Lord Herbert's reference to "that part of knowledge with which we were endowed in the primeval plan of Nature." Rather like Leibniz, Hume regarded such innate knowledge as "a species of instinct."

These ideas are, I think, basically correct. We can now just begin to flesh them out in various domains. Suppose we are presented with a plane figure perpendicular to the line of vision, rotating until it disappears. Suppose that under a certain range of conditions, we take it to be a rotating plane figure, not a plane figure shrinking to a line. Given a series of visual presentations, we perceive a rigid object moving through space, not an object changing its shape. The judgments we dismiss are consistent with the evidence presented, but they are rejected by our system of interpretation of objects in visual space. If the judgments we make are correct, then we have true knowledge, propositional knowledge that the plane figure is rotating, that a cube is moving through space, and so forth. Similarly, we have propositional knowledge that sentences mean so-and-so.

How do we derive such knowledge? In the case of perceptual space, it seems that the visual system is designed to implement the tacit assumption that objects are rigid—Shimon Ullman's "rigidity principle" (1979). Roger Shepard (1982) argues that the perceptual system has, "over the eons of vertebrate evolution, internalized the most important invariants and constraints in the external world," including properties of rigidity and symmetry of objects. In the language case, it seems that our propositional knowledge derives from the interaction of principles of UG once parameters are fixed. What the evolutionary origins of these principles might be is unknown, although some vague analogies have been considered in terms of hierarchical properties, locality principles, and the like, and there are some suggestions about possible functional properties of efficient processing.[22]

It is known that the character of the visual system can vary over a certain range depending on early visual experience, as the language faculty plainly can, yielding the diversity of languages. Learning is a matter of fixing the system within the permissible range; in the language case, by setting the parameters of UG and adding a periphery of marked exceptions. What we know is then determined by the functioning of the mature system, sometimes involving moderately complex inferencelike computations. Such knowledge that so-and-so is not in general warranted or justified by the presented evidence in any useful general sense of these terms, nor is it self-evident or "self-presented" in Roderick Chisholm's sense. An organism differently endowed, or with the same endowment but with a mature system fixed in a different way by early experience, might have a different range of knowledge, understanding, and belief, and might interpret presented experience differently. Furthermore, various cognitive systems appear to operate in quite different ways, as determined by our biological endowment. It may well be that something similar is true of Leibniz's "built-in principles of the sciences" and practical knowledge, although not in quite the sense he intended. If this is correct, then the paradigms of much traditional and modern epistemology are inadequate, although we can give a plausible reinterpretation of certain classical ideas.

One might ask whether it is proper to use the ordinary language term "knowledge" in this connection. Is it, for example, proper to say that a person who knows a language in the ordinary sense "knows the rules of the language" (the I-language) in the technical sense? In part, the answer is certainly negative, because I-language, like other technical notions of scientific approaches, is not language in the pretheoretic sense, for reasons discussed earlier. It is not clear that much is at stake here; our intuitive concept of knowledge becomes hazy and perhaps misleading at certain crucial points, and ordinary usage in fact differs from language to language; one does not speak of "knowing a language" but rather of "speaking" or "understanding" it in languages very similar to English, although this does not affect our concern to discover the cognitive system—whether we call it "knowledge of language" or something else—that enters into our knowledge of particular facts, say, the facts concerning (2) and (3) of Section 4.2.

I think that for the theory of knowledge, we need a concept that is close to the term "know" where it is clear, but that may sharpen or extend its normal usage, much as in the case of the term "language" discussed earlier. Elsewhere, I have suggested that we make up a term, say "cognize," assigning it the following properties. When we know that p, we cognize that p. Therefore we cognize that the sentences (2) and (3) have the range of meaning they do have. Furthermore, we cognize the rules and principles from which these cases of knowledge-that derive, and we cognize the innately given principles that are further articulated by experience to yield the mature system of knowledge that we possess. The term "cognize" is similar to "know." It is identical with regard to knowledge of specific facts, and also, I think, virtually so with regard to knowledge of the system that underlies them, subject to the provisos noted concerning the difference between the term "language" of ordinary usage and our technical term "language" in the sense of I-language. Let us consider some of the relevant cases.

Knowledge of language involves (perhaps entails) standard examples of propositional knowledge: knowledge that in the word *pin*, /p/ is aspirated, whereas in *spin* it is not; that the pronoun may be referentially dependent on *the men* in (9i), but not in the identical phrase in (9ii), and so forth:

(i) I wonder who [the men expected to see them]   (9)
(ii) [the men expected to see them]

If these are not instances of knowledge, it is hard to see what is. In this case, the person who knows the language knows these facts, and cognizes them.

Suppose that R is a rule of English grammar that states that verbs cannot be separated from their objects by adverbs, so that in accordance with R, the sentence "I read often the newspaper on Sunday" is unacceptable; rather, we say "I often read the newspaper on Sunday." Suppose that John, a speaker of English, follows the rule, but Pierre, who is learning English, does not and regularly produces and accepts the sentences R marks unacceptable, as in his native French. What we would say, in this case, is that John knows that verbs cannot be separated from their objects by adverbs, but Pierre has not yet learned this and does not know it. Thus John knows that R, but Pierre does not know that R. Of course, we cannot assume that John knows that R holds, obtains, is a rule of his language. John quite probably does not know this, although some linguist may. In other words, there is no legitimate "semantic ascent" from "John knows that R" to "John knows that R holds."

Suppose, however, that R is not itself a rule of English but rather a consequence of the rule R' that states that Case assignment in English observes a strict adjacency requirement: The value for the Case assignment parameter in English is *strict adjacency*. This seems a plausible conclusion, as we have seen. Would it then be proper to say that John knows that R', but Pierre does not—that is, that John knows, but Pierre has not yet learned and does not know that the value for the Case assignment parameter in English is *strict adjacency*? I think many people would be reluctant to say this of John and Pierre, although I would not. The reason for the difference between attributing knowledge of R and R' does not lie in the nature of the state of knowledge of John or Pierre, but rather in the familiarity of the notions verb, adverb, and object, which enter into R, as compared with the unfamiliarity of the notions Case assignment and adjacency parameter, which enter into R′. But this is irrelevant to the description of John's or Pierre's state of knowledge: These states are what they are, independently of our knowledge of linguistic theory.

In fact, there is nothing about the case that is specific to knowledge of language. Suppose that the sun emits light because of processes of fusion internal to the sun. The statement that this is so is not a meaningful statement of my language if I do not know the meaning of the word "fusion," unless we allow, as perhaps we should, that the meaning of the term for me is expressed in terms of the knowledge of others in my speech community (see p. 18). In this case, however, I think we should attribute knowledge that R′ to John, but not Pierre, on the same grounds.

Assuming this to be correct, let us return to examples (9). Suppose our best theory asserts that speakers know the facts of referential dependence in these cases because their language provides the representations (10i) and (10ii) for (9i) and (9ii), respectively, with the interpretation discussed earlier, and contains the principles assumed earlier—in particular the principles of the binding theory and those determining the presence and character of empty categories in mental representations:

> (i) I wonder [who the men expected [e to see them]]   (10)
> (ii) the men expected [**PRO** to see them]

As we have seen, there is good reason to suppose that something like this is correct. Should we then say that the person who "has" this language "knows the binding theory principles" and so forth? The case is very much like that of R′ in the preceding example, and a positive answer seems consistent with normal usage.

If this reasoning is accepted, then "know" is very much like "cognize." If not, then "know" departs from "cognize" in this respect and is not an appropriate term for the theory of knowledge, because the correct account of the state of knowledge attained by John and Pierre should be independent of what we know; it is a statement about them, not us. I do not think that the question is a very important one. If we continue to use the term "know" in the sense of "cognize," as seems reasonable, then it is proper to say that a person knows that R, where R is a rule of his or her grammar.

The same is true in many other cases. Let R now be the rule that stops in English are aspirated in initial position but not after /s/. If John observes this rule, I would have no hesitation in saying that he knows that R: and if Pierre does not, that Pierre has not yet learned and does not know that R, although he may come to know that R with further experience. Someone unfamiliar with their terms "stop" and "aspiration" would not be prepared to describe the state of knowledge attained by John and Pierre in these terms, but that is irrelevant to the correct attribution of knowledge.

Let us consider now some principle P of UG that is immutable and not parametrized, say, the principle that pronominals cannot c-command their antecedents, one of the principles that entered into the explanation of why the meaning of (11i) and (11ii) is what it is, and of how the facts are known without direct experience:

> (i) John is too stubborn to talk to Bill   (11)
> (ii) John is too stubborn to talk to

Should we say that John knows that P, assuming now that we understand the terms that enter into the formulation of P?

My own rather vague intuition is that there is something strange about this. On the other hand, suppose that some Martian, who does not share the initial state S_0 of the language faculty, is being taught a human language and comes to learn that P. Then I think we would have no hesitancy in saying that before he did not know, and now he does know, that P. But his state of knowledge now could be the same as that of John, so that it would seem that we should say the same about John. The difference, if it is real, again seems independent of the actual states of knowledge of the individuals we are describing, and thus should be eliminated from a principled theory of knowledge. In this case, then, the term we need for the theory of knowledge appears to be something like "cognize," which may abstract from certain features of the term "know" of informal usage.

In most of these cases, there is no way for one to determine by introspection that the rules and principles hold. One cannot become aware that one knows, or cognizes, these rules and principles. If presented with these principles as part of a theory of grammar, we may become convinced that they are correct, but we do so "from the outside," as we may be convinced that a theory of fusion correctly explains the emission of light from the sun. Suppose that the facts were different, and that we could become conscious, by thought and introspection, that we do in fact make use of these rules and principles in our mental computations. Then, I think, one would have no hesitation in saying that we know them. If so, then cognizing would appear to have the properties of knowledge in the ordinary sense of the term, apart, perhaps, from accessibility to consciousness. We might say that "cognization" is unconscious or tacit or implicit knowledge. This seems to me correct, with the provisos given.

It has been argued that it is wrong, or even "outrageous,"[23] to say that a person knows the rules of grammar, even in the sense of tacit or implicit knowledge. As a general statement, this cannot be correct. We do not hesitate to say that John knows, whereas Pierre does not know, that verbs cannot be separated from their objects by adverbs or that stops are aspirated except after /s/—assuming, of course, that we know the meaning of the terms used in these ascriptions of knowledge. Recall that it would be wrong to say that John knows that the rule holds, but that is a different matter. Whether it is also proper to use the term "knowledge" in other cases such as those discussed seems to me unclear, because the concept is unclear, but in any event not very important for the reasons mentioned.

In these and many other cases, it seems that to speak of knowledge of rules, following rules, and so forth is reasonably in accord with normal usage, except, of course, with regard to the normative-teleological aspect of the commonsense notion of language. But again, not much seems to be at stake; different terms can be invented if one is uncomfortable with what appears to conform closely to normal usage (although not various philosophical theories) in these cases.[24]

Let us return to Dummett's questions concerning the concept of unconscious knowledge and his belief that we need much more understanding about "how, in general, unconscious knowledge is manifested if we are to understand or evaluate" the theory that knowledge of language is unconscious knowledge. We "need an account of how unconscious knowledge issues in conscious knowledge," and, he maintains, no such account has been given. But it seems reasonably clear, both in principle and in many specific cases, how unconscious knowledge issues in conscious knowledge, and the literature[25] contains many accounts of what the process might be. Thus, according to the theory that Dummett finds problematic or unintelligible, a person has unconscious knowledge of the principles of binding theory, and from these and others discussed, it follows by computations similar to straight deduction that in (9i) the pronoun *them* may be referentially dependent on *the men* whereas in (9ii) it may not, and that in (11i) the subject of *talk to* is *John* whereas in (11ii) it is not. That this is so is conscious knowledge, among the numerous consequences of principles of UG, which are surely not accessible to consciousness. It does not seem problematic to entertain the hypothesis that the mechanisims of mind permit something akin to deduction as part of their computational character. So we have a reasonably clear account in such cases as these of how unconscious knowledge issues in conscious knowledge.

We do not, of course, have a clear account, or any account at all, of why certain elements of our knowledge are accessible to consciousness whereas others are not, or of how knowledge, conscious or unconscious, is manifested in actual behavior. These questions are interesting and important, but not strictly relevant in this connection.[26] Whatever we take the internal state constituting knowledge of language to be—and surely there is such a state—these questions will arise.

Dummett holds, in particular, that knowledge of meaning is not susceptible to analysis in these terms, because

> though it is conscious knowledge, [it] does not consist in our being able to *state* the meaning. We therefore stand in need of an account of conscious knowledge, and conscious thought, not carried by a linguistic vehicle. Until we can give such an account, we cannot say how much of our linguistic ability can be explained in terms of conscious but unverbalised knowledge; nor can we say how compelling

the case for its resting upon unconscious knowledge, or for
there being such a thing at all, can be made to appear.

The passage seems to me rather obscure. I see no reason to
believe that knowledge of meaning is conscious knowledge, or
that it is in general accessible to consciousness. It is true that we
know the meaning of the word "knowledge," for example,
although we have great difficulty in determining and expressing
this meaning. But in what sense is this conscious knowledge?
Suppose it is true, as has been proposed, that the semantic
analysis of words involves such fundamental conceptual elements as thematic relations including (abstract) position and
its changes, agency, function, constituency, origin, and the
like.[27] Do we have conscious (although unverbalized) knowledge
of the way these elements enter into semantic analysis, if we
know the meaning of the words? Or must we be able, in principle, to determine by introspection, or to recognize when
informed, that these or other concepts are the correct ones? The
answers are negative, throughout. It is true no doubt that there
is such a thing as conscious but unverbalized knowledge: for
example, our knowledge of properties of perceptual space and
the behavior of objects in it. I do not see how this impugns the
attempt to explain aspects of our linguistic abilities in terms of
explicit theories of unconscious knowledge, which appear to
have considerable explanatory force and to be unique in this
respect. Dummett's assumptions as to the burden of proof seem
arbitrary and unjustified.

The attempt to gain some insight into philosophical problems from the careful study of language has been a dominant
theme of modern philosophy and undoubtedly a fruitful one.
One question that has been relatively unexplored until recently
is whether and how the scientific study of language might
contribute to this end. One might ask whether there really is a
"scientific study of language." My own view is that such a field
is beginning to take shape. We can begin to see what the nature
of such an inquiry should be and how it might become assimilated to the main body of the natural sciences. And there are
some beginnings of explanatory theory that seem not inconsiderable. On the basis of these glimmerings of understanding, it
seems that there may well be significant implications with

respect to certain classical problems of philosophy. My own guess is that these implications may prove to be richest with respect to the theory of human knowledge and understanding and more generally with respect to the nature of mind. In particular, what we are now coming to understand suggests that some of the questions of the theory of knowledge should be recast. Certain systems of knowledge that are central to human thought and action do not have the properties that have often been assumed to be paradigmatic.

Of these systems, language appears to be the one most accessible to study. There is reason to believe that knowledge of language, which provides an unbounded range of propositional knowledge and enters into complex practical knowledge, should be regarded as a system of principles that develops in the mind by the fixing of values for certain parameters on the basis of experience, yielding systems that appear to be highly diverse but that are fundamentally alike in deeper respects. The propositional knowledge that results is not grounded or warranted in any sense of these terms that will bear the burdens required in standard ways of thinking about these problems. There may be principles of learning, such as the subset principle (see p. 146), but it appears that the system of knowledge attained is largely preformed, as much a part of our biological endowment as is the general organization of our body. It seems that Plato's problem should be addressed along these lines.

We might speculate that the same is true in other areas where humans are capable of acquiring rich and highly articulated systems of knowledge under the triggering and shaping effect of experience, and it may well be that similar ideas are relevant for the investigation of how we acquire scientific knowledge in those domains where we are capable of doing so, because of our mental constitution. These systems, then, provide the frameworks within which our understanding can develop and flourish. The cost of this richness of potential in certain domains is the existence of limits in others, perhaps even absolute limits.[28] The relationship between scope and limits has traditionally been recognized but often thought to be a characteristic of the nonhuman animal world. It is the richness and specificity of instinct of animals that accounts for their remarkable achievements in some domains and lack of ability in others, so the argument runs, whereas humans, lacking such articulated instinctual structure, are free to think, speak, discover, and understand without such limits (Herder). Both the logic of the problem and what we are now coming to understand suggest that this is not the correct way to identify the position of humans in the animal world.

In my opinion, it is within this larger framework that the technical developments that have taken place within the field of generative grammar should be understood. And is it this range of questions, still on the horizon, that gives them a broader significance that may prove to be far-reaching in the study of human nature and its specific manifestations.

NOTES

1. See Chomsky (1968, 1975b, 1980b).
2. See references of note 1. See also Chomsky (1966) and Bracken (1984).
3. I will discuss these only insofar as they bear on the production problem, without implying that a variant does not arise in the case of the perception problem.
4. Note that one must not assimilate Kripke's notion of "normative" in this discussion to the "normative-teleological" notion discussed in Chapter 2.
5. I have modified Kripke's citation insignificantly to accord with the text in Wittgenstein (1953).
6. What is now sometimes called the "Turing test," understood to provide evidence for possession of higher intelligence.
7. If this is the right approach; it may not be, as discussed earlier.
8. P. 36n. On the significance of these points, see Kirsh (1983).
9. See Gallistel (1980).
10. I am indebted to James Higginbotham, Alex George, and Jerry Fodor for comment on an earlier version of this and the following section.
11. Here and henceforth I will construe the term "behavior" broadly, to include interpretation and understanding, as well as acquisition of language.
12. This terminology seems to me misleading for reasons already discussed; we have little reason to believe that behavior is "caused" in

any well-understood sense of this term. I will, nevertheless, use the terminology, as is conventional, although with this proviso noted.

13. See Dummett (1981). For discussion of Quine's critique and others, see Chomsky (1975b). Dummett's comments appear in a review of Chomsky (1980b); the latter contains a critique of the proposal he outlines and of his own views on the theory of meaning.

14. See Searle's contribution and my response in the peer review journal *Behavioral and Brain Sciences*, 3, 1–61 (1980); see also the further discussion there by various commentators on excerpts from Chomsky (1980b) and my response; see also Chomsky (1980b). See also Searle's unpublished commentary on a version of these remarks presented at the Sloan Conference on Philosophy and Psychology, MIT, May 1984. I am indebted to Searle for clarification of his views in personal communication.

15. We might seek to determine more closely just what kind of "entering into" is relevant here, but although possibly an interesting question, it is not germane in this context.

16. Similar questions arise with no possibility of asking the agent; see Chomsky (1980b), pp. 102–103.

17. See Chomsky (1977, p. 207), and (1981, p. 2).

18. There might be a reasonable interpretation of the latter quest, not strictly relevant to the discussion here; see note 15.

19. On some confusions about the nature and force of the evidence, and the belief that only some categories of evidence serve to confer a mysterious property called "psychological reality," see Chomsky (1980b). See also Gilbert Harman's comments in the reference of note 14.

20. See references of note 14 and Chomsky (1975b).

21. Pylyshyn argues in contrast that we can speak of rules and representations only at the semantic-intentional level. The conclusion seems to me unsound, in fact hardly more than a dubious terminological proposal, although the analysis that lies behind it is informative and enlightening.

22. See Miller and Chomsky (1963), for some early speculation along these lines, and Berwick and Weinberg (1984) for more recent discussion. There is little reason to take for granted that properties of the language faculty have been specifically selected; see Chomsky (1965, 1968). Certainly evolutionary biology is not committed to such a view in general.

23. See McGinn (1981).

24. See White (1982) for a thoughtful and informative analysis of the commonsense concept, although I would question his conclusions about the relation of knowledge to ability for reasons discussed earlier; see pp. 9–13.

25. In particular, the book he was reviewing, Chomsky (1980b).

26. On the first, see Nagel (1969).

27. See, among others, Gruber (1976), Fillmore (1968), Jackendoff (1972, 1984), J.M. Anderson (1972), and Moravcsik (1975). On the possible relevance of sign language in identifying some of these elements and distinguishing their roles, see Gee and Kegl (1982), and Kegl (1984).

28. On this matter see Chomsky (1975b, 1980b) and Fodor (1983).

5   Notes on Orwell's Problem*

In May 1983, a remarkable event took place in Moscow. A courageous newscaster, Vladimir Danchev, denounced the Russian war in Afghanistan over Moscow radio in five broadcasts extending over a week, calling on the rebels "not to lay down their arms" and to fight against the Soviet "invasion" of their country. The Western press was overwhelmed with admiration for his startling departure from "the official Soviet propaganda line." In *The New York Times*, one commentator wrote that Danchev had "revolted against the standards of double-think and newspeak." In Paris, a prize was established in his honor to be given to "a journalist who fights for the right to be informed." In December, Danchev returned to work after psychiatric treatment. A Soviet official was quoted as saying: "He was not punished, because a sick man cannot be punished."

The event was considered to have afforded a glimpse into the world of 1984, and Danchev's act was justly regarded as a triumph of the human spirit, a refusal to be cowed by totalitarian violence.

What was remarkable about Danchev's action was not merely the protest, but the fact that he referred to the Soviet invasion of Afghanistan as "an invasion." In Soviet theology, there is no such event as "the Russian invasion of Afghanistan." Rather, there is a "Soviet defense of Afghanistan" against terrorists supported from abroad. As in the case of most propaganda systems, here too there is a kernel of truth concealed in a massive lie. The Mujahidin do operate from "sanctuaries" in Pakistan, where CIA and Chinese agents oversee the flow of

---

*See the preface, pp. xxv–xxix

arms, and the guerrillas are reported to have destroyed schools and hospitals along with many other acts regarded as "atrocities" by the invaders, who have stated that they will withdraw if Afghanistan is secured from attack from Pakistan. This stance is dismissed by the West on the proper grounds that aggressors should withdraw unconditionally, as the United Nations Security Council insisted, with hypocritical U.S. support that was quickly withdrawn, when Israel invaded Lebanon in 1982. The West has also been justly indignant when the Soviets cynically denounce the "terrorism" of the resistance, or when they claim, absurdly, to be *defending* Afghanistan from these bandits who murder innocents, or when the most disgusting of the Party hacks warn of the violence and repression that would ensue—as it would—if the Soviet Union were to "relinquish its responsibilities" and abandon the Afghans to their fate at the hands of the rebels.

The Soviet Union protests that it was invited in, but as the London *Economist* grandly proclaimed, "an invader is an invader unless invited in by a government with some claim to legitimacy." Only in Orwellian Newspeak can such aggression be characterized as "defense against externally-supported terrorism."

Orwell's *1984* was largely drawn from the practice of existing Soviet society, which had been portrayed with great accuracy by Maximov, Souvarine, Beck and Godin, and many others. It was only in cultural backwaters such as Paris that the facts were long denied, so that Khrushchev's exposures and later Solzhenitsyn's graphic development of the familiar story came as such a revelation, the latter at a time when the intelligentsia were eager to march in a different parade. What was striking about Orwell's vision was not his portrayal of existing totalitarianism, but his warning that it could happen here.

So far, at least, that has not come to pass. Industrial capitalist societies bear little resemblance to Orwell's Oceania— though the terror-and-torture regimes they have imposed and maintained elsewhere achieve levels of savagery that Orwell never depicted, Central America being only the most obvious current example.

Implicit in the press coverage of the Danchev affair was a note of self-congratulation: It couldn't happen here. Here, it requires little courage to defy the government on a point of doctrine. Certainly, no Danchev here has been sent to a psychiatric hospital for calling an invasion an "invasion." But let us inquire further into just why this is the case. One possibility is that the question does not arise because, statistical error aside, there simply are no Danchevs here: Journalists and other intellectuals are so subservient to the doctrinal system that they cannot even perceive that "an invader is an invader unless invited in by a government with some claim to legitimacy," when it is the United States that is the invader. This would be a stage beyond what Orwell imagined, a stage beyond what Soviet totalitarianism has achieved. Is this merely an abstract possibility, or is it an uncomfortably close assessment of our own world?

Consider the following facts. In 1962, the U.S. Air Force began its direct attacks against the rural population of South Vietnam, with heavy bombing and defoliation, as part of a program intended to drive millions of people into camps where, surrounded by barbed wire and armed guards, they would be "protected" from the guerrillas they were supporting, the "Vietcong," the southern branch of the former anti-French resistance (the Vietminh). This is what we call "aggression," "an invasion," when conducted by some official enemy. U.S. officials and analysts recognized that the government installed in the south by the United States (the GVN) had no legitimacy and little popular support, and in fact its leadership was regularly overthrown in U.S.-backed coups when it was feared that they lacked proper enthusiasm for intensified U.S. aggression and that they might even arrange a settlement with the South Vietnamese enemy. Some 70,000 "Vietcong" had already been killed in a U.S.-directed terror campaign before the outright U.S. invasion in 1962, perhaps more than twice that number by 1965 when the full-scale U.S. land invasion began along with the systematic and intensive bombardment of the south and (at one-third the level) the bombing of North Vietnam. After 1962, the U.S. invaders continued to block all attempts at political settlement and neutralization of South Vietnam, and in 1964 began preparations for the vast escalation of the war against the south in early 1965, combined with an attack against North Vietnam, Laos, and later Cambodia.

For the past 22 years, I have searched in vain for even a single reference in mainstream U.S. journalism or scholarship to a "U.S. invasion of South Vietnam," or U.S. "aggression" in South Vietnam. In the U.S. doctrinal system, there is no such event. There is no Danchev, although in this case it took no courage to tell the truth, merely honesty. Even at the peak of opposition to the U.S. war, only a minuscule portion of the articulate intelligentsia opposed the war on grounds of principle—that aggression is wrong—while most came to oppose it, well after leading business circles did, on the "pragmatic" grounds that the costs were too high. Popular attitudes, incidentally, were rather different. As late as 1982, over 70 percent of the population (but far fewer "opinion leaders") regarded the war not just as a mistake, but as "fundamentally wrong and immoral," a problem known as "the Vietnam syndrome" in U.S. political discourse.

These facts should give us pause. How was such astonishing subservience to the doctrinal system achieved? It is not that the facts were unavailable. Although the U.S. attacks against Laos and Cambodia were indeed suppressed by the media for a long period, a fact that continues to be suppressed until today, the U.S. war against South Vietnam was reported with reasonable accuracy from the start—except that it was not described as what the plain facts indicated it was, but rather as a defense of South Vietnam against terrorists supported from abroad. Arthur Schlesinger, in his history of the Kennedy administration, went so far as to write that 1962—the year when the direct U.S. aggression against the south began—"had not been a bad year," with "aggression checked in Vietnam"! Scholarship, textbooks, and the media with very rare exceptions adopt the assumption that the U.S. posture was defensive, a reaction, perhaps unwise, to "Soviet-supported aggression," or to "internal aggression," as Adlai Stevenson termed the "aggression" of the indigenous population against the foreign invader and its clients.

We can begin to understand the mechanisms of indoctrination by looking more closely at the debate that finally developed in mainstream circles when things began to turn sour. The debate pitted the "hawks" against the "doves." The hawks were those, like journalist Joseph Alsop, who felt that with sufficient dedication the war could be won. The doves agreed with Arthur Schlesinger that it probably could not, although like him, they took for granted that "we all pray that Mr. Alsop will be right"—we all pray, in short, that the United States will succeed in its aggression and massacre; and if it does, as Schlesinger wrote in a book that established his reputation as an "antiwar leader" (Leslie Gelb) in the eyes of mainstream commentary, "we may all be saluting the wisdom and statesmanship of the American government" in conducting a war that was turning Vietnam into "a land of ruin and wreck." The same position is commonly reiterated today with regard to the U.S. support for various thugs and butchers in Central America and its proxy war against Nicaragua. The U.S. war in Indochina was regarded by the doves as a "hopeless cause," as critic Anthony Lake observed in early 1984. There is widespread agreement that the war was "a failed crusade" undertaken for motives that were "noble," although "illusory" and with "the loftiest intentions," in the words of Stanley Karnow in his recent best-selling history, the companion volume to the PBS television series, highly regarded for its critical candor.

Strikingly omitted from the debate is the view that the United States could have won, but that it would have been wrong to allow aggression and massacre to succeed. This was the position of a very large part of the American people and of the authentic peace movement (if the war was a "hopeless cause," why bother to protest and disrupt the war effort, why suffer the consequences of that protest, which were often severe, particularly for the youth who were in the forefront of the antiwar movement?). But it is a position that is excluded from the debate between the hawks and doves.

This quite typical commentary illustrates the genius of democratic systems of thought control. In a system based on violence, it is required only that official doctrine be obeyed. Propaganda is easily identified: Its source is a visible Ministry of Truth, and one may believe it or not as long as it is not openly rejected. The penalties for dissidence vary in accord with the commitment of the state to violence: in the Soviet Union today, it may mean internal exile and imprisonment under grim conditions; in U.S.-supported charnel-houses such as El Salvador or Guatemala, the dissident is likely to be "disappeared" or to be found decapitated in a ditch after hideous torture.

The democratic systems of thought control are radically different in character. Violence is rare, at least against the more privileged sectors, but a much more profound form of obedience is required. It is not enough that state doctrine be obeyed. Rather, it is deemed necessary to take over the entire spectrum of discussion: Nothing must remain thinkable apart from the Party Line. The doctrines of the state religion are often not expressed, but rather presupposed as the framework for discussion among right-minded people, a far more effective technique of thought control. The debate, therefore, must be between the "doves" and "hawks," the Schlesingers and the Alsops. The position that the United States is engaged in aggression, and that such aggression is wrong, must remain unthinkable and unexpressed, with reference to the Holy State. The "responsible critics" make an estimable contribution to this cause, which is why they are tolerated, indeed honored. If even the critics tacitly adopt the doctrines of the state religion, then who can reasonably question them?

The nature of Western systems of indoctrination was not perceived by Orwell and is typically not understood by dictators, who fail to comprehend the utility for propaganda of a critical stance that incorporates the basic assumptions of official doctrine and thereby marginalizes authentic and rational critical discussion, which must be blocked. There is rarely any departure from this pattern. Perhaps the sharpest critic of the American war in mainstream journalism was Anthony Lewis of *The New York Times*, who argued that the U.S. involvement began with "blundering efforts to do good" although by 1969—1969!—it was clear that it was "a disastrous mistake." Few academic scholars were more critical of U.S. policy than John King Fairbank of Harvard University, who informed the American Historical Society in his December 1968 presidential address—a year after the Tet offensive had convinced much of the corporate elite to abandon the effort to subjugate South Vietnam—that we entered the war in an "excess of righteousness and disinterested benevolence," but it was a mistake to do so, as events showed. Few dictators can boast such total conformity to Higher Truths.

The devices used to ensure such obedience are effective although not overly subtle. Consider, for example, what is universally called the "peace process" in the Middle East, which culminated in the Camp David accords of 1978–79. Few ask why the inhabitants of the territories under Israeli occupation reject the "peace process" with virtual unanimity and regard it as detrimental to their interests. A moment's thought suffices to provide the reason. As was obvious at once, the "peace process" served to remove Egypt from the conflict so that Israel would then be free, with massive U.S. material and diplomatic support, to extend its settlement and repression in the occupied territories and attack Lebanon, exactly as it has been doing since. But such elementary observations were excluded from responsible discussion at the time, and still are, although the facts, clear enough throughout, are transparent in retrospect. The United States is committed to the creation of a powerful and expansionist Israel as a "strategic asset." Anything that contributes to this end is, by definition, the "peace process." The term itself eliminates any further discussion: Who can be against peace?

There are thousands of similar examples. The U.S. Marines in Lebanon were the "peace-keeping force," and actions taken against them were "terrorism." Many Lebanese saw them as simply consummating the Israeli invasion with its "new order": the rule of right-wing Christians and privileged Muslim sectors over the poor and disadvantaged, whose "terrorism" in their own eyes is resistance—a point of view excluded from discussion here. Similarly, Israeli references to "terrorist villagers" who attack Israeli occupation forces are blandly reported here, with no comment—and no historical memory about similar usage in the past. When Israel bombs villages near Baalbek with 500 casualties, mostly civilians, and including 150 schoolchildren, as it did in early January 1984, or when it hijacks ships in international waters and kidnaps their passengers (as it did a few months later and frequently before), that is not "terrorism" but "retaliation"—or perhaps "legitimate preemptive action"— and it receives no comment or censure here: As a U.S. client state, Israel inherits the right of violence, terrorism, and aggression. Often, unwanted facts are simply suppressed. As noted earlier, the "secret bombings" of Laos and Cambodia were "secret" because the media refused to report the ample evidence available. The U.S.-backed Indonesian aggression in Timor, leading to the death of perhaps 200,000 people and a Biafra-style famine, was almost totally suppressed for over four years. A 1983 Rand Corporation study by Brian Jenkins asserts: "Since

1975 there have been twelve conflicts involving substantial commitments of conventional forces"; the U.S.-backed invasion of East Timor, which began in 1975, is not among them, though the Indonesian troop commitment has been—and remains—"substantial," as has been the flow of U.S. arms dispatched in the certain knowledge that they would be used to implement the massacre. The continuing atrocities today are barely reported, and when some comment is made, after many years of silence, the crucial and quite purposeful U.S. role is pointedly ignored.

The media can be an awesome force when mobilized in support of the state propaganda system. One of the most spectacular public relations triumphs of recent history followed the shooting down of KAL 007 by the Soviet Air Force on September 1, 1983, sure proof that the Soviets are the most barbaric devils since Attila the Hun, so that we must develop the MX-missile, place Pershing II missiles in Germany, and step up the war against Nicaragua. At the same time, as a corporate aerospace analyst quoted in *The New York Times* happily observed, "The Korean jetliner incident provided a spark for a more positive reappraisal of the defense industry, and virtually all defense stocks have gone up." Few events have elicited such outrage, and few stories have received such massive coverage in the U.S. press. The densely printed *New York Times* index devotes seven full pages to the atrocity in September 1983 alone. The administration version subsequently collapsed, and it was conceded that the Soviet military probably did not know that the aircraft was civilian, but the successes had already been achieved.

Within a few months, some questions had been raised about the KAL 007 flight. An article in the British military journal *Defence Attaché* (No. 3, 1984) produced evidence suggesting that the penetration of sensitive Soviet air space by the KAL flight may have been timed to permit U.S. space vehicles to monitor the Soviet response, citing earlier examples of the tactic. The author observed that "If there has been a failure in the West, it is on the part of investigative journalism which has not pursued the enquiry with anything like the vigour that might be expected"; he urged that "It is in the United States itself that the free press should take up the challenge." As of the time of writing (September 1984), the challenge has not been accepted. *The New York Times* did not even report the charges, apart from a cursory reference to a U.S. government denial several weeks later and a few phrases indicating that the charges were "a contention by the Soviet Union," an easy way to dismiss them.[1] A few months later, David Pearson provided evidence that the U.S. government was fully aware that KAL 007 was far off course and "heading toward Soviet territory while a major Soviet missile test was in the making there, and that the airliner was thus in grave danger," and that U.S. agencies "had the time and means to communicate with K.A.L. 007 and correct its course, but not one of them did so." It can be presumed, he argues, that the White House and the Pentagon also had ample information and opportunity "to issue instructions to civilian air-traffic control authorities to correct the jetliner's course, but did not do so." Former U.S. diplomat John Keppel, who had taken part in the attempted cover-up of the 1960 U-2 incident, stated that "his investigation of the Soviet downing of the Korean Air Lines plane convinced him the United States suppressed evidence indicating the plane was on a spy mission" and called for a congressional investigation.[2]

These charges and the information provided to back them up appear to merit attention. For the most part, they have passed in silence, apart from occasional reports of official denials, specifically, the claim that "No agency of the U.S. government even knew the plane was off course and in difficulty until after it was shot down," and that "The crew of the RC135 [the U.S. spy plane equipped with the most advanced technology that passed near the Korean airliner] was totally unaware" of the plane's presence[3]—this in a highly sensitive area subjected to intensive U.S. surveillance that was enhanced at just that moment because of impending Soviet missile tests. Those who credit the official denials should be calling for a different kind of congressional investigation, namely, into the amazing incompetence of U.S. intelligence and surveillance systems.

There are other intriguing aspects of this incident. It is notable that in the midst of the furor over the Soviet atrocity, UNITA, the "freedom fighters" supported by the United States and South Africa, took credit for downing an Angolan jet with 126 killed. There was no ambiguity, the plane was not off course flying over sensitive installations, there was no U.S. reconnaissance jet nearby confusing the issue. It was simply premeditated murder, joyously announced by our heroes. The incident received 100 words in *The New York Times* and apparently no comment anywhere in the media. UNITA's further claim to have downed an Angolan civilian jet with 100 killed in February 1984 received virtually no mention; not a single news item was devoted to it, to my knowledge, anywhere in the U.S. press.

Those with good memories will recall other cases. In October 1976, a Cuban airliner was bombed by terrorists with long-standing CIA connections, and 73 civilians were killed. This was a period when the 20-year campaign of international terrorism against Cuba was reaching a peak. In 1973 Israel downed a civilian plane lost in a sandstorm over the Suez canal, two minutes flight time from Cairo, toward which it was heading, with 110 killed. There was little protest, only editorial comment that "No useful purpose is served by an acrimonious debate over the assignment of blame" (*New York Times*). Four days later, Prime Minister Golda Meir visited the United States where she was troubled with few embarrassing questions and returned with new gifts of military aircraft. Contrary to recent claims put forth in an effort to distinguish this case from the Soviet atrocity,[4] Israel refused to pay compensation or to accept any responsibility whatsoever; it offered only *ex gratia* payments, funded by the usual generous donor from abroad. In 1955, an Air India plane carrying the Chinese delegation to the Bandung conference was blown up in the air in what the Hong Kong police called a "carefully planned mass murder." An American defector later claimed that it was he who planted the bomb in the service of the CIA.[5] None of these incidents demonstrate "barbarism"; all were quickly forgotten. None qualified as "one of the most infamous and reprehensible acts in history" in the words of the resolution in which Congress unanimously denounced the Soviet atrocity, inspiring Senator Moynihan to extol "the most important concept in the evolution of the concept of crime since the Geneva Convention."[6]

One can offer a long series of such examples. In such ways, history is shaped in the interests of those with privilege and power.

All of this falls under the rubric of what Walter Lippman, in 1921, called "the manufacture of consent," an art which is "capable of great refinements" and will lead to a "revolution" in "the practice of democracy." This art has been much admired in the social sciences. The well-known American political scientist Harold Lasswell wrote in 1933 that we must avoid "democratic dogmatisms," such as the belief that people are "the best judges of their own interests." Democracy permits the voice of the people to be heard, and it is the task of the intellectual to ensure that this voice endorses what far-sighted leaders determine to be the right course. Propaganda is to democracy as violence is to totalitarianism. The techniques have been honed to a high art, far beyond anything that Orwell dreamt of. The device of feigned dissent, incorporating the doctrines of the state religion and eliminating rational critical discussion, is one of the more subtle means, although simple lying and suppression of fact and other crude techniques are also widely used and highly effective in protecting us from knowledge and understanding of the world in which we live.

It should be noted that ideological control (Agitprop) is far more important in the democracies than in states that rule by violence, and is therefore more refined, and quite probably more effective. There are few Danchevs here, except at the remote margins of political debate.

For those who stubbornly seek freedom, there can be no more urgent task than to come to understand the mechanisms and practices of indoctrination. These are easy to perceive in the totalitarian societies, much less so in the system of "brainwashing under freedom" to which we are subjected and which all too often we serve as willing or unwitting instruments.

NOTES

1. William Broad, *The New York Times*, 1 Sept. 1984; also 8 July, 31 Aug. *The Washington Post* did carry a report of the *Defence Attaché* article, June 19.

2. David Pearson, *Nation*, 18 Aug. 1984; UPI, *Boston Globe*, 27 Aug. 1984. Tom Wicker describes the failure of the press to report or investigate Pearson's charges as evidence of "the depressing complicity

with Government into which the free American press has sunk since Vietnam and Watergate"—in fact, then and before as well ("A Damning Silence," *The New York Times*, 7 Sept. 1984; the *Times* has been one of the worst offenders).

3.   The words of an unidentified senior State Department official (Fred Kaplan, *Boston Globe*, 29 Aug. 1984). Virtually none of this has been reported in *The New York Times*, which, as the "newspaper of record," has special responsibilities, although some space has been devoted to government denials. The pattern is not atypical. Often, official denials are a useful lead toward otherwise unreported facts, as careful readers of the free press are aware.

4.   Martin Peretz, *New Republic*, 24 Oct. 1983; Michael Curtis of the American Professors for Peace in the Middle East, letter, *The New York Times*, 2 Oct. 1983.

5.   Brian Urquhart, *Hammarskjold* (New York: Knopf, 1972).

6.   Cited by Randolph Ryan, "Misusing the Flight 7 Tragedy," *Boston Globe*, 16 Sept. 1984. The lesson Ryan draws is that the administration and Congress cannot be trusted, that "President Reagan and Congress both did violence to the truth." The more significant question, rarely addressed, concerns the press.

References

Anderson, J.M. (1972). *The Grammar of Case* (London: Cambridge Univ. Press).

Anderson, M. (1979). "Noun Phrase Structure." Ph.D. dissertation, University of Connecticut.

———. (1983). "Prenominal Genitive NP's." ms., University of Connecticut.

Aoun, J. (1982). "The Formal Nature of Anaphoric Relations." Ph.D. dissertation, MIT.

———. (1985). *A Grammar of Anaphora* (Cambridge: MIT Press).

Aoun, J. & Sportiche, D. (1983). "On the Formal Theory of Government." *Linguistic Review* 2.3.

Aoun, J. & Lightfoot, D. (1984). "Government and Contraction." *Linguistic Inquiry* 15.3.

Baker, C.L. (1970). "Notes on the Description of English Questions," *Foundations of Language* 6.

Baker, C.L. & McCarthy, J., (eds.). (1981). *The Logical Problem of Language Acquisition* (Cambridge: MIT Press).

Baker, M. (1985). "The Mirror Principle and Morphosyntactic Explanation." *Linguistic Inquiry* 16.3.

Baltin, M. (1978). "Toward a Theory of Movement Rules." Ph.D. dissertation, MIT.

Barton, E. (1984). "Toward a Principle-Based Parser." ms., MIT.

Belletti, A. (1982). "'Morphological' Passive and Pro-drop: The Impersonal Construction in Italian." *J. of Linguistic Research* 2.1.

———. (1984). "Unaccusatives as Case Assigners." ms., MIT/Scuola Normale Superiore, Pisa.

Belletti, A. & Rizzi, L. (1981). "The Syntax of 'ne': Some Theoretical Implications." *Linguistic Review* 1.2.

Bergvall, V. (1982). "WH-questions and Island Constraints in Kikuyu: A Reanalysis." In J. Kaye, (ed.), *Current Approaches to African Linguistics*, Vol. II, (Dordrecht: Foris).

Berwick, R. (1982). "Locality Principles and the Acquisition of Syntactic Knowledge." Ph.D. dissertation, MIT.

Berwick, R. & Weinberg, A. (1984). *The Grammatical Basis of Linguistic Performance* (Cambridge: MIT Press).

Bever, T.G. (1983). "The Nonspecific Bases of Language." In E. Wanner & L. Gleitman, (eds.), *Language Acquisition: The State of the Art* (Cambridge: Harvard).

Bickerton, D. (1984). "The Language Biogram Hypothesis." *Behavioral and Brain Sciences* 7.2.

Bloomfield, L. (1928). "A Set of Postulates for the Science of Language." *Language* 2. Reprinted by M. Joos (ed.), *Readings in Linguistics*. Washington: American Council of Learned Sciences, 1957.

———. (1933). *Language* (New York: Holt).

———. (1939). "Menomini Morphophonemics." *Travaux du cercle linguistique de Prague.*

Borer, H. (1983). "The Projection Principle and Rules of Morphology," *Proceedings of the Northeastern Linguistic Society (NELS)* 14.

———. (1984a). *Parametric Syntax* (Dordrecht: Foris).

———. (1984b). "I-Subjects." ms., UC–Irvine.

Borer, H. & Wexler, K. (1984). "The Maturation of Syntax." ms., UC–Irvine.

Bouchard, D. (1984). *On the Content of Empty Categories* (Dordrecht: Foris).

Bracken, H. (1984). *Mind and Language* (Dordrecht: Foris).

Bresnan, J., (ed.). (1982). *The Mental Representation of Grammatical Relations* (Cambridge: MIT Press).

Brody, M. (1984). "On Contextual Definitions and the Role of Chains." *Linguistic Inquiry* 15.3.

Burge, T. (1984). "Individualism and Psychology." ms., UCLA. Paper presented at Sloan Conference on Philosophy and Psychology, MIT, May 1984.

Burzio, L. (forthcoming). *Italian Syntax: A Government-Binding Approach* (Dordrecht: Reidel).

Cartmill, M. (1984). "Innate Grammars and the Evolutionary Presumption." *Behavioral and Brain Sciences* 7.2.

Chomsky, N. (1962). "A Transformational Approach to Syntax." In A.A. Hill (ed.), *Proceedings of the Third Texas Conference on Problems of Linguistic Analysis in English (1958)* (Austin: University of Texas Press).

———. (1964). *Current Issues in Linguistic Theory* (The Hague: Mouton).

———. (1965). *Aspects of the Theory of Syntax* (Cambridge: MIT Press).

———. (1966). *Cartesian Linguistics* (New York: Harper & Row).

———. (1968). *Language and Mind* (New York: Harcourt, Brace & World); extended edition (1972).

———. (1975a). *Logical Structure of Linguistic Theory* (New York: Plenum); drawn from an unpublished 1955–56 manuscript.

———. (1975b). *Reflections on Language* (New York, Pantheon).

———. (1977). *Essays on Form and Interpretation* (Amsterdam: North-Holland).

———. (1980a). "On Binding." *Linguistic Inquiry*, 11.1.

———. (1980b). *Rules and Representations* (New York: Columbia University Press).

———. (1981). *Lectures on Government and Binding* (Dordrecht: Foris).

———. (1982). *Some Concepts and Consequences of the Theory of Government and Binding* (Cambridge: MIT Press).

———. (forthcoming). "A generalization of X-bar theory," in A. Borg, S. Somekh & P. Wexler, eds. *Studia linguistica et Orientalia Memoriae Haim Blanc dedicata* (Wiesbaden: Verlag Otto Harrassowitz).

Chomsky, N., Huybregts, R., & Riemsdijk, H. van. (1982). *The Generative Enterprise* (Dordrecht: Foris).

Chomsky, N. & Lasnik, H. (1977). "Filters and Control." *Linguistic Inquiry* 8.3.

Crain, S. & Nakayama, M. (1984). "Structure Dependence in Grammar Formation." ms., University of Connecticut.

Demopoulos, W. & Matthews, R.J. (1983). " On the Hypothesis that Grammars are Mentally Represented." *Behavioral and Brain Sciences* 6.3.

Dennett, D. (1983). "Styles of Mental Representation," *Proceedings of the Aristotelian Society*, pp. 213–226.

Dummett M. (1981). "Objections to Chomsky." *London Review of Books*, 3–16 September.

Emonds, J. (1976). *A Transformational Approach to Syntax* (New York: Academic Press).

Enc, B. (1983, May). "In Defense of the Identity Theory." *J. of Philosophy* 80.5.

Epstein, S. (1984). "Quantifier-pro and the LF Representation of PRO$_{ARB}$." *Linguistic Inquiry* 15.3.

Evans, G. (1980). "Pronouns." *Linguistic Inquiry* 11.2.

Fabb, N. (1984). "Syntactic Affixation." Ph.D. dissertation, MIT.

Fillmore, C. (1968). "The Case for Case." In E. Bach & R. Harms, (eds.), *Universals in Linguistic Theory* (New York: Holt, Rinehart & Winston).

Finer, D. (1984). "The Formal Grammar of Switch-Reference." Ph.D. dissertation, University of Massachusetts.

Fodor, J. (1983). *The Modularity of Mind* (Cambridge: MIT Press).

Fodor, J., Bever, T., & Garrett, M. (1974). *The Psychology of Language* (New York: McGraw-Hill).

Freidin, R. (1978). "Cyclicity and the Theory of Grammar." *Linguistic Inquiry* 9.4.

———. (forthcoming). "Fundamental Issues in the Theory of Binding." In B. Lust, (ed.), *Acquisition Studies in Anaphora* (Dordrecht: Reidel).

Gallistel, C.R. (1980, July–August). "From Muscles to Motivation." *American Scientist* 68.

Gee, J. & Kegl, J. (1982, September). "Semantic Perspicuity and the Locative Hypothesis." *J. of Education*.

Giorgi, A. (1983). "Toward a Theory of Long Distance Anaphors." ms., Istituto di Psicologia. CNR, Rome.

Gleitman, L. (1981). "Maturational Determinants of Language Growth." *Cognition* 10:1–3.

Grimshaw (1981). "Form, Function and the Language Acquisition Device." In C.L. Baker and J. McCarthy, (eds.), *The Logical Problem of Language Acquisition*, (Cambridge: MIT Press).

Gruber, J.S. (1976). *Studies in Lexical Relations* (Amsterdam: North-Holland) [MIT Ph.D. dissertation, 1965].

Gunderson, K., (ed.). (1975). *Language, Mind and Knowledge* (Minneapolis: University of Minnesota Press).

Harris, R. (1983). "Theoretical Ideas." *Times Literary Supplement*, 14 October.

Heilbron, J.L. (1964). *A History of the Problem of Atomic Structure from the Discovery of the Electron to the Beginning of Quantum Mechanics*. Ph.D. dissertation, UC–Berkeley.

Higginbotham, J. (1983a). "Logical Form, Binding and Nominals." *Linguistic Inquiry* 14.3.

———. (1983b). "Is Grammar Psychological?." In L.S. Cauman, I. Levi, C. Parsons, & R. Schwartz, *How Many Questions?* (Indianapolis: Hackett).

———. (forthcoming). "On Semantics." *Linguistic Inquiry*.

Hockney, D. (1975). "The Bifurcation of Scientific Theories and Indeterminacy of Translation." *Philosophy of Science*, 42.4.

Hornstein, N. (1984). *Logic as Grammar* (Cambridge: MIT Press).

Hornstein, N. & Lightfoot, D. (eds.). (1981). *Explanation in Linguistics* (London: Longman).

Hornstein, N. & Weinberg, A. (1981). "Case Theory and Preposition Stranding." *Linguistic Inquiry* 12.1.

Horwich, P. (1984). "Critical Notice: Saul Kripke: Wittgenstein on Rules and Private Language." *Philosophy of Science* 51.1.

Huang, C.-T.J. (1982). "Logical Relations in Chinese and the Theory of Grammar. Ph.D. dissertation, MIT.

———. (1983). "A Note on the Binding Theory." *Linguistic Inquiry* 14.3.

Hyams, N. (1983). "The Acquisition of Parametrized Grammars." Ph.D. dissertation, CUNY.

Jackendoff, R. (1972). *Semantic Interpretation in Generative Grammar* (Cambridge: MIT Press).

———. (1984). *Semantics and Cognition* (Cambridge: MIT Press).

Jaeggli, O. (1982). *On Some Phonologically Null Elements in Syntax* (Dordrecht: Foris).

Jespersen, O. (1924). *The Philosophy of Grammar* (London: Allen & Unwin).

Johnson-Laird, P. (1983). *Mental Models* (Cambridge: Harvard University Press).

Joos, M., (ed.). (1957). *Readings in Linguistics* (Washington: American Council of Learned Societies).

Katz, J. (1981). *Language and Other Abstract Objects* (Totowa, NJ: Rowman & Littlefield).

Kayne, R (1975). *French Syntax* (Cambridge: MIT Press).

———. (1984). *Connectedness and Binary Branching* (Foris: Dordrecht).

Kegl, J. (1984). "Locative Relations in American Sign Language." Ph.D. dissertation, MIT.

Keyser, J. & Roeper, T. (1984). "On the Middle and Ergative Constructions in English." *Linguistic Inquiry* 15.3.

Kiparsky, P. (1982). *Some Theoretical Problems in Panini's Grammar* (Poona: Bhandarkar Oriental Research Institute).

Kirsh, D. (1983). "Representation and Rationality: Foundations of Cognitive Science." Ph.D. dissertation, Oxford University.

Koopman (1984). *The Syntax of Verbs* (Dordrecht: Foris).

Koster, J. (1978). *Locality Principles in Syntax* (Dordrecht: Foris).

———. (1984). "On Binding and Control." *Linguistic Inquiry* 15.3.

Koster, J. & May, R. (1982). "On the Constituency of Infinitives." *Language* 58.1.

Kripke, S. (1982). *Wittgenstein on Rules and Private Language* (Cambridge: Harvard University Press).

Lasnik, H. (1976). "Remarks on Coreference." *Linguistic Analysis* 2.1.

———. (1982). "On Two Recent Treatments of Disjoint Reference," *J. of Linguistic Research* 1.4.

———. (1984). "A Note on Illicit NP Movement." ms., University of Connecticut.

Lasnik, H. & Saito, M. (1984). "On the Nature of Proper Government." *Linguistic Inquiry* 15.2.

Lebeaux, D. (1983). "A Distributional Difference between Reciprocals and Reflexives." *Linguistic Inquiry* 14.4.

Levin, J. (1983). "Government Relations and the Structure of INFL."
In I. Haik & D. Massam, (eds.), *MIT Working Papers in Linguistics*, vol. 5.

Lewis, D. (1975). "Languages and Language." In K. Gunderson,
(ed.), *Language, Mind and Knowledge* (Minneapolis: University
of Minnesota Press).

Lightfoot, D. (1979). *Principles of Diachronic Syntax* (London:
Cambridge University Press).

———. (1981). "Review of G. Sampson, *Liberty and Language.*" *J. of
Linguistics* XVII.1.

———. (1982). *The Language Lottery* (Cambridge: MIT Press).

Longobardi, G. (1983). "Connectedness, Scope and C-Command."
ms., Scuola Normale Superiore.

Manzini, M.R. (1983a). "On Control and Control Theory." *Linguistic
Inquiry* 14.3.

———. (1983b). "Restructuring and Reanalysis." Ph.D. dissertation,
MIT.

Marantz, A. (1984). *On the Nature of Grammatical Relations* (Cambridge: MIT Press).

Marcus, M. (1980). *A Theory of Syntactic Recognition for Natural
Language* (Cambridge: MIT Press).

Marr, D. (1982). *Vision* (San Francisco: Freeman).

May, R. (1977). "The Grammar of Quantification." Ph.D. dissertation,
MIT.

———. (forthcoming). *Logical Form* (Cambridge: MIT Press).

McGinn, C. (1981). "Review of Chomsky (1980b)." *J. of Philosophy*
78.5.

Miller, G.A. & Chomsky, N. (1963). "Finitary Models of Language
Users." In R.D. Luce, R. Bush, & E. Galanter, (eds.), *Handbook
of Mathematical Psychology*, vol. II (New York: Wiley).

Montalbetti, M. (1984). "After Binding." Ph.D. dissertation, MIT.

Moravcsik, J. (1975). "Aitia as Generative Factor in Aristotle's Philosophy," *Dialogue*.

Nagel, T. (1969). "Linguistics and Epistemology." In S. Hook, (ed.).
Language and Philosophy (New York: NYU Press).

Newmeyer, F.J. (1980). *Linguistic Theory in America* (New York:
Academic Press).

———. (1983). *Grammatical Theory* (Chicago: University of Chicago
Press).

Ney, J., (1983). "Review of Chomsky (1982)." *Language Sciences* 5.2.

Ogle, R. (1980). "Two Port-Royal Theories of Natural Order." In K.
Koerner, (ed.). *Amsterdam Studies in the Theory and History of
Linguistic Science III: Studies in the History of Linguistics*, vol.
20 (Amsterdam: John Benjamins B.V.).

Osherson, D., Stob, M., & Weinstein, S. (1984). "Learning Theory and Natural Language. *Cognition* 17.1.

Perlmutter, D. (1983a). "Personal vs. Impersonal Constructions," *Natural Language and Linguistic Theory* 1.1.

———. (1983b). *Studies in Relational Grammar* (Chicago: University of Chicago Press).

Pesetsky, D. (1983). "Paths and Categories." Ph.D. dissertation, MIT.

Pica (1984). "Subject, Tense and Truth: Towards a Modular Approach to Binding." ms., CNRS, Paris.

Picallo, C. (1984). "Opaque Domains." Ph.D. dissertation, CUNY.

Pollock, J.-Y. (1983). "Accords, chaînes impersonnelles et variables." *Linguisticae Investigationes* 7.1.

Popkin, R. (1979). *The History of Scepticism from Erasmus to Spinoza* (Berkeley, University of California Press).

Postal, P. (1964). *Constituent Structure* (The Hague: Mouton).

———. (1971). *Cross-Over Phenomena* (New York: Holt, Rinehart & Winston).

Postal, P. and G. Pullum. (1982). "The Contraction Debate," *Linguistic Inquiry* 13.1.

Putnam, H. (1975). "The Meaning of 'Meaning'." In K. Gunderson, (ed.), *Language, Mind and Knowledge* (Minneapolis, University of Minnesota Press).

———. (1981). *Reason, Truth and History* (Cambridge: Cambridge University Press).

Pylyshyn, Z. (1984). *Computation and Cognition* (Cambridge: MIT Press).

Quine, W.V. (1960). *Word and Object* (Cambridge: MIT Press).

———. (1972). "Methodological Reflections on Current Linguistic Theory." In G. Harman & D. Davidson, (eds.). *Semantics of Natural Language* (New York: Humanities Press).

Radford, A. (1981). *Transformational Syntax* (Cambridge: Cambridge University Press).

Reinhart, T. (1983). *Anaphora and Semantic Interpretation* (London: Croom Helm).

Reuland (1983a). "Governing -ing." *Linguistic Inquiry* 14.1.

———. (1984). "Representation at the Level of Logical Form and the Definiteness Effect." ms., Groningen.

Reynolds, A.L. (1971). "What *Did* Otto Jespersen Say?" *Papers of the Chicago Linguistic Society*.

Riemsdijk, H. van. (1978). *A Case Study in Syntactic Markedness* (Dordrecht: Foris).

———. (1981). "The Case of German Adjectives." In J. Pustejovsky & V. Burke, (eds.), *Markedness and Learnability*, University of

Massachusetts Occasional Papers in Linguistics, 6 (Amherst).

Riemsdijk, H. van & Williams, E. (1985). *Introduction to the Theory of Grammar* (Cambridge: MIT Press).

Rizzi, L. (1982a). *Issues in Italian Syntax* (Dordrecht: Foris).

———. (1982b). "On Chain Formation." ms., Universita della Calabria.

Roeper, T. (1984). "Implicit Arguments and the Projection Principle." ms, University of Massachusetts.

Ross, J. (1967). "Constraints on Variables in Syntax." Ph.D. dissertation, MIT.

Rothstein, S. (1983). "The Syntactic Form of Predication." Ph.D. dissertation, MIT.

Rouveret, A. & Vergnaud, J.-R. (1980). "Specifying Reference to the Subject." *Linguistic Inquiry* 11.1.

Safir, K. (1984). "Multiple Variable Binding." *Linguistic Inquiry* 15.4.

———. (forthcoming). *Syntactic Chains* (London: Cambridge University Press).

Saito, M. (1985). "Some Asymmetries in Japanese and their Theoretical Implications." Ph.D. dissertation, MIT.

Sapir, E. (1921). *Language* (New York: Harcourt, Brace).

Schachter, P. (1984). "Auxiliary Reduction: An Argument for GPSG." *Linguistic Inquiry* 15.3.

Shepard, R. (1982). "Perceptual and Analogical Bases of Cognition." In J. Mehler, M. Garrett, & E. Walker, (eds.), *Perspectives in Mental Representation* (Hillsdale, NJ: Erlbaum).

Soames, S. (1984). "Linguistics and Psychology," *Linguistics and Philosophy* 7.2.

Sportiche, D. (1983). "Structural Invariance and Symmetry in Syntax." Ph.D. dissertation, MIT.

Stent, G. (1981). "Cerebral Hermeneutics." *J. Social Biol. Struct.* 4.107–124.

Stowell (1978). "What Was There Before There Was There." In D. Farkas, W. Jacobsen, & K. Todrys, (eds.), *Papers from the Fourteenth Regional Meeting*, Chicago Linguistics Society.

———. (1981). "Origins of Phrase Structure." Ph.D. dissertation, MIT.

Tomas, V. (editor) (1957). *Peirce's Essays in the Philosophy of Science* (New York: Liberal Arts Press).

Trager, G. & Smith, H.L. (1951). *An Outline of English Structure (Studies in Linguistics* Occasional Papers 3).

Travis (1984). "Parameters and Effects of Word Order Variation." Ph.D. dissertation, MIT.

Ullman, S. (1979). *The Interpretation of Visual Motion* (Cambridge: MIT Press).

Vergnaud, J.-R. (1982). *Dépendances et Niveaux de Representation en Syntaxe*, Thèse de Doctorat d'Etat, Université de Paris VII.

Wanner, E. & Gleitman, L. (eds.). (1982). *Language Acquisition: The State of the Art* (Cambridge: Harvard).

Wasow, T. (1979). *Anaphora in Generative Grammar* (Ghent: E. Story-Scientia Gent.).

Wexler, K. (1982). "A Principle Theory for Language Acquisition." In E. Wanner & L. Gleitman, (eds.), *Language Acquisition: The State of the Art* (Cambridge: Harvard).

Wexler, K. & Culicover, P. (1980). *Formal Principles of Language Acquisition* (Cambridge: MIT Press).

White, A. (1982). *The Nature of Knowledge* (Totowa, NJ: Rowman & Littlefield.)

Whitman, J. (1982). "Configurationality Parameters." ms., Harvard.

Whitney, W.D. (1872). "Steinthal and the Psychological Theory of Language." *North American Review*.

Williams, E. (1980). "Predication." *Linguistic Inquiry* 11.1.

———. (1982a). "Another Argument that Passive is Transformational." *Linguistic Analysis* 13.1.

———. (1982b). "The NP Cycle" *Linguistic Inquiry* 13.2.

Wittgenstein, L. (1953). *Philosophical Investigations* (Blackwell: Oxford).

Yang, D.-W. (1983). "The Extended Binding Theory of Anaphora." ms., MIT.

Zagona, K. (1982). "Government and Proper Government of Verbal Projections." Ph.D. dissertation, University of Washington.

Zubizarreta, M.-L. (1982). "On the Relationship of the Lexicon to Syntax." Ph.D. dissertation, MIT.

Index

Index

About the Author

Dr. Noam Chomsky is an Institute Professor at the Massachusetts Institute of Technology. The publication in 1957 of *Syntactic Structures* launched what has been called the Chomskyan revolution. This book marks a fundamental break with the American tradition of structural linguistics by turning away from the description of certain features of natural languages to inquiring into the general properties of any system of rules that may serve as a basis for human language, that is, to study of the general *form of language* that underlies each particular realization, each particular natural language. Central to Chomsky's analysis is the distinction which he draws between a person's linguistic *competence* (knowledge of the system of rules that govern language) and a person's actual *performance* as a user of language.

As a linguist, Professor Chomsky's aim is not limited to making a technical contribution with his generative theory of language. His thought integrates this into a wider view of the relationship between language and the human mind, the main feature of which is his hypothesis that human beings are born with an innate knowledge of universal principles underlying the structure of human language. Chomsky's views and his ideas have exerted a powerful influence on other disciplines by restoring language to a central position in cognitive psychology and in the philosophy of mind. And the wider impact of his redefinition of the subject gives him a permanent place in the intellectual history of the twentieth century.

About the Founder of this Series

Ruth Nanda Anshen, Ph.D., and Fellow of the Royal Society of Arts of London, founded, plans, and edits several distinguished philosophy of culture series, including World Perspectives, Religious Perspectives, Credo Perspectives, Perspectives in Humanism, The Science of Culture Series, The Tree of Life Series, and Convergence. She also writes and lectures on the relationship of knowledge to the nature and meaning of man and to his understanding of and place in the universe. Dr. Anshen's book, *The Reality of the Devil: Evil in Man*, a study in the phenomenology of evil, is published by Harper and Row. Dr. Anshen is a member of the American Philosophical Association, the History of Science Society, the International Philosophical Society, and the Metaphysical Society of America.